The author respectfully acknowledges the Wardandi People, past and present traditional guardians of the land on which this book was written.

GEORGIANA MOLLOY
the mind that shines

BERNICE BARRY

Pan Macmillan Australia

First published 2015 by Redgate Consultants
This Picador edition published 2016 by Pan Macmillan Australia Pty Ltd
1 Market Street, Sydney, New South Wales, Australia, 2000

Copyright © Bernice Barry 2016

The moral right of the author has been asserted.

All rights reserved. No part of this book may be reproduced or transmitted by any person or entity (including Google, Amazon or similar organisations), in any form or by any means, electronic or mechanical, including photocopying, recording, scanning or by any information storage and retrieval system, without prior permission in writing from the publisher.

Cataloguing-in-Publication entry is available
from the National Library of Australia
http://catalogue.nla.gov.au

Cover and internal design by Lauren Wilhelm Design
Typeset in Garamond by Kirby Jones
Printed by McPherson's Printing Group
Cover photo credits: The Board of Trustees of the RBG, Kew;
Cumbria Archive Centre; Cambridge University Herbarium;
Botanical Garden and Botanical Museum of Berlin

The author and the publisher have made every effort to contact copyright holders for material used in this book. Any person or organisation that may have been overlooked should contact the publisher.

For Patrick Richardson-Bunbury

and

Georgiana Theodosia Bisdee née Hale

But it's not her air, her form, her face,

Tho' matching beauty's fabled queen,

But the mind that shines in ev'ry grace.

An' chiefly in her sparklin' een.

The Songs of Robert Burns 1824[1]

The Molloy & Kennedy Family Tree

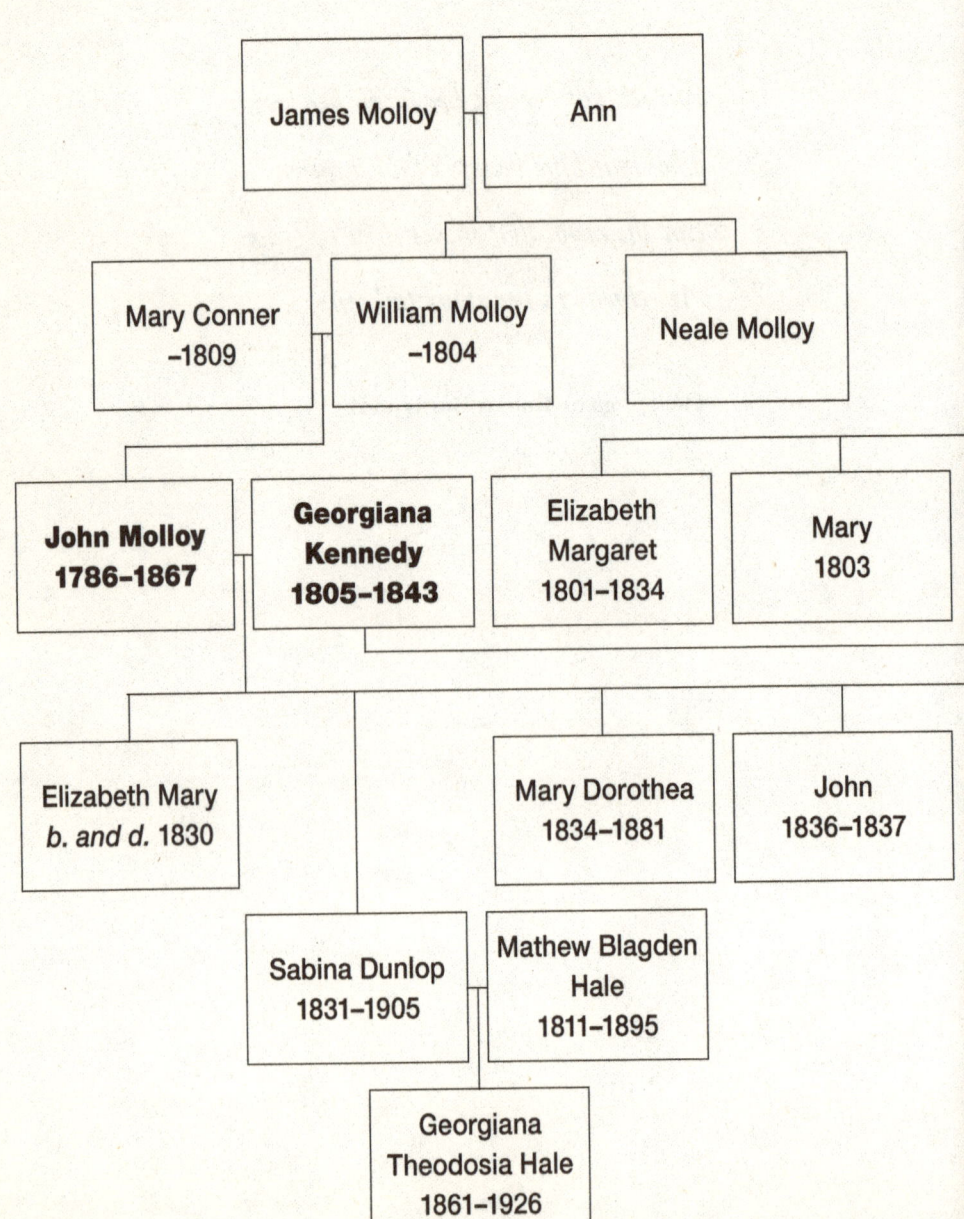

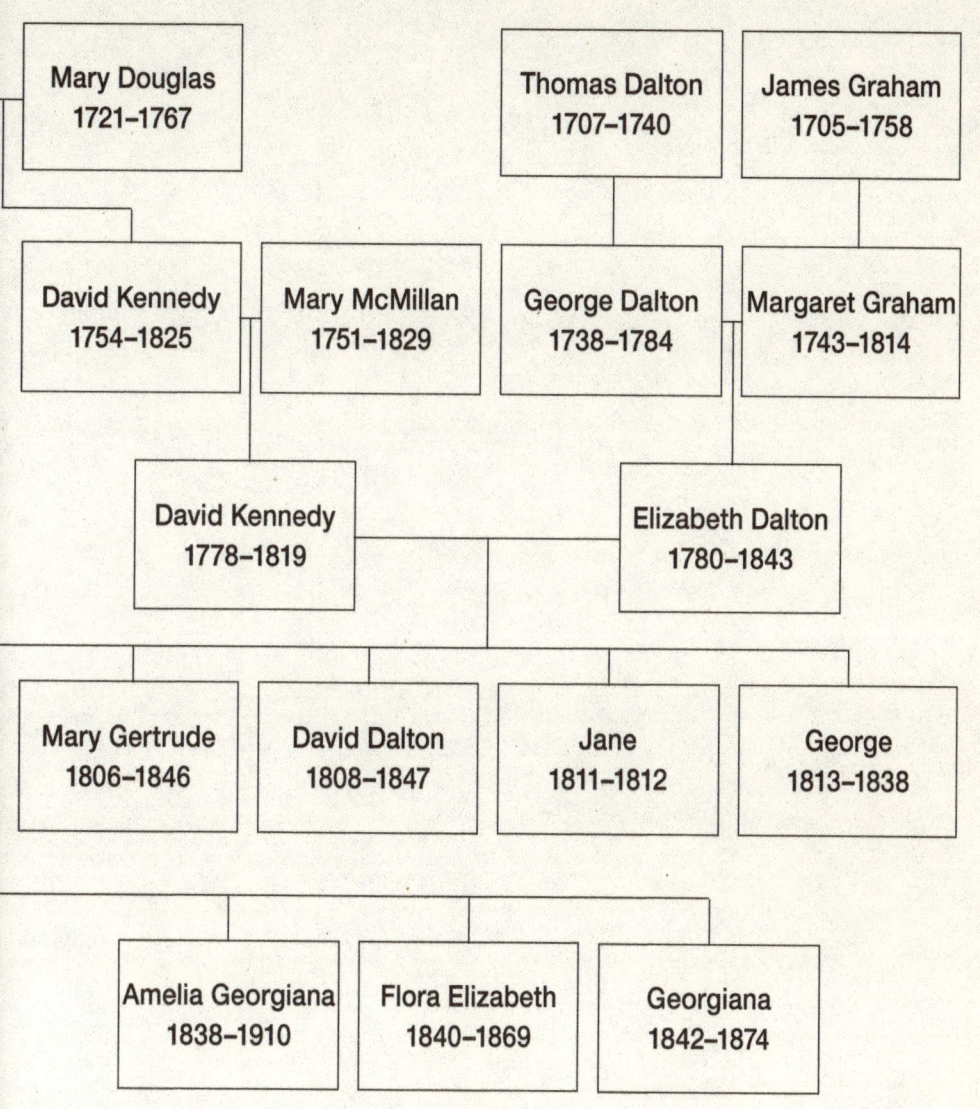

Contents

Preface	1
England	**5**
A childhood in Eden	7
John Molloy, London boy	28
Sisters and secrets	42
Scotland	**59**
An unbroken spirit	61
Portugal, Spain, France, Belgium	**83**
King George commands	85
Scotland	**101**
May the end be blest	103
Western Australia	**127**
Adieu, my native land!	129
Cottage on the Killiter	153
Mending and making	174
Botany by the Blackwood River	206
A garden in Busselton	239
Life after Georgiana	281
Maps	299
Endnotes	301
Image credits	328
Index of names	329
Acknowledgements and Sources	334

Preface

After a month of mild winter days, things were about to change. Early on the morning of 1 December 2009, three weather fronts were gathering energy to begin their icy journey across the United Kingdom. Near Manchester, just before dawn, temperatures dropped suddenly to minus five degrees. A band of rain was already sweeping the last crisp remnants of autumn leaves into wet brown piles that clogged drains along the streets.

All this went largely unnoticed by the first travellers of the day, including me. Arriving at London's Euston railway station, it was the departures board not the weather that was on my mind. With a window of just twenty-four hours for my round trip to the northwest of England, the delay or cancellation of the 7.30 from London to Carlisle would have felt like a disaster.

I had been living in Western Australia for ten years and London no longer felt like home. I bought a take-away coffee at my usual place. It had been my usual place on and off for half a lifetime and although the brand name had changed yet again the hot, bitter coffee still tasted good. After four weeks in the city, with a packed work diary behind me, there were just three days left before the flight back to Perth. I would usually have planned to spend my free time window-shopping in Covent Garden, visiting the Victoria & Albert Museum and then enjoying dinner Turkish-style in St Christopher's Place. But this time there was something that drew me away from the pleasures of the capital, something I was searching for. I hoped to find it in the northern county of Cumbria, in a 900-year-old castle, three and a half hours away by high-speed train.

About an hour into the journey I first began to notice the chill. Warmth blew lightly across my feet from heating vents but the temperature in the carriage was dropping steadily. We travelled further north, city stations flashing by in a blur of bright signage. As the intervals between stops grew longer and the views began changing from buildings to fields, a pale wash of icy air was slowly blanching all colour from the countryside. By the time the land had heaved itself up into the foothills of the Cumbrian fells, a white blanket of curling fog masked not only the high ground but also the spiky crowns of the dry-stone walls.

Around 10.30 the train lost speed to travel through the small station at Penrith. Nestled in the lush Vale of Eden, the town is a gateway to the northern end of the Lake District for thousands of travellers each year. Seeing the grey line of the River Eden valley that morning was a sudden reminder that, when we least expect it, disparate things connect. Like me, the river was heading to Carlisle, but in its onward sweep towards the great Solway Firth estuary, it would first head north and wind through Crosby-on-Eden, just as it had on the moonlit evening in 1819 when the village squire fell from his horse and died, leaving five children fatherless.

With a few lurches, the train moved forward again as a muffled conversation started up somewhere behind me. I looked at my watch and realised that we would soon be pulling into Carlisle station. I also realised that my journey and my search had not begun that morning in a London hotel but seven years earlier, on the banks of the beautiful Blackwood River in Western Australia, where I first went looking for Georgiana Molloy.

We both travelled to the other side of the world to make a new home in Australia's far southwest, but I arrived with the new millennium and she packed up her life in 1829 as one of the first European settlers in a colony that was still a collection of tents. Georgiana is known today as the first internationally successful female botanist in Western Australia, a pious and brave pioneer. Like so many other readers interested in history and botany, I first came to know her as a demure person of extreme religious fervour with a husband typical of so many in the nineteenth century, a social climber who had been handed the good things in life on a plate. But my initial tentative investigations threw up more questions than answers and it was not long before a trail of conflicting evidence grew about the woman beneath the pale, ringleted exterior depicted in her portrait, so widely used in books and on websites. As I began to search more rigorously for the missing pieces in her story, personal correlations between us became apparent in ways that forced me to think about my own past. I looked back with new clarity on childhood memories and family relationships, and thought again about the emotional journey that migrants experience. Things that moved Georgiana and ideas that touched her belonged in the life of someone quite different from her public image.

What began for me as an interest in local history grew rapidly into an all-consuming pursuit of the truth about Georgiana's life. At first there were more dead ends than breakthroughs but as months turned into years, my research methods improved and new pathways began to appear. Thousands of searches – each one bringing either success or failure – taught me different thinking strategies. Somewhere between London and Carlisle on that long, cold train journey, I decided to find a way of passing on not just the narrative of Georgiana's life but also what I had learned about exploring the past. The telling of a quest is one of the most ancient and widely shared connections between people within and across different cultures: a way of understanding how others live their lives and what that means for each of us. A making sense of who we are. A history. A story.

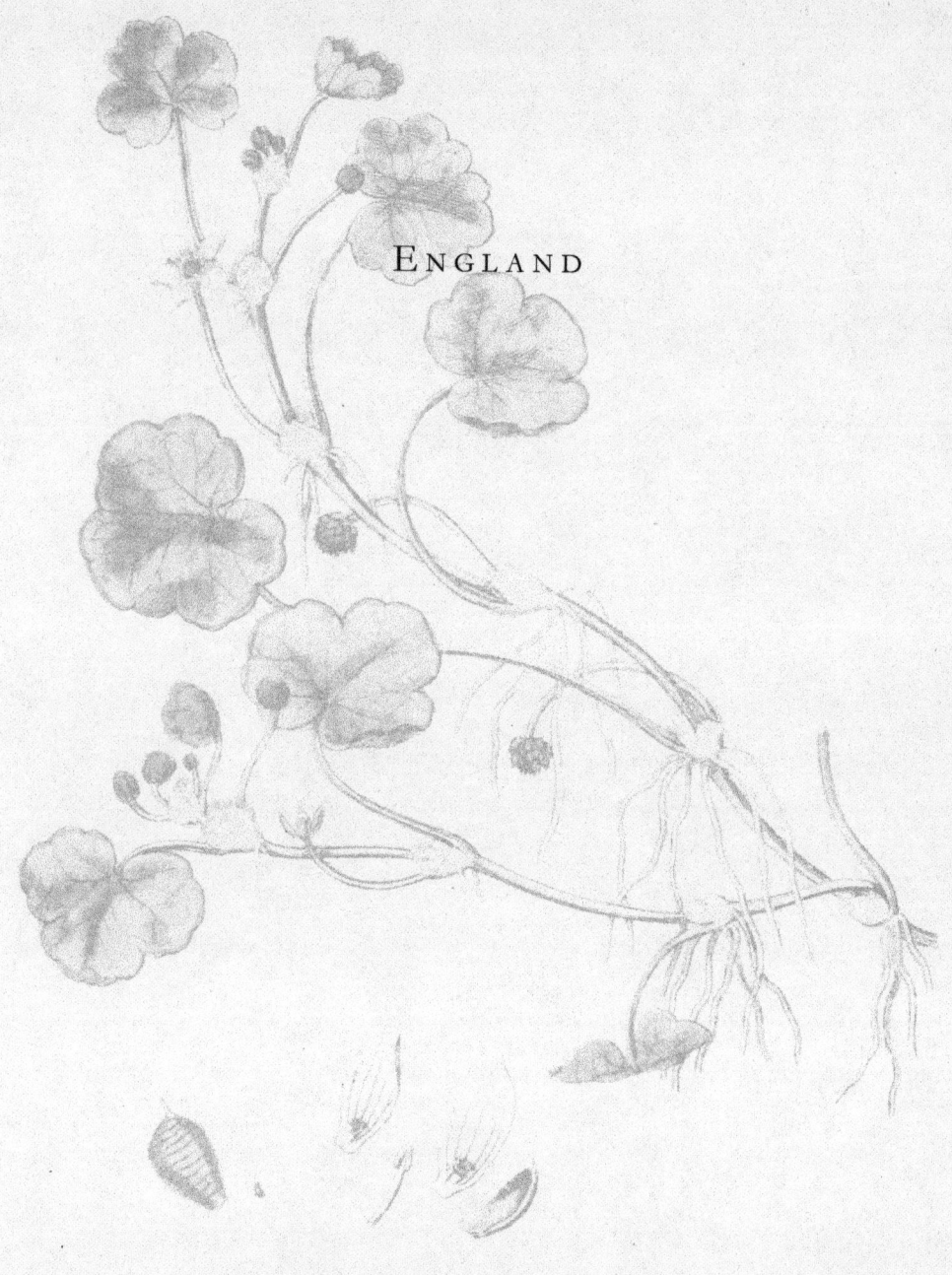

Ranunculus Lenormandi   Lenormand's Water-crowfoot

A CHILDHOOD IN EDEN

Georgiana Kennedy was born in the ancient city of Carlisle at two o'clock in the morning on Thursday, 23 May 1805, in her grandmother's house in Abbey Street.² Her life began where England and Scotland meet, near the wide mouth of the Solway Firth that slices a deep notch into the coast and defines the narrow waist of an island once made up of many tribal kingdoms. But her history began generations earlier, in families who lived in the wild and lawless lands on either side of this natural belt, borders that were controlled by clans and 'reivers' who fought with legendary ferocity.

Georgiana's family tree retells the history of centuries. A direct bloodline travels back through Scottish names with French connectives that reflect the noble lineage of her distant ancestors and the eleventh-century invasion of Britain by Normans: Gilbert Macdowell de Carrick and Fergus, Lord Dunbar of Galloway. She probably never knew that her great-grandfather twenty generations earlier was the first Norman king of England, William the Conqueror. He won the Battle of Hastings in 1066, began building the Tower of London and made his French barons into landowners and lawmakers, changing the English language forever. William's son, King Henry I, built the first stone castle in Carlisle in 1122, at a high defensive point in the west. It still stands like an old sentinel looking out across the ruins of Emperor Hadrian's Roman wall, guarding the old boundary between two countries.

A few steps from the site of the Kennedys' home in Abbey Street, a pedestrian walkway across the Millennium Bridge provides a bird's-eye view in every direction, revealing the landscape of Georgiana's early childhood. At one end of the street the brooding shape of the castle dominates the horizon and at the other end the towering red sandstone walls of the twelfth-century cathedral overshadow houses built by her grandfather in the 1700s. To the east, a medieval marketplace still bustles with the daily business of buying and selling and, to the west, far below city walls made from Roman stonework,

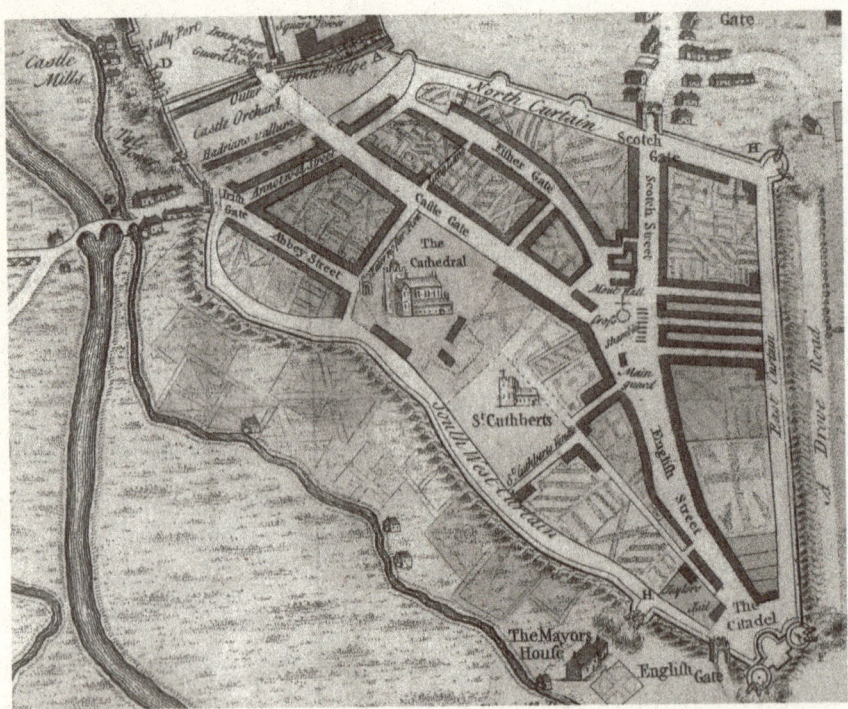

The city of Carlisle in 1746 showing Roman remains of a section of 'Hadrian's vallum' [wall] by the castle entrance, a few steps from Georgiana's birthplace at the end of Abbey Street. The 'moat hall' and cross show the site of the market place.

Extract from A Plan of the City of Carlisle *by G Smith reproduced with the permission of Cumbria Archive Centre ©Cumbria County Council 1995*

a wide expanse of Cumbrian wilderness disappears into the distance. The same as the little girl's view from her window: four sides of a square around the family home. The first influences in Georgiana's early life were formidable and enduring: military power, religion, society, nature.

***

The small collection of books that crossed the oceans with the newly wed Georgiana Molloy was the first mystery. I had read that her sisters found her 'tiresomely pious' and that 'religion became her total response to life'.[3] There are plenty of examples of conversations with friends, family, servants and even strangers where she tried to influence their behaviour, and I had the impression that her rigid Christianity made her severely judgemental of others. But when I saw the titles of the books she brought with her on board the ship to Western Australia, the story they told about their owner did not match what I had learned about her.

We all like to browse a friend's reading collection when we visit their home for the first time, to find out what matters to them and what has shaped them. The books from my own past gather dust and most of them are rarely opened, but the titles that line my shelves reveal the complexity of what lies beneath. Each one is like a single pixel in a coloured image that merges to create a portrait, and all the layers are there. Things from the past can hold great importance for migrants and Georgiana chose to keep those tiny, leather-bound volumes close to her during a six-month journey.

Her library included the *Holy Bible*, *The Force of Truth*, *Sacred Poetry* and *Letters on the Elementary Principles of Education*.[4] No surprises there, but in August 1829 she also packed a copy of *The British Album*, a volume of boldly romantic love poetry.[5]

The book was an anthology of poetry by the Della Cruscans, a small group of English writers living in Italy. It narrates a poetical correspondence between a man and a woman, declaring their love and describing their romantic encounters. The poems describe physical passion, only lightly veiled by erotic imagery. This was not a title I was expecting to see on Georgiana's reading list and it was not the only surprise. She had also placed in her trunk a copy of *The Songs of Robert Burns*.[6]

The first verse of Burns's poem 'Auld Lang Syne' welcomes the new year in many homes but 'the bard of Ayrshire' also wrote in vernacular Scots language about the lives of ordinary folks: love and loss; family and community; power and patriotism; the roles of men and women; poverty and inequality. And, of course, the delights and dangers of love and liquor as celebrated by the old voices of Scottish ballads, handed down through generations.

For the last year before leaving for Australia, Georgiana was often a guest in the home of a clergyman and his wife, where they cooked the food in advance and served it cold on Sundays so that no-one worked on the Sabbath day. They cleared away children's toys on Saturday evenings to make sure the youngest members of the congregation could focus only on Bible stories. The church was bare of colour, comfort and music. In contrast, Georgiana's copy of Burns's poems included reworkings of traditional tunes with lyrics that leave no doubt, even for a twenty-first-century reader, about the subject matter. She could not have missed the bawdy content and the explicitness of Burns's protestations of love for the many ladies in his life. In the poems unmarried couples frolicked among the hay rigs and had the kind of illicit fun that a woman with a very strict Anglican lifestyle would have condemned as sinful behaviour. These books were the first clues to emerge about Georgiana's true character and I had no idea there were so many still ahead.

Sometimes fragments from the past turn up so easily they tumble over one another, but many of them dissolve quickly into nothing. I had accumulated a folder of information about Georgiana's childhood friend, Elizabeth Senhouse. Letters showed that Georgiana's mother stayed with the Senhouse family in Cumberland, and the two daughters were corresponding regularly between 1828 and 1830. A collection of original documents held at the Carlisle Archive Centre (CAC) includes Georgiana's letters to her mother as well as family papers dating back to the sixteenth century. A search in 2009 had randomly thrown up another record: Elizabeth Senhouse's diary for 1828, the year Georgiana suddenly left home. My last-minute train journey to Carlisle on the coldest day of the year was all in the hope that Elizabeth might have written about something that could explain why Georgiana became estranged from her family.

I arrived in the early afternoon with snow falling from a blue-black sky. At that time the CAC was located in the castle and the freezing wind turned to sharp shards of ice against my face as I walked down Abbey Street. There were still a few hours left before closing time and I knew exactly what I was looking for. I settled into an empty seat, turned off my mobile phone and waited for the archivist to deliver the record I had ordered. She arrived within minutes, with a manila envelope tied up and ribboned like a gift with coloured cotton tape. The diary was very delicate. The cover was worn and damaged but what mattered were the contents of that little book. I looked at the first page, a frontispiece showing the year and an etching, then turned to the first entry for January 1828. Before I had read a single line, a hand came down on my shoulder. 'I'm sorry,' the archivist said. 'We've just noted that this is too fragile to be viewed. It should never have been brought out.' The diary was gently folded back into its acid-free tissue paper, tied up once again in the folder and carried away. I was left alone.

What had been so close had been snatched away. Just before I left the centre, I stopped one of the staff who was passing and told her what had happened. 'Look, it's just a try,' I said, 'but do you think there's any chance that someone might be able to make digital copies of the diary and have them emailed to me in Australia?' The woman smiled kindly, she had seen a desperate researcher before. 'We're moving into our new premises in a few weeks so it might be a while before anything's organised. Write your email address for me,' she said and handed me a scrap of torn paper. Later, in the early northern darkness of a winter afternoon, I walked around shops that glittered with Christmas decorations then went back to a narrow room and ate a sandwich in front of the TV.

Four months later, an email arrived on my computer at home in Western Australia. That scrap of paper had been passed on, survived the corporate move into a new, state-of-the-art building, made it through the reorganisation of an archive containing thousands of records and ended up placed carefully on the flat-bed of a digital scanner. Copies of every page of Miss Senhouse's diary were ready to order online. They arrived almost instantly but told me nothing at all.

***

It was clear to everyone who met her that Georgiana was raised as a lady. When she arrived in Australia her manners, bearing and the words she used in conversation suggested a background of wealth, education and privilege. But Georgiana and Captain Molloy were both something of a mystery from the beginning. They arrived in style and mixed with the Governor and his friends, they had servants, valuable livestock and enough capital to acquire large land grants from the British Government, but as time passed it became obvious there was no family money or inherited wealth behind them. When hard times fell on the settlers, Georgiana went hungry alongside her neighbours, made and mended the family's clothes and worked on the farm beside her servants. If supplies were available, she bought only what was necessary for survival. When boxes arrived from her family in England, they contained basic, inexpensive items, not gifts of money.

Local people put two and two together and guessed that John Molloy, apparently a gentleman with high connections but without any fortune, was keeping a secret about his background. Georgiana herself must have helped to fill out the rumours that began to circulate: a suitable wife for a man who was an illegitimate child of royal parentage; ladylike and genteel but inexplicably poor in comparison with other women in the same social class. The rumours were wrong about Captain Molloy, and the etiquette of class distinction meant that Georgiana did not discuss the full story of her family history with the other settlers. Doing so would have explained everything.

Her mother, Elizabeth, descended from families who had been acquiring farming estates and city houses in Cumberland since the 1500s. One of her grandfathers was the apothecary James Graham of Knells, a Mayor of Carlisle in 1746 and related to the Graham baronets of Netherby. Her other grandfather, Thomas Dalton, was a wealthy Carlisle merchant who married into the Gregg family of Oulton Hall, securing even more land and incomes.

Elizabeth's father, George Dalton, owned many properties including a farming estate at High Crosby, a few kilometres outside the city, and had two stylish new houses built in Abbey Street, one of the finest areas in town. Dalton was an example of the rising upper middle classes, families who acquired capital from the business opportunities of mechanisation and the wealth it channelled into cities like Carlisle. The late eighteenth century was a time when men without titles could become powerful and influential if they invested profits back into property and married into other up-and-coming families. George Dalton was the son of a 'grocer' and went to the local grammar school, but he inherited from his great-grandfather at a young age and when he married Margaret, 'the amiable Peggy Graham', he was ensuring a very comfortable future for any children they might have.[7] He became a prominent businessman, deputy lieutenant for the whole region, a captain in the local militia, Keeper of the King's Peace for Cumberland and Mayor of Carlisle twice.[8]

In 1771 he was the founding master of a new Masonic lodge that met at the Blue Bell Inn in Scotch Street, a ten-minute walk from his

George Dalton's 1771 application to be master of a new Masonic lodge in Carlisle.

Library and Museum of Freemasonry GBR 1991 HC 1/G/4

home along the old city walls.[9] He had aspirations too, and created a family crest for his bookplates by adapting the Dalton arms and replacing the family motto with a new one, *'Amor, honor et justitia'* (love, honour and justice) a phrase used by the brotherhood of Freemasons.

Elizabeth Dalton's background meant that she inherited a large collection of assets from both sides of the family, including farming estates, shops and a public house. She was an heiress with very high expectations for her own lifestyle and she had to think carefully about who would share her fortune through marriage.

Her father died when she was three and his cousin John Mitchinson became her guardian; Mitchinson was a wealthy conveyancer, influential in the city and, like her father, a collector of rare books.[10] He was also a Quaker and he held parental responsibility to Georgiana's mother for twenty years. The large Quaker community in Carlisle was not the only influence on Elizabeth's young life. She had close social links with the writers who spearheaded the Romantic Movement in Britain, including Robert Southey, William Wordsworth and Samuel Taylor Coleridge.

Georgiana's father was David Kennedy, heir to the Craig and Millenerdale estate, in Ayrshire, Scotland. It was little more than a collection of farms and villages, including Colmonell in the valley of the River Stinchar but the Laird was powerful because his many tenants relied on his favour for their homes and incomes. Tiny rural communities did not produce riches for their landlord. The Kennedys were landed gentry but not nobility and over several generations their capital had dwindled. Compared with Elizabeth's family in Carlisle, they were a family going in the opposite direction on the success ladder. David Kennedy was the eldest son in a family of eleven children. He grew up in Balhamy farmhouse by the river believing that one day everything he saw around him would be his. He was wrong.

In 1793, France declared war on Britain and a military force of 'defencible' regiments meant battle-ready troops could be deployed quickly if there was an invasion.[11] Two months after Kennedy's seventeenth birthday he bought a commission into the Princess Royal's regiment of the 'fencible' cavalry, serving under Colonel Andrew McDouall.[12] Their fathers were friends and neighbours, so it was a secure step onto the military ladder, but by the time Kennedy married Elizabeth, the same defence troops who proudly wore the traditional highland kilt as their uniform were being disbanded. Britain needed to build up a full military force ready to face the increasing threat of Napoleon Bonaparte, so Kennedy's regiment was closed down in 1799 and he went home to his father's farm. By the following summer he was in love with Elizabeth Dalton and wrote her a poem called 'The Adieu'. He described her as 'formed with every grace of person and of mind' and told her his heart was 'in chains confin'd'.[13]

On 31 August 1800, Elizabeth Dalton married her well-connected young Scot in Carlisle cathedral expecting to become lady of Craig eventually and, a few weeks later, France surrendered the island of Malta to the British, sowing the first seeds of the Napoleonic War. Further south, Colonel Coote-Manningham was gathering an experimental corps of marksmen to be trained in a very different approach to warfare. The first 'chosen men' were volunteers from the old fencible regiments and, as the 95th Regiment of Foot, they would soon become legendary heroes of the Napoleonic War, dressed in their striking dark green uniforms with black facings. They were the sharp-shooting men of the Rifle Brigade.

For the first six years of their marriage, Captain and Mrs Kennedy lived in the Dalton family home in Abbey Street with Elizabeth's widowed mother on the site of what is now number five. It was a street of affluence then and little has changed today; the street is still surfaced with square, grey stone sets and bears the unmistakable features of urban Georgian architecture.

Carlisle's position made it a powerful centre for trade and industry, revealed by the pattern of roads that all seem to lead towards the marketplace. In 1800, the manufacture of cotton cambric was turning the place into a boom town, and the value of land and buildings that would be Mrs Kennedy's inheritance was soaring. David Kennedy became a captain in the Carlisle militia, commander of the 1st Company of the Loyal Carlisle Volunteers, and immersed himself in his new role, one of influence and respect that came to him with marriage into a family such as the Daltons. The couple's first child, Elizabeth Margaret (Eliza), was born in 1801 and another girl, Mary, arrived in 1803 but lived for only a day. Georgiana arrived two years later and on 24 June she was baptised, as her sisters had been, in the lofty magnificence of the cathedral, which performed the role of parish church for St Mary's, where the family lived.[14]

The Dalton 'mansion house' was just one part of the layering of Carlisle's long history. The house was built on the site of a Roman fort constructed around 80CE and stood opposite a medieval gateway in the city's western walls. With a street frontage of thirty-six metres, three floors above street level and symmetrical rows of five windows across the front façade, it was an impressive brick-built home, double-fronted with steps to a central door, and a cellar. The family owned a large plot including a small house next door and extending about forty-two metres around the corner into Annetwell Street, so that even in the centre of a busy town there was plenty of room for a coach-house, stables and outbuildings.[15] Behind the house was the first garden in Georgiana's life.

She was a town child for two years but already knew what it was to have space around her at a time when it was not unusual for a whole family to live in one room. Apart from the servants' area and kitchens, the house had ten bedrooms, a dining room, drawing room and two dressing rooms. There was also the library that housed her grandfather's collection of expensive books. The landscape on the other side of the street was empty, wide and wild. In spring, the steep vista down across the valley of the River Caldew and out towards the Solway Firth can still bring a rush of upward-scooped air that smells of moss, or tastes of salt, or promises snow.

The bridegroom David Kennedy had moved into his mother-in-law's home and although it was still a symbol of George Dalton's wealth and influence in the town, it was not enough. Kennedy's expectations of becoming a well-regarded, powerful landowner were frustrated after leaving the army and there was still no income from Scotland. He wanted a home of his own that matched his status as heir to the Craig and his wife's position in Carlisle's wealthy elite. Through his marriage he acquired buildings, land and farms at Brunstock, Jerristown, Bassenthwaite and Oulton Hall, a total of 400 acres of rentable property with additional income, but of most interest to him was the land he now owned at High Crosby in the village of Crosby-on-Eden.[16] Margaret Dalton had always intended it to be a legacy for her daughter and it was the perfect site for a country house. He did not waste any time. In 1802 he employed local 'joiners and cabinet makers' John Graham and William Nicholson to demolish the old farm buildings and build new ones, with instructions for them to give William Johnston, the tenant, time to move out before they began knocking down the old house and barn. The new 'offices' for the estate were the outbuildings and services he would need to run an impressive, efficient farm: a cottage, barn, stable, byre, granary, coal house, calf house, cart house, sheds and a yard.

In 1806, the Kennedys moved from Abbey Street to live on William Troutbeck's estate at Ennim Bank (also known as Ennom Bank) and Mary Gertrude Kennedy was born there on 9 September 1806, a little sister for Eliza and Georgiana. Troutbeck's son, George, was six years old, a perfect matrimonial match for Georgiana in the future, something that both of them would realise before too many years had passed.

Kennedy enjoyed the life of a country landowner at Ennim, buying and selling rams and discussing the price of horses. He decided to push ahead and complete the grand plan to move his family into a new home at Crosby, so he commissioned the specification for his country house from Nicholson and Graham with Paul Nixson, a successful local surveyor and stonemason, as the architect. The contract was signed on 21 January 1807 with an agreed total price of £1100 and a promised finish date of November the same year. In February 1808, ceilings were being plastered and on 25 April, Kennedy paid £1134 as the final account.[17]

He paid each instalment on time but his collection of receipts closely matches the amounts in his mortgage notes and bonds. At the age of thirty he had not yet inherited the Craig and the fortune in capital assets his wife could expect was already dwindling. Her mother had sold off properties in 1801, giving notice to thirty-nine tenants. As David Kennedy was raising the specification on his house and increasing the bill, he was borrowing month by month to pay the builders and then the local craftsmen who fitted out the house.[18] Everything was of the highest quality. Ironworks such as cranks for the servant bells were bought from local foundries but all the internal fittings were handmade on site by carpenters, including chairs, a linen press in the nursery, and library shelving. In July 1808 the family moved into Crosby Lodge, 'a place of his own making & loved seat'.[19]

The home Georgiana knew as 'Crosby' was small in comparison with the country homes of the nobility but it was modern, well-proportioned and elegant enough to impress. Kennedy had a shelf-lined library of books, including rare volumes. Stairs from the wine cellar led up to the butler's pantry with direct access to the dining room. In keeping with fashion, the house was built on a high point to make the most of the views across its gardens to the landscape beyond. Three main reception rooms along the front, each with full-length windows, gave family and guests a panorama of gently rolling fields, low hills and a sweeping informal lawn enhanced by the elegant curve of the drive. Visitors had a full view of the building's stylish design as they approached. Just as importantly, they could be seen clearly from the drawing room, allowing the ladies time to prepare themselves for receiving guests.

The children's new playground on the banks of the River Eden must have seemed as heavenly as its name implied: a garden and a time of innocence. There were cornflowers and poppies on the slope between the house and the river in summer and when thick autumn mist came down over the hedges there were blackberries to be picked. The first winter at Crosby brought silver sheets of sharp hoarfrost then heavy snow for days, isolating the village completely from the outside world.[20] Most wonderful were the wildflowers of spring, some so small that the children had to hunt for them in shady places under trees or muddy overhangs along the riverbank. However cruel the winters, Cumberland bloomed again every year and the view of meadows from the nursery window became a wide green quilt, brightly embroidered with ribbons of colour.

The natural setting was picturesque but lacked order, so it needed landscaping to be fashionable. Kennedy spent large sums of money importing thousands of trees, including unusual specimens and a wide range of imposing firs. Then he paid to have the land prepared and the trees planted. Crosby Lodge was the place where Georgiana's early horticultural skills were nurtured, and it was her father she learned from. Kennedy worked outside with his daughters, and together they planted the ancestors of crocuses and daffodils that still appear in spring on a steep, grassy bank along the lane.[21]

In November 1808 he completed the second plantation, a broad border of trees along the Carlisle road with a meandering pathway through its centre; a walking route for the family between the house and the village church. Kennedy marked the occasion with a 'memorandum' among his papers: 'Be it remembered'. His note contains the earliest evidence that connects Georgiana with anything botanical. Family and friends ceremonially planted a tree each and three-year-old Georgiana somehow managed to plant a Balm of Gilead, its fragrant leaves said to have medicinal properties.[22]

The original simple shape of the house has changed a lot in two centuries with extensions added on both ends and ornamental roof castellation. In 1809 an old survey of the land was out of date, with the new outline of Crosby Lodge added in pencil, so Kennedy proudly commissioned a new one. A contemporary watercolour painted as part of his 1810 survey by Nicholson and Reid shows the house as it was when Georgiana lived there and the original route of the drive curving up from the road, still visible today as a shadowy line when the meadow is dry.[23] The painting shows a couple walking arm in arm. She wears a bonnet in the 'cottage' fashion and carries a parasol. He wears a hat and a tailcoat, with breeches and white stockings in the old style, as Kennedy did.[24] Ahead of them, a smart carriage approaches the house. Georgiana's parents had just taken delivery of an expensive new carriage from London.[25] David and Elizabeth Kennedy are walking up the drive to their new home.

Kennedy's marriage made him a landowner. As deputy lieutenant of the county his days were always full. It was a short ride on horseback into the city, through the village of Stanwix and across the old stone bridge over the River Eden, entering through the Rickergate. For a few years family life was privileged and comfortable but wealth did not protect them from sadness. David Dalton Kennedy (known as Dalton or Doe) was the first child born at Crosby Lodge, on 31 July 1808, and in 1811 when Georgiana was six another little sister, Jane, was born but she lived only ten weeks. In 1814 there was another death at Crosby and another family journey to the Dalton vault at the cathedral, to bury Georgiana's grandmother. As an only child, Mrs Kennedy inherited all the family property in Carlisle and the country estates, and her husband added them to his property portfolio.

George Kennedy was born on 5 May 1813 and always thought that one day Crosby would be his because Dalton, as the eldest, would become Laird of Craig. As young boys, George and Dalton had a role in life: to become well educated and honourable. They learned Latin and Greek and the formal conventions of public speaking because they were destined for a military career, the law or the church. Their sisters' priorities were social etiquette and charm. With servants to do all the household work, ladies chose how to spend their time. Mothers busied themselves preparing their daughters for a suitable marriage and girls were grateful for the social opportunities their parents allowed them at garden parties, musical evenings or house visits. Mrs Kennedy's advice to her own daughters was clear from the beginning: they should marry an older, 'steady, sober, religious man' and one with money because 'when poverty comes in the door love flies out the window'.[26] In the nineteenth century, girls like the Kennedy sisters spent long days at home acquiring wifely skills: sewing, singing, dancing, playing the piano, speaking French and the newly fashionable language of travel and literature, Italian. In our world of instant communication it's hard to appreciate the importance of letters, particularly for women with wealth and status. Their lives were cushioned from hardship but most had no profession to take them outside the home. Personal letter books were kept as drafts of every message; notes were sometimes exchanged more than once a day and Carlisle post office was open from 9am until 9pm. It was not unusual to send a letter by hand and receive a reply by return, delivered by a servant.

Young women gossiped with their friends through a network of notes they called *billets*. They shared a cumulative knowledge about the ways men and women behaved in one another's company because, in an age of obsession with propriety, girls trod a dangerous pathway when a potential husband came into their sights. They should appear dutiful and innocent but, to catch a fiancé in the face of competition, a sharp intellect and some subtle flirting were also required. Too much piety and a girl might be seen as boring, losing her suitor to someone more entertaining. But a lady too free with her talents might not only damage her marriage prospects permanently but also shame her family. Before long Georgiana realised that those close to her found it harder than she did to maintain this balance.

There's no doubt that 'Miss Georgy' achieved all the social graces she needed.[27] Friends described her as 'enchanting' and 'charming' and a neighbour in Australia later wrote of her as 'a remarkably <u>fine</u> woman of the magnifique class.'[28,29] The possibility of marriage into a title was every mother's dream for a daughter. The names that appeared in the Crosby social calendar were all-important: who acknowledged you in public, who invited you to their home, who asked you to dance. Georgiana's friends were among the 'principle inhabitants' of Carlisle, but she was never quite part of the highest circle of lords and ladies, viscounts, baronets and dukes.[30] Mrs Kennedy knew the art of name-dropping and social climbing and made sure her family mixed with the right people. Henry Birkett and his wife, Frances, lived at Etterby Lodge, not far from town. They were old friends of the Kennedys and Georgiana never forgot her childhood attachment to them. The Birketts were well connected. In 1795, their daughter, Frances, married Sir James Robert Grant, who became Inspector General of Army Hospitals and served in every campaign of the Peninsular War; just the kind of hero a girl might have dreamed of for a husband when 'Burky' told stories about Grant's adventures at Waterloo, the battle people said had changed the world.

The connections in Georgiana's life at Crosby went far beyond house calls. Her growing interest in the natural world was an effortless extension of religious belief and love of landscape. With its dramatic extremes of physical beauty, the Lake District was the geographical centre for new 'Romantic' ideas in art, literature and music, pioneered by the Lake Poets, among them Wordsworth and Coleridge. A wide circle of writers flowed in and out of the area, connected by an intricate web of social and literary strands as well as marriages and romantic affairs. Wordsworth's wife, Mary, was a niece of Robert Southey, a future Poet Laureate. Coleridge, already married, fell in love with Mary's sister, Sara Hutchinson, and she moved in with the Wordsworths, where he often stayed. Mrs Kennedy was a friend of Southey and his wife, Edith, whose sister, another Sara, was Coleridge's wife. The Coleridge and Wordsworth families stayed at a Cumberland farm belonging to the Calverts and some of the most well-known poems in English were written there. William Calvert was a close childhood friend of Wordsworth and left him the legacy that financed the poet's early career. Mary Calvert was a daughter of John Mitchinson, Mrs Kennedy's guardian.

She was almost the same age as Mrs Kennedy and shared the same group of friends so it is unsurprising to find Mrs Kennedy featuring in their gossip. Sara Hutchinson reported to a friend something she had heard about Dr Bell, a well-known Carlisle figure: 'I must tell you that Mrs Calvert says that the dear Doctor actually offered himself to Mrs Kennedy – she being an heiress – Mary had forgot the Lady's name but it must have been Miss D. from the time, her being an heiress, having a mother, and being a ward of old Mitchinson of Carlisle.'[31]

The influences around Georgiana resonated with her young mind. The new wave of thinking matched her grandfather's humanitarian values and the simple, secular pillars of Freemasonry. By the time she was at school, early criticism of the Romantic writers had turned into praise and fame. Their poems described a spiritual source of renewal through the beauty of mountains, lakes, trees and plants. What she read acknowledged the emotional response she felt, and feared, in the face of her God's creations. William Wordsworth's views about his connections with nature, described in his 1798 poem 'Tintern Abbey', echoed her own so closely.

> And I have felt
> A presence that disturbs me with the joy
> Of elevated thoughts; a sense sublime
> Of something far more deeply interfused,
> Whose dwelling is the light of setting suns,
> And the round ocean and the living air,
> And the blue sky, and in the mind of man;
> A motion and a spirit, that impels
> All thinking things, all objects of all thought,

> And rolls through all things. Therefore am I still
> A lover of the meadows and the woods,
> And mountains; and of all that we behold
> From this green earth; of all the mighty world
> Of eye and ear, both what they half create,
> And what perceive; well pleased to recognize
> In nature and the language of the sense,
> The anchor of my purest thoughts, the nurse,
> The guide, the guardian of my heart, and soul
> Of all my moral being.[32]

Maintaining the practices of Christianity was an expectation as well as a comfort at a time when so many children died before their third birthday and cholera was endemic. The average life expectancy for those who survived childhood was about fifty years for the most privileged and for the poor it was around twenty. The Kennedys regularly attended the village church at the end of their drive; as concerned as others with safeguarding their souls, that did not stop them from enjoying life and it certainly did not mean that they drank no alcohol.

Any evidence that Georgiana's father was a Freemason has disappeared along with missing Lodge records but her grandfather's household ran on Masonic fraternal principles, which hold that all people are equal regardless of religion or ancestry. The movement originated in Scotland, near David Kennedy's birthplace, and was an important feature of commerce and social life for businessmen and their families. His Ayrshire countryman, the poet Robert Burns, was an influential Freemason and the words of his most famous poem ('Auld Lang Syne') strongly reflect the concept of brotherhood. Whether or not they derived from Freemasonry, Georgiana admired the principles she saw reflected in her father's behaviour towards his children and his wife. They were reasons enough for her to adore him.

Her personal writing echoes not only the cornerstones of Freemasonry but also reveals a bold simplicity in her relationship with

Christianity that closely matches the Quaker values held by so many in Carlisle in the nineteenth century, including Mitchinson, her mother's guardian. Along with others in the family, both male and female, Mitchinson was a supporter and financer of the movement to abolish the slave trade. The 'Religious Society of Friends' follows a way of life rather than a set of beliefs. The principles that underpin Quaker life read much like the reasoning behind Georgiana's own ideas:

- Individuals find God within themselves by waiting silently and do not need a minister to receive spiritual guidance.
- The 'Peace Testimony' resolves conflicts without violence; God is part of everyone so all human life is sacred.
- God gave equality to human beings regardless of race, gender, faith, or social status so respect is due to all.
- Life should be unpretentious and truthful. Quakers live and dress simply, and use plain speech.

Lines from Georgiana's writing exemplify these Quaker testimonies of truth, peace, equality and simplicity. The deeply held views she expressed so eloquently in her Australian letters and journals reveal the range of influences on her young life. She was a devout Christian but she was also a widely informed, independent thinker and understood that there were many ways to know God.

Georgiana's time in her valley of Eden was coming to an end. In 1819, all was not well at Crosby. Her mother was described as an heiress but two generations later her family found no evidence of any fortune.[33] Yet in the Cumbrian archives the ancient documents she kept safe, written in Latin on vellum scrolls and weighted with heavy wax seals, record the vast wealth in property her parents inherited and acquired. Land deeds for Crosby and other Cumberland estates date from 1597 and documents of rental, accounts and farm plans from 1694.

David Kennedy was accumulating debts that would soon create complications for his wife and cast a shadow of social embarrassment over the next generation. Ten years earlier, he had borrowed £500 from his commanding officer, Andrew McDouall, and still had not paid off the ever-increasing account despite the colonel's regular written requests.[34] It was a large amount and was one of many loans. His mother-in-law had sold off houses and businesses before she died, thereby reducing the rental income his wife inherited but Kennedy did not stop spending. On 21 January 1819 he arranged three new mortgages that allowed him to borrow a total of £1100.

On a summer evening in June that year, he was riding home from a Yeomanry dinner where he had spent the evening with other landowners.[35] Not far from Crosby Lodge he fell from his horse and was brought home unconscious. Mrs Kennedy sent for Georgiana, who took her father's hand and asked him to squeeze her own if he could hear her, but there was no response. Ten days later, soon after dawn on 30 June, Elizabeth Kennedy became a widow.[36] Her youngest child, George, was six years old.

Georgiana's 'dearest Papa' was buried in the graveyard at St John's church, a few steps from the end of his own drive, with the grave facing towards Crosby Lodge.[37] Georgiana had just turned fourteen and his death left an empty space around her that was not filled for ten years.

John Molloy, London boy

Not long after David Kennedy's death, Georgiana met the man she would marry. Captain John Molloy was the reason why she sailed to a distant colonial encampment with just a few weeks' notice and why she stayed in Australia when the plan was to return home after a period of financial success. His influence on her was significant, but historically he has been a shadowy figure beside his wife the botanist. John Molloy's personal history and the circumstances of their meeting have remained a mystery. Rumours of a secret regal bloodline in his family seem compelling and have endured, but evidence to support the stories has yet to be provided. When new facts from primary sources are aligned, a less mysterious but equally enthralling personal history comes into view for the first time.

John Molloy and Georgiana Kennedy could not have experienced more different childhoods. Born into a community where poverty had extreme effects on families, Molloy was lucky to survive. In the three weeks after his birth, a third of the people buried in England were less than two years old. Before he met Georgiana he had been shipwrecked, fought in sea battles and captured pirates. By the time they married, he had spent twenty-seven years on active military service, twenty of them in the most dangerous brigade in the British army, and seven of those fighting Napoleon Bonaparte's forces in the Peninsular War. He had been wounded twice and, unlike thousands of others, survived the carnage that was the Battle of Waterloo.

John Molloy was born on 5 September 1786 and baptised in St Martin-in-the-Fields, London, on 8 October, the same church where his parents, William Molloy and Mary Conner had married on 30 January that year.[38,39] It was, and still is, the parish church of Buckingham Palace, and the area in front of the building marked the junction of the main routes through the fast-growing city of London. On the Sunday of John's baptism there was 'vast rain' as the bells of St Martin's rang out over a crowded public walkway next to the royal stables.[40] As they walked down the wide steps of the church with their baby son, the Molloys could not have guessed that within his lifetime the whole area in front of them would be demolished to become Trafalgar Square, the most iconic public gathering place in London, commemorating Lord Nelson's victory over Napoleon Bonaparte's navy at the Battle of Trafalgar. Nor could they have known that at

In 1786, John Molloy was baptised in this seventeenth-century font in St-Martin-in-the-Fields. An example of fine Renaissance marble work, it was made in 1689.

seventeen their boy would be serving in the King's Royal Navy, sailing to support Nelson's flagship as the British fleet prepared for that very battle.

Molloy's early life has been a mystery for more than 150 years. There are several different theories about a possible link to the royal line of Hanover and speculation about a perceived facial likeness to the Duke of York. The birth of illegitimate children to members of the royal family was not uncommon, and usual practice was to place such babies with families whose discretion could be relied upon given the benefits that came with the arrangement. There are claims that Molloy never knew his mother or father, that he received an anonymous annual payment while studying at Oxford University, that he was given a £20,000 cheque on his twenty-first birthday to purchase a commission into the navy and that a commission into the army was purchased anonymously for him at the outbreak of the Peninsular War.[41] When Molloy arrived in Western Australia he never discussed his childhood and gave nothing away about the years before he joined the army. As stories about his parentage circulated, he offered no alternative details, giving strength to rumours that he had secrets to keep about the true nature of his roots. The story of his ancestry is very different.

His father's family were from County Kildare and Kings County (Offaly) in Ireland, an extended lineage that included landowners, merchants, farmers and tradespeople. William Molloy fell out with Catholic members of his family over religion and moved to London, and although there was trouble ahead between Catholics and Protestants on the streets of the city, his relocation proved to be a good decision. By 1788 he had moved from St Martin to a substantial building on St Giles High Street that included a 'dwelling house', a shoe shop and a warehouse with access onto a delivery yard.[42] He owned other properties too, in the Seven Dials area between St Martin and St Giles.[43] Although he was a very successful businessman, his work was considered to be a lowly trade and not a profession.[44] John Molloy never felt able to discuss openly the details of his parents' lives, even with his own children. Questioned by one of his daughters in his old age, he told her: 'My dear, the circus of our family affair & its decadence I am unwilling to record. There are circumstances connected with it which can only be communicated personally – In position we had nothing to boast of. Religion & other matters were unpleasantly connected with it – and I am now the head of the family.'[45]

More than once John Molloy recorded his place of birth as Harrow, a nearby parish to St Giles and in the same county but more prestigious. It is plausible that his mother, Mary Conner, was in Harrow when he was born and was home again in St Martin's parish, a few kilometres away, four weeks later for John's baptism. It's also possible that her son later gently shifted the exact geography of his birthplace to a more affluent area of the same county. His sister Susannah was born in 1789 at the family home, number sixteen, St Giles High Street[46] next door to the White Lion tavern and directly opposite the church where she was baptised on 10 June.

All day the cries of traders and beggars mingled with the noise of wooden carriage wheels and the streets were crowded. The Molloys' other neighbours were a dealer in rags and iron, a tobacconist, a timber merchant, a whip maker and an undertaker. Just around the corner were the cheesemonger, harness maker, stable keeper and several more taverns.[47] Records show that the business thrived for twenty years and William's family were much better off than the workers they employed to make shoes or the children's Irish nursemaid. In 1801 William sold seventy-two pairs of shoes to the same customer within two months.[48] The maze of alleys that backed onto the shop was a refuge for thieves; shoes were very valuable items and worth stealing. In 1801, a man tried to make a large purchase from the shop using forged money, one of many crimes the Molloys experienced.[49] Transcripts of court proceedings where William described cases of theft from his shop are the eighteenth-century equivalent of an audio recording. When his statements over several years are read aloud, the nuances of an Irish accent become almost audible.

The cases tried at the Old Bailey fill in details about the life of young John. The house was lit by candlelight and the family ate their evening meal between six and seven. The shoes, as now, were stored in boxes and the shop had a window to display its goods. Transcripts of trials help to verify John Molloy's age and show that he was living at home in April 1800. As a key witness in one case, William described how a waistcoat belonging to his son 'about fourteen years of age' was stolen. One particular transcript, from a trial held in 1799, describes what may have been the first time that twelve-year-old John Molloy, a future Rifleman, held a gun.

> WILLIAM MOLLOY sworn. – I am a shoemaker, No. 16, High-street, St. Giles's, facing the church: On the fifth of this month, I think, Tuesday, about seven o'clock, I was backwards at tea, and thought I heard something like glass crack: I sent my little boy into the shop, and he said, there was nothing the matter; I told my boy to go and fetch a small gun that I had, and then two men ran away; I followed them, and caught the prisoner at the bar in Compton-street, about one hundred yards from my house, the other got away; ... I said, you have been breaking my shop; you lie, you rascal, says he, I have not; there was a gentleman got hold of him, who brought him back to my shop; ... he begged leave to sit down, and dropped a shoe on each side of him, and I took out of his pocket two odd slippers, and a pair of boy's shoes; I knew them all to be my shoes, from the cutting out of them, and from the workmen that made them.[50,51]

The starkness of contrasts in John's life was extreme during that first decade of the nineteenth century. He lived on the margin of two very different worlds. High Street was the centre of St Giles's parish but it also marked the line where sweet-smelling, up-market Bloomsbury and the damp, squalid slums of Holborn converged. It was the boundary where a notorious triangle of poverty known as the Rookery 'fades into the cleanness of the more civilised districts in its vicinity, by insensible degrees, like the hues of the rainbow'.[52] A densely populated warren of lanes and courtyards, the Rookery was the centre of the Irish community, where the poorest immigrants in London scraped a living on the streets or provided cheap labour for the businesses that surrounded them.

> Whoever ventures here finds the streets (by courtesy so called) thronged with loiterers, and sees through the half-glazed windows the rooms crowded to suffocation. The stagnant gutters in the middle of the lanes, the accumulated piles of garbage, the pools accumulated in the hollows of the disjointed pavement, the filth choking up the dark passages which open like rat-holes upon the highway – all these, with their indescribable sights and smells, leave scarcely so dispiriting an impression on the passenger as the condition of the houses.[53]

Contemporary descriptions convey the unrelenting noise and overwhelming, foul smell of city life: rotting vegetables, fish, horse manure, tobacco and sweat. Abandoned children took to crime. Men and women drowned their sorrows in gin, which could be bought even on a Sunday morning before the church service began: 'Every house in St. Giles's, whatever else they sold, sold gin; every chandler's shop sold gin.' For William Molloy's up-market customers, the crime they experienced in St Giles was linked with poverty and poverty was connected with the Irish community. It was a place that anyone who managed to escape would not want to remember. John was born in London in a time when nationality came from parentage. He grew up on a social frontier between English and immigrant, success and failure. His life could have taken either path depending on the choices he made when childhood ended but, faced with the cruel inequalities of eighteenth-century Britain, it was unlikely he would ever be considered a gentleman.

A friend who knew John Molloy well for many years told his daughter, 'He would never talk about his father.'[54] As the complete story of his early life takes shape, it's easier to understand why he chose to remain silent even in the sparsely populated southwest of Western Australia. To broadcast the fact that the most senior government representative of the region was the son of an Irish immigrant shoemaker would have risked the status of his wife and children in the hierarchical climate of the new colony. Nineteenth-century communities were parochial and biased; a majority still believed that being a gentleman or not was a matter of good breeding rather than character or behaviour. Molloy had earned everything he had achieved; to reveal his humble ancestry openly in order to dispel rumours that deemed him part royal would have been social madness. He simply kept quiet.

* * *

The truth about Molloy's childhood and youth have remained a mystery since the day he walked away from St Giles and began another life. The evidence was just waiting to be found, but the search itself has taught me important lessons about the pitfalls of historical research. As I waded through hundreds of hits from internet searches, stories about secret royal ancestry were recirculating the same information again and again and being requoted in academic papers and on genealogy websites. The number of references to a royal illegitimate birth seemed to lend credibility to apparent facts, but when cross-referenced, most derive from the same limited sources, themselves either anecdotal or circumstantial. With several different theories circulating about Molloy's year of birth, it has been difficult even for family members to know exactly how old he was at any point. An admittance entry for a 'Molloy. Jn.' to Harrow School in 1802 provided a starting point for descendants to piece his story together, but it turned out to be a false lead that had been blocking the way forward all along.

Patrick Richardson-Bunbury, a great-great-grandson of John and Georgiana Molloy, has transcribed many letters and diaries over the years and has often sent me packages containing copies of documents that opened doors to new research pathways. He showed me a copy of the Harrow register and a 1979 letter to him from the school archivist, confirming that John Molloy entered the school in 1802 and left in 1805. Published editions of the registers showed that this boy became a monitor, a position of responsibility in the school community, and gave speeches in Latin and Greek on Parents' Day, alongside Lord Byron.

The record of his entry to the fourth form in February 1802, aged thirteen, described his later achievements in the 95th Foot Brigade (Rifle Brigade) and the fact that he was wounded at the Battle of Waterloo. Believing that John was educated at one of the principal private schools in England added weight to theories about his highborn connections, but as alternative evidence began to grow, it was clear that something was wrong: my research made John fifteen, not thirteen, at that time.

I looked again, more carefully, at the school records and noticed that all other records only gave family names, not first names and I remembered the common practice was to label brothers as either 'Major' and 'Minor' or 'Senior' and 'Junior'. Captain Anthony James Pye Molloy, a discredited navy officer, is sometimes cited as John's real father. Pye Molloy had two sons and both of them went to Harrow School. John William Molloy was thirteen in 1802. 'Molloy Jn.' was not 'Molloy, John' but 'Molloy, Junior', the younger brother of Charles Manners Molloy. The current school archivist confirmed for me how one Molloy could be so confused with another that a reference to his life achievements could be incorrectly published. The school entrance book for that period has disappeared and the lists for 1805–29 were compiled from data in the old account books. Later, published editions of the register added extra personal details from external sources such as the *Dictionary of National Biography*, *The Gentleman's Magazine*, newspapers and university registers. Someone made the same mistake as so many others and confused two Molloys. But if John was not at Harrow School, where was he?

One day, an email arrived from Patrick Richardson-Bunbury with a short statement at the end, added almost as an afterthought: 'Inside the back cover of one of GM's diaries is a note: Ship "Hindostan", JM on board abt. 14.'

I had seen those words before at the JS Battye Library in Perth but had not thought about them again. They were written by Georgiana Bisdee, a granddaughter of the Molloys, and they led the way to the missing years of John Molloy's life and explanations for some family anecdotes. But first, I had to deal with a problem.[55]

No secondary source material brings a closer connection with the past than real things and places, and nothing compares with the magnified experience of reading words written in ink applied two hundred years ago with the cut point of a quill. Emotion becomes evident when the dull, sooty lustre reveals a writer's points of pressure and the physical flow of feelings into the words themselves, but digital resources are sometimes the only option. When the quest becomes impossible from a distance, researchers need the kindness of someone in the right place. I found the *Hindostan* and the location of records for details of her crew, but the books had not been digitised and were on the other side of the world. A friend who lived near the National Archives in Kew offered to help and in the space of a few hours Molloy's naval career was brought into the light for the first time.

With a list of archive numbers as a starting point, my friend looked for entries that matched the sketchy story I had pulled together from online catalogues. With an eight-hour time difference between us, it was the next day before I downloaded her notes. Margaret had connected John's journey from ship to ship and attached photographs of the evidence. One showed the last page in the muster book for HMS *Hindostan*. 'You will have to handle some of these books at some time,' she wrote in her email. 'My hands were black yesterday – most of the books look like they were in a fire and are burnt around the edges.' That book was indeed in a fire and John Molloy was there. I sent her the story by return email.[56]

A miniature portrait of Georgiana Molloy, painted in 1829, in London while the Molloys were preparing for the voyage to Western Australia.

John Molloy also sat for a portrait in London. Georgiana sent both their 'likenesses' to the Dunlop family in Scotland as keepsakes. This may not be the same 1829 miniature of her husband, but it was painted after 1816–17, when the Battle of Waterloo medals were issued. Molloy is wearing his medal in the portrait and wore it, on significant occasions, for the rest of his life.

H. M. O. Hale family collection

Georgiana's parents, David and Elizabeth Kennedy (née Dalton) circa 1800.

The Kennedy sisters (clockwise from top left): Elizabeth, Georgiana and Mary.

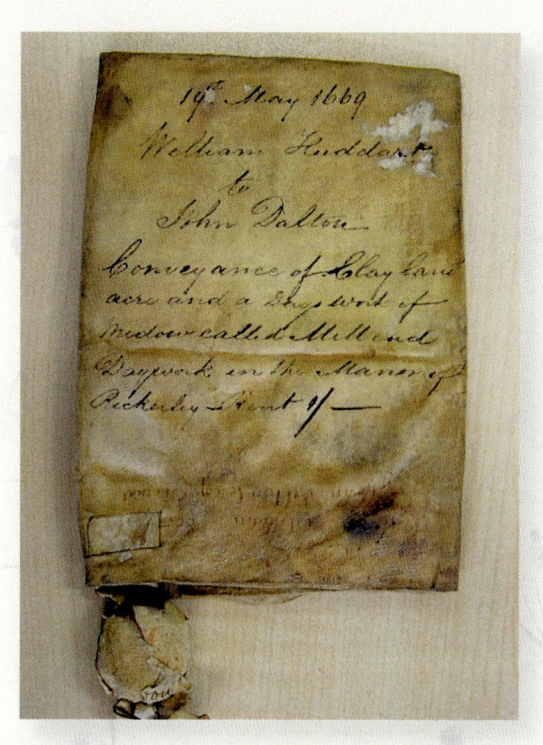

Among many documents in the family archive is this 1669 land conveyance to Georgiana's ancestor, John Dalton, written on vellum and mentioning the manor of Rickerby. The seal on its base has been lost but a faded signature 'John Dalton son of Thomas' can still be seen at the top of this photograph.

The first record of eighteen-year-old ensign John Molloy in the Oxford Militia pay book, June 1805. Ensign was the lowest ranking post for an officer so this was Molloy's first secure step on the ladder to becoming a gentleman.

Carlisle Castle in 2013. The castle, a few metres from the house where Georgiana was born, was already in ruins in 1805. It's unlikely she knew that she was a direct descendant of the man who built the first stone castle on the site in 1122, a son of King William the Conqueror.

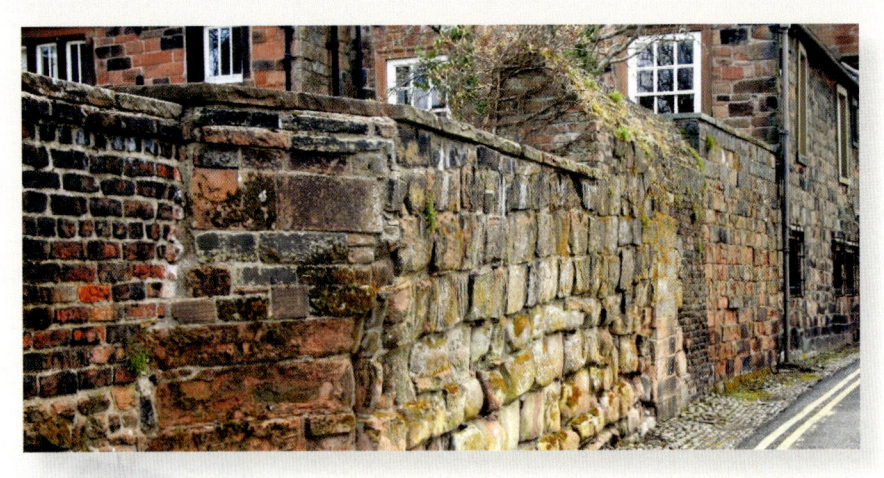

The ancient walls of the city are adjacent to the site of the Kennedy family home in Abbey Street where they provided a roadway for carts, horses and pedestrians. Made from a range of distinctive materials including Roman stonework, they reflect the passing of time.

In 1810, Georgiana's father commissioned an estate plan when the landscaping and planting was completed for his stylish country home, Crosby Lodge, Crosby-on-Eden. This small watercolour sketch shows him walking up the drive with his wife behind their expensive new carriage, recently delivered from London.

Crosby Lodge, as Georgiana knew it, was smaller and less ornate, without the roof castellation and towers shown in this photograph.

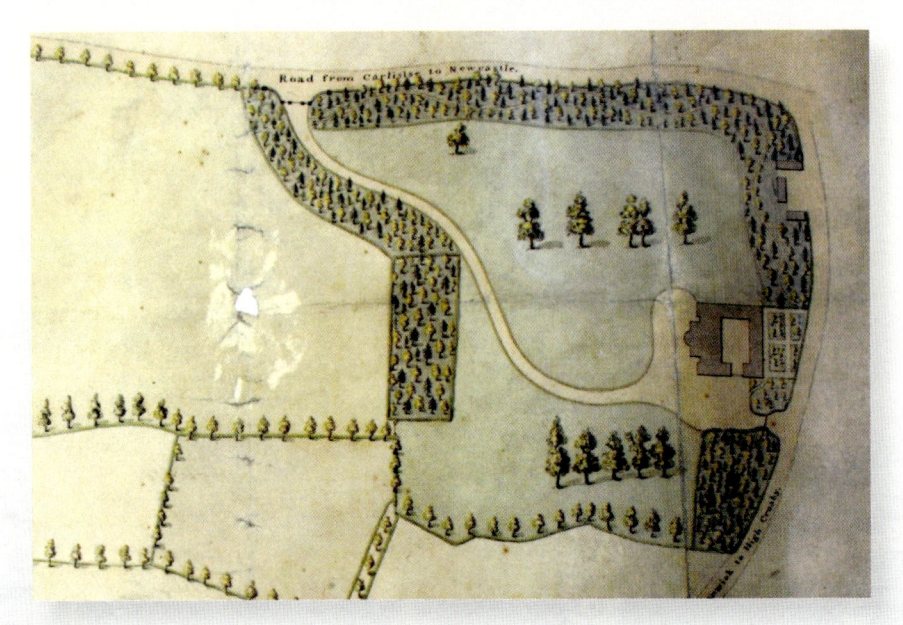

Plan of Crosby Lodge estate, circa 1810, showing the original site of the garden. The walled garden of today was not shown on the 1810 plan and was probably built later as a kitchen garden and a source of cut flowers. The small garden where John Molloy first met his future wife was at the back of the house. It was originally laid out in the same simple cross pattern as Georgiana's first garden in Augusta.

The drawing room in Crosby Lodge, 2013. The proportions and basic features of this room, including the interior wooden window shutters, have not changed since the time when John Molloy stayed there as a guest of Georgiana's mother. It was the place where the family gathered informally in the evenings and where they 'withdrew' with their guests after dinner.

In 1821, Georgiana was at a boarding school on Kensington Square in London. In front of the school was the elegant, tree-bordered garden of Kensington Square. Some of the nineteenth century trees are still standing there today, as shown in this photograph of Kensington Square in 2014.

Mrs Kennedy often wrote a short note on letters she received, a reminder of the content and the date she replied. This letter was about 'Unpleasant family circumstances' and her abbreviation 'Fr. B.' probably means that it was 'from John Besley'. He wrote to her in 1828 about an argument involving himself, Georgiana and her sister Eliza, his fiancée.

Keppoch House was a comfortable, modern country home when Georgiana went to stay there in 1828. Since then, the roof has been raised and bay windows added but the size of the house has not changed. There were also servants' cellars, stable buildings, a walled orchard and a large kitchen garden.

Georgiana often worked in this walled flower garden at Keppoch House. She went there early on the morning of her wedding day to gather flowers for the ceremony, using some to decorate the rooms. A sunken rose garden and a heated greenhouse gave protection from cold Scottish winters.

***

Two months after Molloy's fourteenth birthday the *Hindostan*, a Royal Navy store ship, sailed up the River Thames in London to be refitted for war. By January 1801 she had fifty guns and was ready to carry supplies to the British fleet at war with France. Her captain was Joshua Mulock, from Kings County in Ireland. The Irish Mulocks and Molloys were neighbours and related by marriage. When the captain was billeted in London for three months with a newly fitted ship, life dealt John Molloy a lucky card. It was his chance to take the first step up from being a shopkeeper's son.

The *Hindostan* sailed in January for the Cape of Good Hope via the west coast of Africa. Molloy is not listed as a crew member on that voyage but by March he had arrived in the Cape Verde islands, a critical harbour and navy supply point. On 5 March he signed up at St Jago as a volunteer, 'second class boy', on the eighteen-gun Royal Navy sloop HMS *Penguin*, under Captain Mansel. The ship's record shows that it was his first posting.[57]

The *Penguin*'s job was to escort supply convoys to the British navy at war in the Mediterranean Sea, to search enemy ships she encountered and seize their cargo. It was only days before Molloy's adventures began. He fell seriously ill with a fever 'off the African coast'.[58] Left alone on deck at night without medical care, and 'waves washing over him', he nearly died of 'neglect' and his light hair turned dark.[59,60]

In April the crew boarded a Portuguese schooner carrying slaves to the West Indies then, after running aground in gales, they arrived safely back in Simons Bay, Cape Town, on 5 August. John sailed with the *Penguin* for a year and transferred to HMS *Rattlesnake*. Sailors often followed their captain when he moved ship and Molloy transferred with Captain LeGros to his next posting in August 1802, at the Cape of Good Hope.[61,62] He was back on the familiar deck of the *Hindostan* but not, this time, as a lowly volunteer. John Molloy was given the important role of ship's clerk. He was moving up.

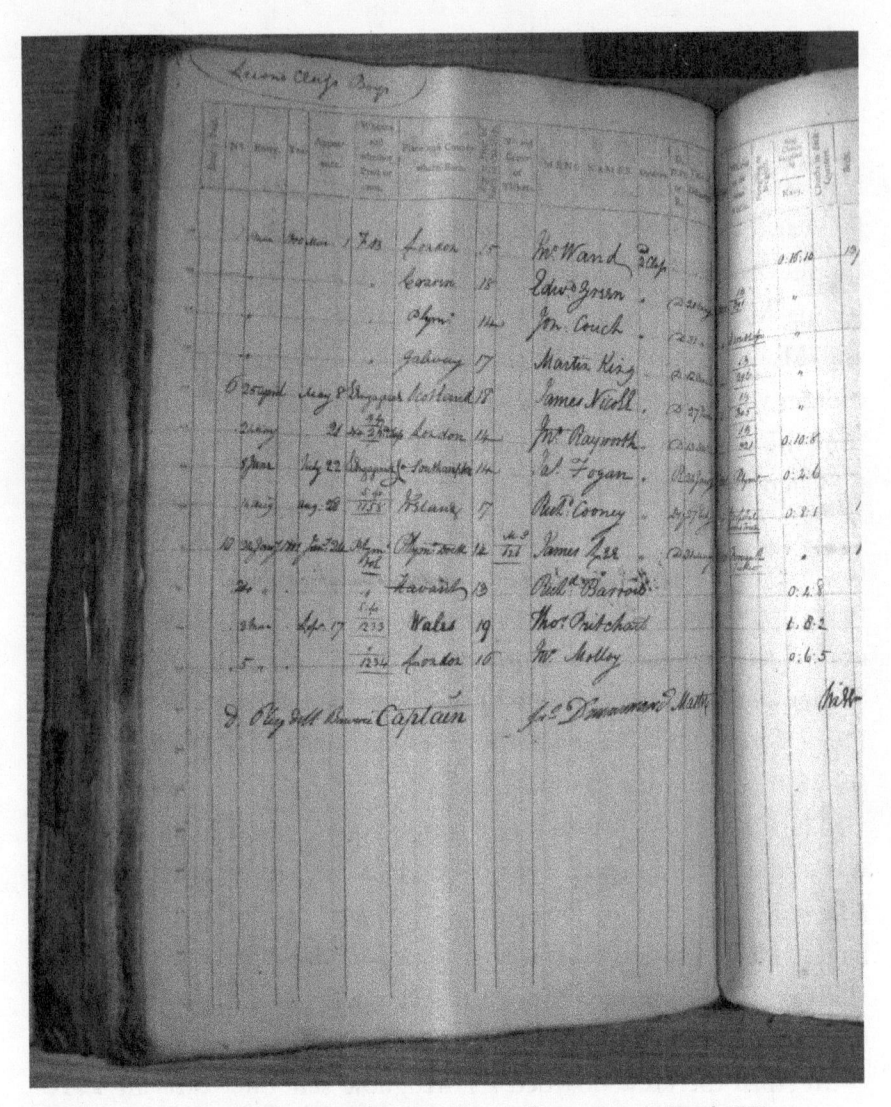

Admiralty records for HMS *Penguin*. John Molloy's name first appears in March 1801 on an unlabelled page after 'Third class boys' but, by the August muster, he has moved up to 'Second class boys', his age recorded as sixteen, born in London.

Crown copyright. National Archives ADM 36/15145

In May 1803, after a short interval of peace, Britain declared war on France once again and navy life was eventful even for a clerk, with prisoners and ladies often on board alongside the crew.[63] But things were about to take a more dramatic turn. In early 1804, the government sent the 1100 ton ship to the Mediterranean, fully laden with supplies for Lord Nelson, then commander-in-chief of the fleet. Among the 259 people travelling on board were civilian passengers including a foreign diplomat, women and children. LeGros had more than just his men to manage on the day that was to be his last as commander of the *Hindostan*.

Early on the morning of 2 April, near Cape St Sebastian, thick smoke began pouring from two of the main hatches. A cargo of hemp rope urgently needed for rigging on Nelson's warships had overheated in the damp conditions in the hold and ignited; the noxious smoke prevented the crew from removing it. LeGros ordered the marines to shoot any man who tried to escape before the passengers were safe. After seven hours of firefighting, he attached weights to his dispatches and threw them overboard in case they fell into enemy hands. With the magazines below still loaded with ammunition, the

Fire damaged pages of the HMS *Hindostan* Pay Book 1799–1804

Crown copyright. National Archives ADM 35 / 787

main mast alight and fire all around him on deck, Captain LeGros gave orders to launch the boats and jumped into the last raft moments before the ship exploded. He was clutching the ship's record books and 200 years later they are still blackened by smoke.

In the ensuing chaos, the men were left to rely on the kindness of local people and family accounts say that Molloy spent some time at nearby Gibraltar.[64] When the sailors mustered again there was a court martial, required automatically when a ship was lost, but Captain LeGros and his crew were cleared of any dereliction of duty and Admiral Nelson himself commented on their bravery: 'The preservation of the crew seems little short of a miracle. I never read such a journal of exertions in my whole life.'[65]

Molloy, like everyone else, was officially discharged on 9 April 1804. Urgently needing another posting, he joined the crew of HMS *Royal William* the next day but not as a clerk. He was listed as AB, an 'able seaman', indicating his experience. During the next few weeks he spent short periods on other ships but it was not long before the job he had been looking for turned up. On 31 July he joined the crew of HMS *Glory*, recorded as 'born in London', and listed as an able seaman and a clerk. He was back in the role that he knew so well, but things were about to change once again. At home in St Giles, John's father knew it was time to write his will. It was signed on 19 November.

John was discharged from HMS *Glory* on 8 November, at Portsmouth, on the south coast of England. The road from there to London was very busy and a young hero returning from active service in the Royal Navy would have had no trouble in finding transport. He arrived home just in time. Many years later, on a less guarded occasion than usual, Molloy told a friend that he remembered his father well. 'Recollect him? Of course I do and (closing his eyes) I can see him as plainly now as I can see you. I recollect too as he lay dying I went to him and said, I think Sir I had better go and join my ship. Yes, he said.'[66]

William Molloy was buried on 4 December, a few steps from the shop, in the small, crowded churchyard of St Giles-in-the-Fields. He left his estate in equal shares to his wife and children, but John and Susannah's capital was set up as a trust fund 'for their education and benefit until they reach the age of 21'.[67] As the family sadly marked the arrival of the new year, 1805, John was not old enough to receive his inheritance. At seventeen he had already experienced war at sea but there was more adventure ahead than he could have imagined. He was about to make the decision that would set his life's course towards Georgiana Kennedy.

Sisters and secrets

Within a few weeks of her husband's death, Mrs Kennedy knew the stark reality of her financial situation. Her friend and adviser, George Leach junior, drew up a simple account, showing what she owned and what she owed. Her husband's debts totalled nearly £11,000 and all her capital assets, including the Crosby estate, were worth £13,000. It was very clear: she did not have enough income from the rent of her properties to pay the debts and keep her family.

Mrs Kennedy quickly arranged a public auction to sell what was left of her husband's crops and stock including horses, cows, heifers, sheep and pigs and then rented out a garden and one room at Crosby Lodge.[68] She advertised her farms on the Crosby estate and held another auction at the Carlisle Coffee House to sell some of her most significant properties.[69] By the end of September she had made nearly £9000 with other estates at Bassenthwaite, Oulton Hall, Brunstock and Jerristown and two more houses in Abbey Street up for sale, but she was still in a desperate situation.[70] After paying household accounts and the interest on his loans, she had £400 left in the bank and that would be eaten up by the next wave of bills and the funeral expenses. She dreaded receiving more demands but most of all she was 'miserable about Crosby Lodge being disposed of'. She said her

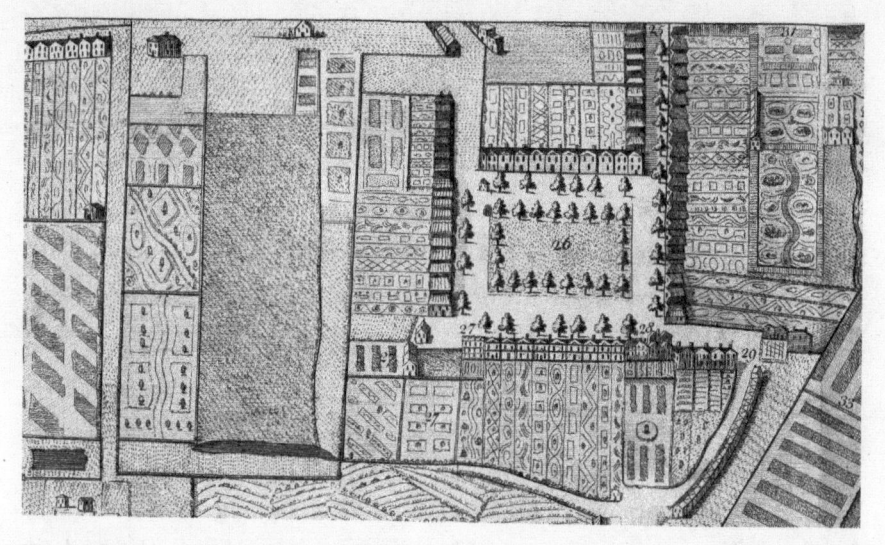

The number 27, marked three times, shows the large house, outbuildings and gardens of the Burnetts' school on Kensington Square.

Extract from A Topographical Survey of the Parish of Kensington *by Joshua Rhodes, 1766. Courtesy of the Royal Borough of Kensington and Chelsea Local Studies and Archives.*

'earthly happiness' depended on keeping the house. 'If my Kennedy knew it was intended to be sold I am sure it would distress his spirit.' The biggest individual debt was her husband's longstanding loan from McDouall and she told him she simply could not pay. Selling Crosby was out of the question, so she began delaying payment of her own bills by ignoring them even when demands became insistent.

Until the early nineteenth century most girls did not have the same opportunities as their brothers to have a formal education, but an increasing number of schools for young ladies were opening to meet the expectations of wealthier families. The schools for young women balanced acquisition of social and feminine arts with a wider, more contemporary education. Between 1820 and 1821 Georgiana and her younger sister Mary were students at 23 Kensington Square, a school in London run by Elizabeth and Esther Burnett.[71] It was the largest building in the square and 'full of fine oak staircases and carvings'.[72]

In 1820 the neighbourhood was an upmarket place to live, with expensive railings and plenty of street lamps. There were fines for beating carpets, exercising horses or letting pigs run loose, and watchmen to make sure the rules were followed. The original building where Mary and Georgiana lived has been replaced but the quiet square in front of it, with its lawns and flowerbeds, has changed little and several huge trees remain from the original street planting in the 1700s.

* * *

Back in London once again in 2014, I was staying in a hotel not far from Kensington Square. Hurrying to a meeting, three days before I was due to leave, I glanced into a shop window and saw a framed picture showing maps of the square at three different dates, including one from 1820. Time for any research was running out and a sense of urgency directed me for the next forty-eight hours. I asked strangers for help and the results took me to another garden in Georgiana's life.

No-one in the shop could answer my questions but they told me I should try Kensington Library. The next day I found the library and asked for the local studies librarian. He was off duty but invited me in and located some old books for me to look through. Within fifteen minutes I had found a ground-floor plan of the building drawn not long before the Misses Burnett turned it into a school, with its own stables, coach-house and outdoor toilets. I also found a map of the square during the same period showing that behind the school was an extensive garden with a parterre, ornamental outdoor rooms and a wandering pathway through trees.

Walking back to my hotel via Kensington Square for the second time in twenty-four hours, I stood on the street for a while and looked at the building that stands on the same site today, used as a college of the University of London. It has the same dimensions and the same views, probably the same number of steps to the front door and the same number of windows across its front façade. Suddenly the front doors slid open as someone came out and I walked in before they closed. If my first question to the receptionist puzzled him, he did not show it. Yes, there was a garden behind the building and, no, he could not give me permission to see it. As soon as I got back to the hotel I sent an email to the address on the business card he gave me, not expecting to get a reply for weeks during the college holidays but the next morning I received a welcoming invitation to make an appointment. Thanks to the kindness of people who found time to help, on my last day in London I walked into the garden where Georgiana spent her schooldays.

***

Family records show that the Misses Kennedy had lessons in music, dancing and drawing. They went to see 'a French play' and Georgiana purchased her own camera lucida, a portable device used for drawing. But the curriculum was also designed to equip them with the raw material for intelligent conversation. They needed things to talk about and that meant developing views and opinions. The girls went out to attend lectures by eminent scholars on history and other topics, paying for a coach when necessary but often walking long distances. Georgiana got through several pairs of gloves and shoes within a few months, including a white satin pair and 'snow boots'.

In May 1820 Mrs Kennedy was making plans to go to London. She said she was worried about Georgiana but George Leach strongly advised her not to go because her mourning period was not over. To reappear on the party scene in London so soon after her husband's death would have been considered shocking. Perhaps Georgiana was genuinely her mother's reason for wanting to visit London, or perhaps it was the promise of extravagant celebrations for the new king's coronation that was calling Mrs Kennedy. It seemed that the rest of the social world was descending on the city to prepare for the festivities.

Georgiana did not go home for more than a year and stayed at school during every holiday in 1821. Her mother was struggling to make ends meet, juggling income from what was left of her inheritance with the monthly expenses of a family of six. In August that year Mrs Kennedy decided to move out of her home, asking her lawyer to rent it privately. She advertised an estate cottage and field for sale at Crosby to bring in some urgently needed cash and, in October, having run out of all other options, she let out Crosby Lodge for three years.[73] By the time the school closed in early 1823, Georgiana had returned to Cumberland to live with her mother in temporary accommodation in Allonby, a tiny Quaker-built village on the coast and the fashionable place to be during summer. Georgiana was eighteen and she never returned to Crosby.

The spring assizes were held in Carlisle every year, in the week after Easter. For a few days visitors filled the market square and there were dances in the evenings. Apart from the drama of the trials themselves, the week of socialising offered an opportunity for girls to stay in town and meet young men from outside their usual circle of friends; Georgiana was no exception. That year, the son of one of the judges caught her eye and they spent at least one evening in each other's company enjoying the music and dancing.

Sir George Sowley Holroyd was a Justice of the King's Bench and had six sons of a suitable age to attract Georgiana's attention. Whether it was James, Henry, Charles, George, William or Thomas who she set her sights on, one of the Holroyd boys stole her heart. A week later, she was still so captivated by the young man that she confided in a friend and talked about him constantly as they walked together on the wide beach at Allonby Sands. Her notebook for that year no longer exists but before it disappeared one of her granddaughters transcribed a page that Georgiana wrote at Allonby in June 1823.

> The lawyers gay, the Judge's son
> Shone all in courtly splendour
> At night we met, God, God, what fun!
> The music sweet the tale how tender.
> Could I but write the whole *haut ton*
> I'd never end this ditty
> All I lov'd was Holroyd's son
> If he lov'd not the more the pity
>
> The Assizes were over and then
> To the coast we were hurried amain
> On Allonby Sands were women and men
> Sitting like babes on a counterpane
> Oh Holroyd there how oft I thought
> On the pleasures past and gone
> With love for thee my heart was fraught
> I sat and walked alone.

The notebook also shows there was another, more serious, matter preoccupying Georgiana at the time: 'Never shall I spend such a happy week again al'tho I was leaving my native County and the mortal remains of my dear departed Father.'[74] She knew her mother was moving the family south and their new home would be as far from any coast as it is possible to live in England. Mrs Kennedy said the change was for the sake of her sons' education. By the time ten-year-old George started at the school in May 1823, her address had changed to Rugby.[75] The move was not a good one for the Kennedys.

Rugby school dominated the town. The streets were crowded with boys and their teachers, known as 'masters'. There was one bank, run by family friend William Butlin, but with fifteen different places to buy alcohol and nine different hat makers, it seems there was more demand for wine, beer and fashion than financial advice.[76]

The family drama that was about to unfold took place on the stage of this unremarkable town. Letters and hastily written notes tell the story of a family who were faced with difficulties that are strikingly familiar today. For Georgiana, the years between 1824 and 1828 were distressing and life changing. Her hatred of Rugby never left her and she went away whenever she had the chance.[77]

Georgiana's mother had no hope of buying her own home so she used her connections and the family stayed with friends. Their host, Abraham Caldecott, was Lord of the Manor of Rugby and his home was conveniently close to the school.[78] His brother John was married to Ann Caldecott, an old friend of Mrs Kennedy's, and Georgiana often stayed with the couple at their home, Holbrook Grange, a short journey from town in a beautiful setting on the River Avon.

Things seemed to go well at first. Kennedy Major and Kennedy Minor learned drawing and dancing as well as Latin, and their French teacher was hired to give lessons to their sister Mary. School costs soon began to grow because, as well as the fees, Mrs Kennedy had to pay for every candle, pen and book the boys used but she was saving money thanks to the hospitality of her friends. Abraham Caldecott was a fellow of the Horticultural Society and lavished money on the extensive gardens of Rugby Lodge. Georgiana must have seen the innovative addition he described in his letter to *The Gardener's Magazine*, 'a combined pinery, vinery and succession pit', which was used as a heated winter greenhouse.

But it was not the town garden that interested Georgiana. Holbrook Grange was a comfortable rural home with beautifully crafted interiors and also the centre of a working farm with stables, vegetable gardens and a creatively stocked flower garden where she saw proteas in flower for the first time.[79,80] When she stayed at the grange, she was watching and learning and later, in her new home in Western Australia, she applied what she had learned.

After an auction of stock and household goods at Crosby, all that remained of Mrs Kennedy's furniture and belongings was shipped to Rugby in 1826[81] and she rented a house there. With no apparent reason for Georgiana's dislike of the town, it's been suggested that she disapproved so strongly of her sister Eliza's fiancé that she left 'for the sake of peace'.[82] Other theories maintain that her Christian beliefs made it difficult for her to accept her family's lifestyle. Georgiana was pious but she was far from being a prude. There is evidence that she moved out because of dramatic scenes she witnessed as a result of her sister Eliza's misuse of alcohol, and because of the way their mother chose to manage the situation.

For a while, Georgiana and Eliza enjoyed the usual innocent flirtations of young, single women. In February 1828, Mrs Kennedy's friend the Reverend William Spencer Phillips wrote to advise her on the girls' behaviour.[83]

> Reports reached me in Oxford of little indiscretions by their flirting with the boys – who (I think wrongly) were permitted to come to your house but this is nothing – but I would let it operate for the future as a caution not to let George bring the bigger boys home with him as he grows older.

There was also some gentle advice to Georgiana in a note from Ann Caldecott, about a visit from a single man while Mrs Kennedy was away.

> My dear Georgiana
>
> I certainly am very sorry that the Gentleman is coming in your Mamma's absence and you may recollect I recommended you in your answer to his first letter not to give him encouragement to visit you at least without her sanction; and I am quite sure if he does come there will be remarks made that neither you or I should wish to hear.[84]

Mrs Caldecott's advice was not heeded and the gentleman was welcomed, suggesting that prudishness and innocence were not the reason for Georgiana's decision to leave home. But while Georgiana's conduct was within the limits of public acceptability, her elder sister's was growing more extreme. Whatever its underlying cause may have been, Eliza's alcohol-related illness became increasingly distressing for Georgiana to witness.

A clever and successful man and a Fellow of Trinity College, Oxford, William Phillips had funded the building of St John's church in Cheltenham, an elegant spa town.[85] He advised Mrs Kennedy on her sons' education and his connection with the family lasted for at least fifteen years. A note written in 1827 indicates that the thirty-two-year-old Phillips was probably the girls' guardian rather than an admirer of Eliza or Mrs Kennedy. By the time Georgiana penned the vehement lines that provide the first clues to growing discord, he was an influential figure to the Kennedy children.

Georgiana's hurriedly written message to her mother reveals the strength of her feelings in the hard indentation of the pen strokes.

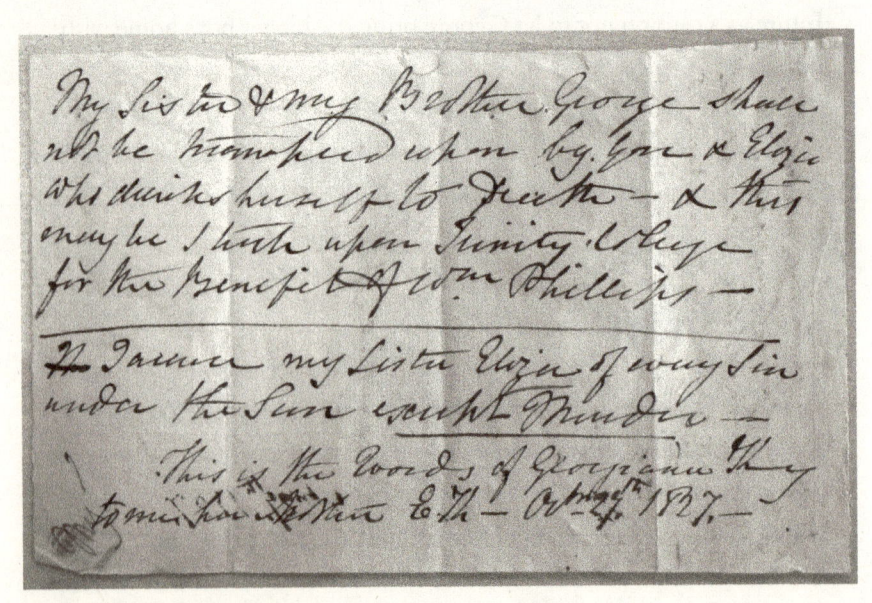

Georgiana's note to her mother, Mrs Kennedy, in April 1827

Cumbria Archive Centre D KEN 3 / 26

My sister and my brother George shall not be trampled upon by you & Eliza who drinks herself to death – & this may be stuck upon Trinity College for the Benefit of Wm Phillips –

I accuse my sister Eliza of every sin under the Sun <u>except Murder</u> – This is the words of Georgiana Kennedy to my (her) mother E. K April 7th 1827[86]

In April 1827, Mrs Kennedy wrote to Ann Caldecott to say there had been another incident to disturb the family's 'peace and comfort' and the timing suggests that it is the same event. Mrs Caldecott wrote straight back reminding her friend that she had already commented on Eliza's 'unbecoming conduct' but her comments had not been welcomed and she did not expect to be forgiven for interfering.[87]

It is not hard to imagine the scenes that might have taken place in that elegant home in Rugby when Eliza had drunk too much, perhaps even in public during dinner parties or social visits. Whatever the details were, her problems became more obvious to outsiders. Georgiana felt frustrated that their mother refused to acknowledge the situation and deal with it before things escalated. With the best intentions, friends did what they could to advise without offending, but Georgiana's embarrassment grew into anger and frustration, and by the late autumn she could no longer control her feelings. Raised to be truthful, to see things simply, to expect fairness and to judge people only by their actions, she would not be silenced by society's expectations of her age and gender.

Eliza had recently become privately engaged to a very eligible clergyman, the Reverend John Besley from Bradninch in Devon. At sixteen he won a scholarship to Balliol College, Oxford, and was obviously destined for a great career.[88] Mrs Kennedy must have been relieved. She should also have been concerned.

In early November, while Besley was staying with the Kennedys, there was another incident. There are no details in the correspondence; perhaps something happened while Besley was alone with Eliza or perhaps Eliza was drunk in public. Whatever Georgiana considered her sister's 'sin' to be, she was a witness and lost her temper. When Besley took sides with his fiancée a serious confrontation took place. Matters that had remained unspoken were laid bare. Reverend Besley left immediately, leaving a letter for Mrs Kennedy to explain his hasty departure.[89]

> My dear Madam
> I am very sorry to have to inform you that an accusation of extremely ungentlemanly conduct which has been laid against me this evening will prevent my continuing my stay with you as long as I intended – the circumstances Miss G. Kennedy will no doubt inform you of but I must say that such insinuations against Eliza were thrown out as I could not lamely brook nor could I sit by & witness the domineering conduct of her younger sister without remark. While I do stay I shall carefully avoid being present at any times but when you are able to receive me in person – as from you I am always sure of a kind reception.

Besley's relationship with Eliza had reached the point where an understanding must be followed through to the commitment of marriage, however uncomfortable the circumstances had just become for an unwilling suitor. He wrote to Mrs Kennedy again a few days later, still defending Eliza's conduct, but the letter hints at his disappointment that news of their engagement had become public.

> I regret to learn from them that yet some disquietude prevails in your house; as I had hoped that in my departure those feuds would have been allayed, the main cause of them being removed – It is a satisfaction to me to learn that Eliza's conduct under these trying circumstances has met your approval, and I have no doubt that by an adherence to it she will at length have the pleasure of finding that it has softened those feelings of irritation which she appears (how, I know not) to have excited –

> An unfortunate enquiry of Miss Southey's addressed to Moberly in the course of his sojourn in the Lakes, has made my engagement quite known to all the Fellows.

Mrs Kennedy did what she could to give the impression of a smooth-running household. Maintaining her social status and reputation was vital, but her correspondence shows that Eliza's behaviour had not changed. Ann Caldecott was an honest confidante. She sent notes almost daily and did not hide her views about the urgent need to deal with Eliza's 'repeated misconduct'. In one letter, addressing her friend Mrs Elizabeth Kennedy as 'Eliza', Ann commented on the effect that the harrowing situation was having on Besley.[90]

> For your sake alone dear Eliza I have patiently waited long – will even wait longer – but do not ask me to take her to my bosom until I have better assurance of amendment than occasional abstinence from the dreadful vice evinces. I was sure the first moment I beheld you last night that all was not right and I turned my sorrowing eyes from the unhappy parent to the object on whom her child had fixed her affections. His silent sorrow was too evident to be obscured and I would only offer up my prayers that the cause, by God's restraining grace, might effectively be removed.

Months passed and Mrs Kennedy quietly managed her eldest daughter's escalating problem, the awkward scenes she caused and the gradual destruction of family relations as Eliza's siblings struggled to deal with the consequences of her illness. The mother chose to direct her support, her energies and her loyalties to the child who was suffering in the most obvious way. She turned a blind eye to the severity of incidents that took place and disregarded the kindly meant advice of friends. She ignored Georgiana's pleas for recognition of the true state of affairs, seeing her heated interventions as a lack of loyalty, or jealousy, or childish wilfulness. Dalton, Mary and Georgiana began to take sides.

Many years later, the niece of a close friend described how Georgiana felt about her relationships at the time:[91] '[Georgiana's] home was not a happy one. I fancy her mother petted one daughter & was not kind to the other.'

Mrs Kennedy's friends rallied around her to offer support but their own priority was not to be tarnished socially by scandal. Even William Phillips was so worried about 'the world's gossip' that he begged her to put everything in a letter with an envelope to prevent discovery of the contents and said that it would be 'most indiscreet' for them to meet. At the same time as he assured her that he was 'grieved to the heart's core' to hear about her problems, he also told her emphatically to destroy his letter.[92]

Mrs Kennedy relied heavily on men she trusted and described as friends, but these confidants — bankers, land agents, lawyers and accountants — were usually working for her in some way or other. William Butlin met with Phillips and the two men devised a support plan for Eliza.[93] After lengthy discussions they came up with a course of action which, Butlin told Mrs Kennedy, 'may be hard but is highly desirable and will ultimately give the most satisfaction & comfort to the mind'.[94] There had been some 'progress of amendment' in Eliza's behaviour but, he regretted, not enough to prevent them from arranging some help.[95] In another frank piece of advice, the ever-cautious William Phillips advised Mrs Kennedy to keep the truth from Besley, Eliza's fiancé. The content of his letter gives the first hint of Eliza's mental health issues.

> It is one of those unaccountable things that baffles all human calculation — & tho' an affliction of no ordinary magnitude yet like all others it must be borne with patience & time may & I earnestly hope, will remedy the evil — My opinion is that he should not be informed of it at present but I am equally decided in opinion that if the fatal malady should continue a full disclosure ought to be made. This if represented to the individual most concerned will I should

trust go far to remove all further anxiety especially as I understand the best resolutions have been formed.⁹⁶

The same letter is also the first evidence of Georgiana's decision to leave home. Phillips pointed out that Mrs Kennedy had a second 'cause of uneasiness & distress' to address, the growing anger and frustration of her second daughter who was already talking openly about leaving, and the limited options available to her. This was a surprising decision given the choices she had, with no money to live on, no immediate prospect of marriage to provide financial support and, like most other young women in her social circle, no career to give her an income. Phillips decided that Georgiana was 'at liberty to depart' as soon as she found a suitable place to go and another home that would be 'more agreeable to her views'. He showed a little sympathy, aware of the shocking things she'd seen, and he thought that a few weeks away from home would bring her 'to her senses'. He could not have been more wrong.

> I see much to <u>excuse</u> & even to <u>admire</u> in <u>some</u> <u>part</u> of Georgiana's conduct – Poor Girl! She could not possibly endure the scenes that she has been destined to witness. Much allowance is to be made for exhibition of temper at such a moment.⁹⁷

Mrs Kennedy continued to make excuses for Eliza's behaviour and found fault with Georgiana for attaching blame on her sister. Focusing her maternal support on one daughter while dealing sharply with another left Georgiana feeling even more isolated. Many years later, Elizabeth Dunlop wrote a poignant letter to a family member, recalling how Georgiana had confided in her. It reveals that Georgiana's unease around her mother and elder sister had been growing for years.

> The details have faded, the general impression remains that her own home was unhappy – her mother the source of her unhappiness –

that she had been devotedly attached to her father, whose death had been a bitter and permanent affliction to her. That her former home, Crosby Lodge in Cumberland, where she had lived with him, was still very dear to her & Rugby, to which place they had removed for the education of her two brothers Dalton & George, was intensely hated. I cannot tell exactly why – her misery at home seemed always associated with her mother and I heard afterwards among mutual acquaintances in Cumberland that Mrs Kennedy was an attractive woman, fond of adulation, and particularly addicted to flirtation with any officers who happened to be stationed at Carlisle Castle.[98]

Georgiana began thinking of distant shores. Foreign places and unknown horizons held no fear for her even then. Among her papers for 1828, a printed, loose sheet describes the items that a young lady would need if travelling to India.[99] Phillips was against the idea unless she had the right companion and Butlin, ever the banker, said it would be far too expensive.

Biographers have concluded that Georgiana's hurried departure from Rugby resulted from intense religious piety that distanced her from the family, but the pen and ink remnants of her story show that she removed herself as a matter of emotional survival. The fact that she ended up staying with one particular family in Scotland was just convenience and chance. Her escape route from Rugby was another family friend, Jane Carus.

Miss Carus was the daughter of a gentleman and she had been a regular visitor to Crosby Lodge. On one of her visits she met Alexander Dunlop, another of Mrs Kennedy's guests. He'd been widowed twice and had five daughters still living at home. Jane Carus was invited to become the Dunlop girls' governess, and she moved to their home in Dunbartonshire, Scotland. She was in her early fifties, a caring woman and loved like a mother by the youngest member of the family, sixteen-year-old Elizabeth. Miss Carus kept up her communication with the Kennedys and as months passed, the Dunlop girls began writing too. When they realised their new friend was 'very unhappy at home', they asked Miss Carus to invite Georgiana for a visit so she could meet the girls she knew only through their letters.[100]

Alexander Dunlop agreed to the arrangement and sent a formal invitation at the beginning of February 1828.[101] Phillips and Butlin reassured Mrs Kennedy that her daughter would soon be brought to her senses by a stay away from home, especially in the calming presence of Miss Carus. They expected a holiday in Scotland to 'change the present feelings & teach a duty which appears at present not much considered'. They hoped it would 'lay the foundations of right & dutiful feelings & create a content in that home than which she will never find any other place so comfortable'.[102]

Through the timely intervention of her friend, Georgiana got her way and packed her bags. On 27 February 1828, she visited the Caldecotts at Holbrook Grange for the last time and the next morning she set off on a week-long journey to Keppoch House, Alexander Dunlop's country home in Scotland.[103,104]

Still young enough to marry again, and even without her fortune, Mrs Kennedy's old status as an heiress made her an eligible partner. But moving socially on the edges of wealthy circles rather than within them, she worried terribly about the gossip surrounding her family. Isolated in a country town, burdened with the prospect of Dalton's inheritance but unable to benefit from it and with a financial situation that was not improving, she left Rugby soon after Georgiana and moved her family to fashionable towns where she had friends or relatives. She began spending time among the university community in Oxford, in Leamington, a spa town, and in Cheltenham, where William Phillips was part of high society.

When travelling she could not imagine life without luxury and there were always ways of finding money, including borrowing from friends.[105] Her invoices record the predictable purchases of nineteenth-century life – rush lights, candles, leeches, yellow soap and large supplies of peas and sugar – but her shopping expeditions also included more frivolous things.[106] She was fond of coffee and chocolate, expensive luxuries in 1828, and was a regular customer of the Crown Hotel in Leamington for bottles of pale sherry. By 1832 her milliners and bootmaker were writing repeatedly, demanding money, but she managed to delay repayments for two years.

Georgiana's mother spent the rest of her life travelling from one temporary home to another, her fortune gone and her children a disappointment. Her family had secrets so she did what she had learned to do since childhood and acted on the behaviour code of generations of Grahams and Daltons: kept up appearances. Her clothes were designed for dancing beneath the flattering light of hundreds of candles at a grand ball in Leamington Spa. She waved to acquaintances with her latest purchase, a pink gauze handkerchief, and when she left at the end of the evening, her black cloak trimmed with crimson was perfectly matched with handmade black satin slippers.

Scotland

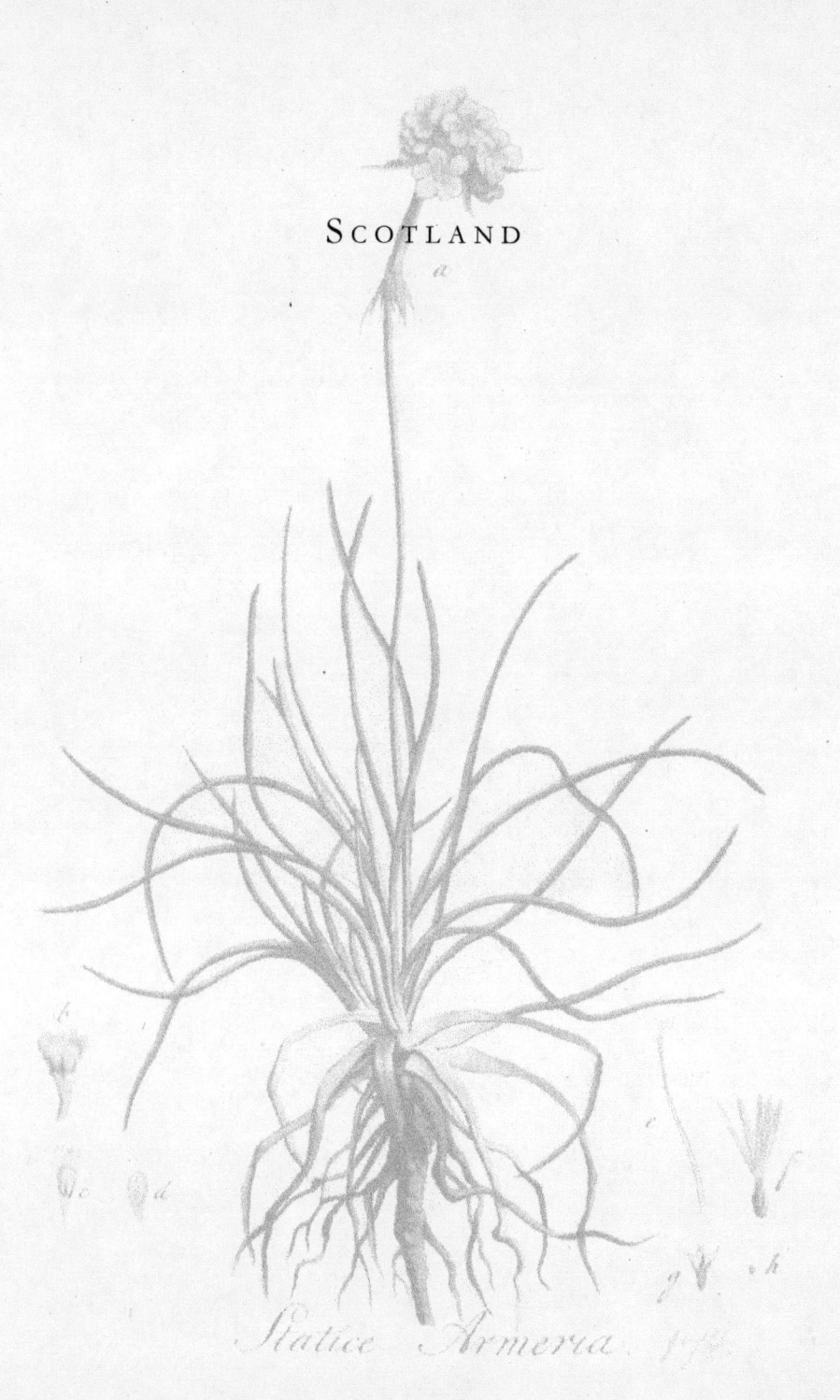

AN UNBROKEN SPIRIT

Georgiana stepped off the Clyde steamer near Keppoch House at the end of winter in 1828 after her journey from Rugby. What she saw on her arrival could not have been more different.

The Gareloch stretches across the west coast of Scotland like a long, narrow shard of broken mirror. In a flat band of reflections, billowing white clouds race by, hawks slide from east to west without a wingbeat and sunbeams ride the wind-roughened surface. Against a landscape of muted colours, browns and purples are laid and overlaid along the shoreline. In the distance, a humpback line of dark hills holds land and sky together from horizon to horizon. Carved deep into the earth millions of years ago, the loch itself looks like an inland sea, tidal but gently so in the north and more fiercely pulled by the great Firth of Clyde at its southern end, where the cracked landscape of lakes and headlands still traces the journey of the ice-sheets: the Isle of Bute, Loch Long, Loch Fyne, the isles of Jura, Arran, Islay and Mull.

In 1820, Alexander Dunlop, a banker and businessman from Greenock, acquired the Keppoch estate close to the shore of the Gareloch and built a fine country home there outside the small town of Cardross.[107] The house is grand without being large and remains today, with its new additions and higher roofline, elegant in the simple Georgian style with a central door flanked by tall windows. The rooms are large with wide doors and high ceilings, so in spite of Dunbartonshire's mild winters, the enormous fireplace in the entrance hall was a necessity. In March, the comforting glow of coals from Newcastle would have been Georgiana's first welcome but the reception she received from the Dunlops was even warmer.

They were a family of wit and learning. A son of Alexander Dunlop founded the first Temperance society but their home was not at all solemn. There is plenty of evidence to show they knew how to have a lot of fun. Mr Dunlop belonged to an exclusive 'whist and supper' club called the Board of Green Cloth. At one meeting in 1810, twenty-three men drank forty-three bottles of wine during dinner, in addition to the port, ale, punch and spirits they also consumed.[108] There was gambling, too. At a meeting in May 1809, Dunlop made a bet – on a bottle of rum – that a certain lady and gentleman would not be married by 8 July. Another bottle of rum was lost in 1814 over a bet about the contents of a toasted cheese sandwich.

The six youngest Dunlop children were living at Keppoch in 1828 and the three girls nearest in age to Georgiana – Margaret, Mary and Helen – became her close friends, with a foundation based on several years of letters. The girls, like their brothers, discussed ethics, politics and religion and their opinions were valued. Conversation respected all views and affection was shown freely. These were liberating experiences for Georgiana, who had not felt that her feelings and opinions had been considered since her father died a decade earlier. Through ten formative years when her intellectual capacity was craving debate, challenge and growth, she had been expected to join in with discussions about fashion and flirting. But exercise for the mind was not the only attraction at Keppoch. After dinner in the evenings, old Scottish songs were sung and often a foursome jumped up and danced a reel. The young people teased one another and Miss Carus was often the brunt of the boys' 'good-humoured badinage'. When Elizabeth tried to join in the game and defend her governess she was always 'drowned in a chorus of laughter'.[109] It was years since Georgiana had experienced such light-hearted family fun. The worlds of intellect and spirit, philosophy and education were all part of the daily dialogue and she felt that, at last, she belonged.

Alexander Dunlop had so much in common with Georgiana's father that she quickly grew fond of him. As a young man, he rose through the ranks of the Greenock volunteer army to become a colonel and was greatly respected by his men. Like David Kennedy, he was a well-loved member of the community with a bloodline to be proud of and, also like Kennedy, he had known financial difficulty, but by the time Georgiana arrived he was a wealthy man again. Keppoch was not Crosby Lodge and he was not her father but he was a protector and a solace.

A short stay turned into weeks, then months, and Georgiana was happier than she had been for years. Surrounded by the wild, coastal beauty she remembered from her childhood in Cumberland and enriched by intellectual friendship, she found herself in a place that seemed perfect. For a while she was able to forget that it was a temporary arrangement.

Georgiana always wrote about that first spring and summer with great affection. She had moved from a landlocked town with a flat skyline of grey roofs to an expanse of silver water in one of the most beautiful places on Earth. Travellers who visit the Gareloch today are struck by its dramatic natural beauty and descriptions from the nineteenth century show that little has changed.

> Whether it be in summer, when not a cloud rests on the blue ether of the sky, or is embosomed in the calm loch, with all nature quivering in the hot, impalpable haze, – or in winter, with a soft shroud of snow enveloping mountain, field, and garden alike, – the picture is radiant with loveliness. Spring has its own peculiar elements of beauty, the first suffusion of the glow of mingling colour, which

afterwards pervades the spot. Autumn's rich mosaic flames over wood and brake, and the deep crimson of the setting sun flushes over sky and strand.[110]

Keppoch was a quiet place, untouched by the Industrial Revolution and the mild climate meant a profusion of plant and animal life. There were bottle-nosed whales, otters and seals in the loch, and deer, badgers and martins in the fields. The landscape of flora and fauna richly rewarded visitors who had the time or inclination to linger. Georgiana had both.

She walked almost daily on the coast and the hills behind the house but she also spent time closer to home. Her diary for 1828 is full of references to gardening. Not yet the botanist that history recognises, she was learning more about horticulture: the ways that seeds were set, the conditions of their growing time, pruning and feeding. On days when the Scottish sky was cold and grey, gardening warmed her spirit with digging and weeding and planting. 'I raked some leaves and made a Bonfire.'[111] These activities were a ladylike way to spend her time and felt natural. They were also a strong, practical foundation for the more meticulous work of a botanical collector – but that life was eight years away.

Georgiana's love of plants grew first from her appreciation of the visual changes in their appearance from buds to blooms, the subtle variation between different varieties and, the gardener's most personal reward, their fragrances. But when there was a garden available to become the medium for these pleasures, her interest expanded; her connection with flowers became not just emotional, but intellectual. The plants were more beautiful if their needs were taken care of, from preparing for the season of growth to protecting them for the cold, dormant months of the northern winter.

Walks were punctuated by calls on friends and neighbours, and in summer there were sightseeing expeditions and boating regattas. In winter there were parties and long walks in the snow. The entries in Georgiana's journal reveal that she enjoyed company as much as she enjoyed time alone.[112]

> Thursday 10th July 1828[113]
> set off for Inverary and waited until 12 for Edward Grant who was to form one of the party, he arrived in a profound sleep & the difficulty of getting him out of the noddy caused Margaret & I considerable laughter.[114]

The ladies often called at Ardandan House, near the gates of Keppoch and sometimes walked further along the Helensburgh Road to visit Camis Eskan, the stately mansion home of the Dennistouns of Colgrain. The Dennistouns had royal lineage and had owned lands near Cardross for generations. James Dennistoun senior was deputy lieutenant of Dunbartonshire and his eldest son, also James, was another member of the Board of Green Cloth. A handsome and wealthy young lawyer, James junior was two years older than Georgiana and had already graduated from both Glasgow and Edinburgh universities. He could not have appeared more attractive to her.

Recently returned from a long tour of Italy, Dennistoun was deeply interested in European literature, music and art. His family often called at Keppoch and Georgiana took any opportunity to return the compliment by walking the road to Camis Eskan, even in the snow. She was honest enough to record her feelings several times for 'il mio favorito' [my favourite].[115]

This time in Georgiana's life has been viewed by other biographers as a religious 'retreat' but the reality was quite different.[116] She attended church once a week and although she showed great interest in the sermons, they did not dominate the way she spent her days. On the other side of the River Clyde, the busy port of Greenock was within easy reach by paddle-steamer. Thirty-five kilometres by boat from Glasgow, it was the point where the rest of the world connected with life on the Gareloch. On clear days, the view across the open water from Keppoch House to Greenock was the view out towards the world of travel and commerce. With more steamers carrying passengers along the coast as each month passed, there were adventures on offer. Within weeks of arriving in Scotland, Georgiana went on a trip that combined handsome, eligible young gentlemen, explorations at sea, nature walks, beautiful scenery and culture.

She set off from Gourock on 5 July with Margaret Dunlop and her brother Hutcheson Dunlop for an extended tour to Inverary, passing the western isles of Arran and Bute. The group who boarded the *Rothesay Castle* that day should have included Captain Duncan Darroch. Five years older than Georgiana and unmarried, he was the future Baron of Gourock. She was disappointed when Duncan sent a note at the last moment to say he would not be able to join them.

The journey had a few false starts due to rough weather but the young people eventually boarded the *Rothesay Castle*, a wooden paddle-steamer, and left behind the familiar view of Kilcreggan on the other side of the Clyde. The adventure was an innocent one, climbing mountains, collecting wildflowers and exploring a castle. Finding the inn at Inverary full, they slept on floors and sofas. They ate picnics and drank beer, sitting daringly on the paddle box of the steamer as it cruised through some of the most beautiful coastal scenery in Europe, and Georgiana kept a travel journal of the whole trip.[117]

* * *

On the last day of a visit to the west coast of Scotland with my husband, Mike, there were a few hours of daylight left and we took the narrow road down the far side of the Roseneath peninsula which forms the other side of the Gareloch, to see some of the views described in Georgiana's journal. The western end of Loch Long begins as a narrow stretch of water but soon opens to the scenery that she described so eloquently, the wide panorama of the Firth of Clyde

Ruins of the old Kilcreggan pier in 2014

and the vast sky it mirrors. Always close to the loch's stony edges, we followed the road on to Kilcreggan, a place Georgiana knew well from visits to the Campbells at Portkill Farm. I wanted to look for any remnants of the old pier that was a stopping-off point for the local packet-boat (or 'wherry') that transported stock, provisions and passengers between Roseneath and Kilcreggan in the 1820s.

From a distance the solid shape of the pier was unmistakable, tumbled and uneven but still resting its full, grey weight across the beach and out into the loch, a gigantic stone arm curved slightly in a protective gesture. As I stood alone in the absolute calm of twilight with no sound or movement, apart from the gentle shifting of the water, the moment was loaded with the potential for nostalgia. I thought about how the energy of human purpose seems to linger in some places for centuries, and the way an unexpected connection between past and present can take you by surprise. It was an invitation to visualise another summer afternoon with a boat off-loading its cargo of sheep and passengers, among them a well-dressed young woman wearing a straw bonnet. Georgiana's observations often feel sharply familiar, and her descriptions in the journal she kept on board the *Rothesay Castle* perfectly captured my own feelings about the view in front of me. There is so much that's timeless in the words she left behind and many of the opinions she held were startlingly progressive. It's easy to think of her as a contemporary who shares a twenty-first-century view of the world but a lifetime of intellectual shaping by much older influences is always there, dimly lit but present, in the way she gave voice to her feelings. In subtle ways, her writing was influenced by a life lived entirely in the nineteenth century. That afternoon, standing where she stood on the old Kilcreggan pier, I remembered that her journal also clearly reveals the differences fashioned by 200 years that separate us. It was a moment of realisation and a reminder why I decided to tell her story always through the historical context of her own time and place.

* * *

Georgiana sketched the views and wrote in detail about the changing panoramas as the boat travelled past the mouth of Loch Long to Rothesay on the Isle of Bute and on to the head of Loch Fyne. She was overwhelmed by 'scenery so exceedingly wild and beautiful and only wished for as beautiful an habitation on its shores as suited to my kind, as the herons which first I saw there had for their refuge'.[118] The remote, untamed mountains and seascapes were exactly what she wanted to see and with plenty of time to think and write, she rewarded herself with sentences that feel luxurious in their complexity.

Georgiana's letters and diaries are packed with sensitively expressed observations about the natural world around her. The wide range of vocabulary she chose and the inventive imagery she used show how important it was to her to communicate not just what she saw but also to capture the thinking that was part of looking. She was born at a time when views about people's relationships to the world around them were changing; a shift was taking place from the old admiration of all things ordered and controlled by men, including gardens. In the eighteenth century, a neatly manicured formal garden was a daily reminder of effective human dominance, nature under control, but in 1828 the outcomes of that control were beginning to seem less desirable. After years of enforced enclosures, huge areas of countryside were changing. Wide, open spaces with winding lanes were being transformed into a criss-cross pattern of straight roads between small, regular fields demarcated with hedges. The travelling people and peasants who populated rural landscapes were disappearing along with the traditional work they did. Industry flourished, towns grew bigger, straight roads and man-made shapes appeared over horizons where there had once been trees and winding lanes. As industrialisation spread its effects further into the wild places of Britain, a popular nostalgia for the 'rustic' scenes of the past began to grow, nurtured by writers, artists and composers such as Sir Walter Scott, John Constable and Hector Berlioz, who captured the sense of loss by depicting a new kind of ideal landscape in poetry, music and painting – untamed scenes where the natural world was left without interference. Places that were wild and even dangerous were considered beautiful again, and what became thought of later as typically English gardens were beginning to appear, with their deliberately planted randomness and irregularity of form. Travellers began to seek out places with wide horizons and unlimited views, mountains and crags, unexplored valleys and forests. Paintings depicted people living in harmony with the natural world and old forms of agriculture where manual labour had little visual impact on its pastoral setting. This view was a romantic one and its proponents became known as the Romantics. They developed new, shared understandings of what could be described as 'beautiful', 'sublime' and 'picturesque'; the line between wild and ugly was a thin one.[119]

Georgiana's relationship with the wilderness around her in Cumberland, Scotland and Western Australia was an integral part of her nature but it was also very, very fashionable. The Romantic Movement was her sibling, born and matured during the years of her lifetime. Two of the most significant influences on the development of Romanticism and its 'language of description' were William Wordsworth and Samuel Taylor Coleridge.[120] The two poets developed, through their creative partnership, highly influential theories about the connection between natural landscapes and the human mind. Through poetry that was at first controversial, they introduced new ways of writing and talking about 'visual images for the poetic imagination they cared so much about'.[121]

But for Georgiana, the influence of Romantic writing and thinking was more than a matter of literary fashion. Both Wordsworth and Coleridge were part of her local social group. Cumberland itself was the precise, dramatic backdrop for their poetry of 'the language really used by men', where 'low and rustic life' was the surprising choice of content because 'in that condition the passions of men are incorporated with the beautiful and permanent forms of nature'.[122] The poems they published together in 1798 shocked critics at first but are often cited today as the beginning of the Romantic Movement in literature.[123]

The poets began to use written images of pure light moving and changing on landscapes as a metaphor for their theories about imagination and the unity of all living things. They developed their ideas into an allegorical language that soon permeated literature and art. It is no accident that Georgiana's writing leans in the same direction: moonlight and sunlight, reflections on water, the contrasts between bright colours and dappled shade are often embedded like 'the poetry of nature' in her contemplations about life and her Scottish journal is an example.[124]

> I had never seen Dumbartonshire from the Greenock side before and the beautiful shades which a bright July evening cast over those blue and varied mountains can only be imagined by those of a warm and ardent temperament whose mind is just recovering from many painful circumstances. This evening was particularly bright; the fertile point of Roseneath formed a rich contrast to the grey parts of the mountains receding from it and called the Duke of Argyle's

Bowling green, a misnomer as the summits of each form a sort of rude and uneven crater. The Clyde was unrippled and of a palish sapphire blue, two or three skiffs lay moored off the Beach, and the dark smoke emitted by some steam vessels plying from Greenock lighted on the dark green woods of Roseneath and was lost to the sight, the sky all the while, most beautifully blue and mingled with soft white clouds.[125]

The same pages written in her first Scottish summer show that Georgiana shared Wordsworth's dislike of the visual effects of human intervention in landscapes. He wrote about the ugliness of signs of human control and order that had been deliberately placed into settings for effect. Wordsworth particularly disapproved of buildings that spoiled rural views and the planting of trees that were not indigenous to their new surroundings. The subject matter of the Lyrical Ballads pushed home these new ideas, which helped to influence the swing in public opinion away from symmetry and management to the nostalgic attraction of wild, random scenes. Although Georgiana grew up with cotton mills on her doorstep in a town that became wealthy from industry, she expressed strong views about man-made scars on the natural environment. Her opinion was progressive and enlightened in 1828, but these comments, written during her Scottish voyage would not seem out of place today.

Mr. Hutcheson & I went up the Shawes, which are large Waterworks on Sir Michael S. Stewart's property immediately above the west end of Greenock for the purpose of erecting Cotton Mills, (what Goths & sordid beings men are!) on that beautiful hill.[126]

We passed several slips into the water which is conveyed from a reservoir 8 miles distant, being Sunday the water was not an inch in depth. The Engineer was Mr. John and the works cost £30000. They are worth seeing. I wish the ground that is designated for such a purpose belonged to me and I would save it from such profanation.

Each day looked 'if possible more beautiful than yesterday', but the sharp memories of other scenes stayed lodged in her mind. A constant flow of letters from Rugby meant that although she had left the source of her problems behind, she had not escaped from the legacy of duty and guilt. A letter from her mother made no bones about where, in Mrs Kennedy's opinion, the blame should be laid and who was the real sufferer.

> My dear Georgiana,
> I was not aware that I took a cold leave of you but I am nearly driven to that pitch of misery by all of you for you are all three wrong in your various ways that I fear my mind will not stand it long. I carried you all in my womb, done all in my power for you my children. I trust it will please the Almighty to help <u>me</u> through this accumulated sorrow and June of discontent and uncharitable feeling towards each other which is undermining my constitution and that He will forgive you all for the misery you have & are causing to a mother who wd. not have injured any one let alone my own flesh and blood for all this world can give is my sincere prayer – For nothing but prayer I find will do. May God bless you all and send you better minds,
> Yr afft. mother,
> E. Kennedy[127]

Georgiana's reply asked her mother to be thankful that Eliza's marriage to Reverend Besley was going ahead in a few weeks and hoped 'that this said marriage may instantly take place for our sakes, certainly not for Mr Besley's'.[128] But what her letter conveys most is the strong spirit of a young woman who refused to bend to propriety if that meant abandoning her convictions about the importance of truth. The behaviour expected of her was hypocrisy and she was unwilling to sacrifice personal values. 'I know I have all along been too outspoken for you. I do not wish to feign the spirit of conciliation for the purposes of deception.'[129]

Although adamant and confident in letters to her mother, her heart was uneasy. As she recorded the daily events of the boat trip around the Scottish islands, she included personal comments that expose her inner turmoil.

> Why did I feel an oppression or rather an indescribable alloy to this scene, as if my mind & desires were grasping at more than I was permitted to enjoy in the first place, I recurred to past scenes at Rugby and then in the second I know I shock and think too much of this sublunary world.[130]

She added that she was feeling 'much depressed from an unbroken spirit of pride and independence' and believed herself unworthy of the joy she found in her new situation. But she still refused to allow her spirit to break.

Surrounded by her new 'sisters' at Keppoch House and with a choice of aristocratic friends within walking distance, even the gloomy days of winter seemed perfect. There were sewing jobs and light cooking or mending to be done, books to read and discuss, flowers to be pressed, letters to be written and a journal to keep. When the sun rose late and set again before afternoon was ended, the evenings were long but the family often enjoyed the company of visitors and, later, the women sat together in their high-ceilinged rooms and talked for hours. Georgiana never stopped questioning and analysing her Christian faith and she found a theological counterpart in Mary Dunlop. They prayed together or studied the Bible and debated the new ideas they heard about interpretation of the Gospels. Those heartfelt conversations they shared were long remembered. When she arrived in Western Australia, one of the greatest losses Georgiana mourned was the company of her female friends, other women with whom she could discuss personal, private matters. That was a time when confiding in a servant or a neighbour who was not a 'lady' would have been a social sin.

Travel by boat was a regular part of daily life. The land around Keppoch House was mountainous with very few roads. Steam power was still very new technology but some boats had started carrying passengers and cargo from Port Glasgow to the head of the loch, a view Georgiana could see from the coast at Keppoch. But it was the view in the other direction across the Gareloch that became most significant for her. That misty vista would lodge in her memory for the rest of her life, nurtured and restored for nine years by its twin, the view across the Blackwood River from her cottage in Augusta.

When twenty-three-year-old Miss Kennedy arrived at Keppoch she was in turmoil, burdened with grief, defiance and confusion. Like an answered prayer, Scotland provided all she needed to heal her mind and soul. In Alexander Dunlop she found a father figure but in a tiny community on the other side of the Gareloch she found a spiritual mentor.

In 1824, Helen Dunlop became engaged to the Reverend Robert Story, minister of St Modan's church in nearby Roseneath. He had arrived as assistant to the previous minister, the Reverend George Drummond, and was soon 'a favourite in society. His exceedingly handsome and striking appearance, his cultured mind, and agreeable manners, made the young minister to be courted by the wealthy, and even the titled, in the land.'[131] The reverend was not extravagant but he did not have a head for business. With a salary of £200 a year and debts of £300, he had to withdraw his proposal when Helen's father insisted he should be free of debt before the marriage. Story started returning Helen's letters and called off the engagement.

He worked endlessly for the wellbeing of his parishioners, walked or rowed for hours in all weathers, day and night, to be with them when needed but did not look after himself. By 1827 he had become physically weak and went to England to rest and recover. While he was there he met the charismatic preacher Edward Irving, through their mutual friend Dr Thomas Chalmers.

When Story returned to Scotland in better physical and financial health, Helen's brother helped to change their father's mind and, in September 1828, the wedding took place at Keppoch House. Georgiana's diary for that period has not survived but she must have compared Helen's happy and secure future with her own situation. Their birth dates were only three months apart but Georgiana had no suitor, no income and no home. As always, she put her trust in God and waited for His guidance. Soon after Helen moved to Roseneath Manse, Georgiana received the first of many invitations to stay with the Storys on the other side of the loch and she accepted their offer.

In Roseneath, life had changed little in the previous hundred years on the narrow peninsula between two lochs bordered by mountains. Most people still worked for the local landowner, the Duke of Argyll, or made a living through crofting, fishing or weaving.[132] Very few families owned their cottage and life was hard. They burnt the cheapest fuel, peat dug from the land. After a day that began before dawn there was little to cheer them after sunset except whisky. The small distilleries around Roseneath were illegal but they were 'fatal attractives during the long nights of winter, to the unoccupied fishermen'.[133] Many of the cottagers were involved in smuggling and in 1816, when Story first arrived, the smoke from their fires in all directions was a constant reminder of the spiritual work he had to do.[134] It was not a wealthy parish but in comparison with most towns it was a very healthy environment: a close, isolated community where people supported one another, made the best of things, worked hard and enjoyed life when they could.

Georgiana loved staying at the old manse with its slow lifestyle. A carriage drive to Row or a short walk from the gates of Keppoch to the Drumfork ferry and in a few minutes, if the tide was gentle, she could be on the other side of the Gareloch. When the tide was running heavily it was a different story. There were times when the surface of the loch was completely calm but the fierce swirling of water forcing its way through the narrows by the ferry mooring could be heard a long way off 'like the sound of a cataract'.[135] Tucked in a sheltered spot under the green dome of Campsail hill, the area around the manse was quiet and dramatically beautiful, and it has remained the same. Once seen, Roseneath burns in the memory.

> Great mountain precipices and vast crags seem toppling over in the moving cloudland overhanging the waters. The pale green of the young bracken is in strong contrast with the purple clouds, and light streamers of mist curl themselves round the fir plantations.[136]

The scenery was luxurious but the manse was not. Built in 1770, it was not old but the house stood where rainwater and melting snow gathered on a flat area near the constant, noisy tumbling of the Clachan burn. Damp rose through the walls and the rooms smelled of wet, crumbling plaster.[137] When Story arrived, the house was 'mouldy and out of repair' and 'discoloured wallpaper hung off the walls'. It was just as uncomfortable when Georgiana stayed there in 1828 and 1829.[138]

St Modan's church was bare and frugal, in keeping with the strict beliefs of its minister and parishioners. The church had an earth floor and rough timber pews. An upper gallery ran around three sides with a simple pulpit between two windows on the fourth side. Once painted plain white, the walls were green with mould, altogether 'a forlorn appearance'.[139] The 'dingy barn-like Kirk' was uncomfortable enough but services were often three hours long. The company, however, was warm and comforting.[140]

A small group of closely connected local gentry and professionals walked, dined and worshipped together. The noble Campbell family won Georgiana's heart and she often called on Lorne Campbell, the Duke of Argyll's estate manager at Portkill Farm on the other side of the hill. Helen Campbell and her sister, who lived at Clachan House, had a 'wild Highland accent' and were 'both of a romantic disposition – friendly, warm and generous'.[141,142] Their home was reached by crossing a little wooden bridge over the stream beside the church and walking along an avenue of ancient yew trees; a route that can be traced through the park to a cluster of new houses. To this day, it seems as if all pathways in Roseneath lead to the ruins of the old church. In the nineteenth century, faith provided the framework for daily life and a guide through difficult times but it did not stop people, including men of God, enjoying themselves. When the celebrated preacher Edward Irving visited, Helen Campbell arranged an 'entertainment' for him and the visiting ministers at a picturesque bower near a waterfall in the Clachan glen.

> The large and happy party from the Manse and Clachan House partook of breakfast in the bower, after doing justice to which, one of the gentlemen played an inspiring reel tune on the violin, and no less decorous a reveller than the celebrated Irving danced the Highland fling, with astonishing vigour. After the entertainment was over, and the friends returned to the Manse, Mr. Story enquired, 'What shall we do now?' when Dr. Chalmers, in his characteristic way, exclaimed, 'Come and let us abandon ourselves to miscellaneous impulses!'[143]

The Storys' sheltered cottage garden was another attraction for Georgiana, an opportunity to enjoy what was fast becoming more than a hobby. She put on her gardening gloves and got to work. Years later, close to starvation in Australia and reduced to growing only vegetables to feed her family, she often dreamed of the manse garden.[144]

> O! My dear & lovely Roseneath – my heart bleeds when I think of the happy celestial days I spent there and all the violets & primroses are still fresh in my memory.[145]

It was the unexpected mixture of earnest faith and uncomplicated joy in life that Georgiana found so appealing. After her difficult years in Rugby, the people of Roseneath refreshed her belief that balance could be achieved between the 'different occupations of mind & body'.[146]

She was living the truth, peace and simplicity of a Quaker lifestyle and in later years she cherished the memories, often trying to picture herself back in Scotland enjoying a drive out in the pony cart with Mary Dunlop or tying Ayrshire roses around poles in the garden.[147] If Georgiana ever felt she had a sister in spirit, it was Mary Dunlop. Mary suffered from spinal pain and was the most deeply religious of the sisters but she never gave up her worldly pleasures of singing and music.[148,149] When Georgiana needed a trusted friend, fourteen years later, it was Mary she turned to.

The year 1829 arrived with the usual Hogmanay celebrations, and Georgiana enjoyed her second spring at Keppoch. Her time there overlapped with a significant era for the Church of Scotland. Changes that had been brewing locally for years would soon reverberate beyond the mountains around the Gareloch, but Georgiana was not living in a 'centre of religious fervour' nor was she 'under the influence' of Edward Irving and the contentious ideas he preached.[150] If the things that affected her personal beliefs are examined more closely they can be seen not as a life-changing conversion but a simple affirmation of the religious and moral codes she had aspired to since childhood.

New ideas were germinating in the minds of more than one influential member of the community. They took shape slowly and independently of one another but in the space of a few years between about 1827 and 1831, some basic tenets had been shaped into a different way of believing. Like thousands of others, Georgiana was drawn to the logical purity of these interpretations of Christianity, but there were powerful people who deemed the new thinking as nothing less than heretical. The idea that salvation was attainable for all believers was difficult for some people to accept and what had been a gentle, rolling wave of change became a torrent of concern for the presbytery of Dumbarton. What were those core principles that were considered revolutionary and shocking enough to ban ministers from ever again serving in the church? God loves us all equally and is universally forgiving; our assurance in God's love is the essence of faith and it is not just a chosen few who can go to heaven. Here was the remaining Quaker testimony that Georgiana was looking for: equality.

Spiritual guidance in the region was delivered in the same way it had been declaimed from the pulpit for generations. The congregation heard about God's anger and vengeance but not much about His love. They learned that some of them could hope for salvation but others could not. There was a chasm between the message from the pulpit and the people sitting on the hard wooden benches beneath it. Robert Story and some of his contemporaries were beginning to realise this.

> Alas for the poor people in the hands of many of us! Instead of a message of heart-stirring joy and gladness, a principle of life and peace, of holy and blessed activity in all heavenly pursuits, it is made an embassage of perplexity, of negotiation, of disputation.[151]

Against this backdrop, three things began to happen that made an impression on Georgiana's religious thinking. They were independent events but the fact that they occurred at around the same time is not coincidental.

First, Reverend Robert Story's friend and colleague, Reverend John McLeod Campbell, decided to act on the thinking that had occupied his mind for some time. He was minister of Row, a small parish further along the shores of the loch where Georgiana occasionally went to church, and by 1828 he was preaching only Bible-based teachings. His sermons described the concept of 'assurance', the knowledge of God's prior love for everyone. He told his small congregation 'that God loves every child of Adam and that Christ died for the same'.[152] Georgiana recognised in this something that matched with her deeply felt beliefs. Her grandfather's code for life, the pillars of Freemasonry, provided a model: all people are equal in the eyes of God. Some locals complained that Campbell was preaching contrary to the doctrine of the Church of Scotland and although Robert Story and Alexander Dunlop both publicly defended him, the local church authority lodged and successfully proved a libel against him. A year later, after Georgiana had left Scotland to emigrate to Western Australia, an appeal was approved and in 1831 Campbell's sermons were judged to be 'obnoxious and intolerable' and the 'Row heresy' was denounced in Glasgow and Edinburgh. Campbell was deposed as a minister and forbidden to preach in any Church of Scotland.

Second, Reverend Story was refining the details of his own teaching. He had returned from England with 'the growing reflection in his own heart of the great central heart of love' and was already preaching 'peace in believing'.[153] When he saw an example of his beliefs in the life of a local woman, he began writing a book.[154] Isabella Campbell suffered greatly from illness in the months before she died but she expressed her joy in God's love every day. Story was moved by her faith and added the spiritual insights from their conversations to his writing. Isabella died before Georgiana arrived in Scotland, but her religious doctrine was still a frequent topic of conversation at the manse, and Story's book was among Georgiana's reading material during the long voyage to Australia.

And third, just like the minsters of Row and Roseneath, Edward Irving had worked out that there were better ways to connect with ordinary people. He had become an inspiring, influential speaker and his dramatic sermons were drawing in bigger crowds each week when he visited both parishes to preach in the summer of 1828. Although Story invited his friend to preach in Roseneath, Irving's teachings on supernatural dimensions of the Gospels were becoming more radical and were drifting further from Story's own doctrines. Irving's belief that bodily disease was a direct infliction by Satan and his views about prophecy and healing were topics of heated debate at the manse. Georgiana's diary entries and her full social calendar at Keppoch House show that religion did not become 'her total response to life' and she did not live with the Storys, but she did think Irving was both clever and kind. She heard him preach again in London the following year shortly before she set sail for the new colony, and enjoyed his 'exposition of the 22nd Psalm' so much that she went to his church again the following Sunday.[155]

He prayed for the settlers who suggested that he should think about joining them but the next week he did not return their messages. After Georgiana had left Scotland, Isabella Campbell's younger sister, Mary, suddenly developed what Irving and his followers believed to be the God-given gift of 'speaking in tongues'. She said she was speaking in a language of the Southern Pacific Ocean, that it was 'a manifestation of the power of the Holy Spirit' and an invitation for her to become a missionary.[156] Although the phenomenon soon came to an end, Irving, who was 'in the maelstrom of his impassioned fanaticism', took up her story and introduced her to a wider circle of believers. Their association was the beginning of his demise and distanced him further from Georgiana's friends on the Gareloch, even more so when Mary Campbell confessed to Story that she had lied about the whole thing.

More than any other aspect of Story's teaching, it was the possibility for 'joy' and 'peace' that resonated with Georgiana's own thinking. Christianity taught her as a child that she might not go to heaven if she was not good enough and that meant she could not have full confidence in God's love. Belief without hope gave no reason to be joyful. But in Scotland she found a new assurance that God loved her even though she had sinned. This different interpretation of Christian faith was a relief, but she still often struggled with the depth of her conviction and acknowledged what she thought were her failings. One Sunday, after attending church during her second spring in Scotland, she wrote in her diary: 'My belief very very small & I cannot gain the spirit I Ought to have but God is great.'[157]

Georgiana spent eighteen months in Scotland at a time when there was vibrant debate about the church's teaching and she loved the analytical, scholarly discussion around her. But what drew her in was the theological and spiritual essence of Reverend Story's ministry and it stayed with her until she died.

PORTUGAL
SPAIN
FRANCE
BELGIUM

KING GEORGE COMMANDS [158]

Seven months after leaving the navy, on 17 June 1805, John Molloy purchased the military documents that would make him an officer for the first time. Military posts could be earned through promotion when a position became available or could be purchased, but officer commissions were expensive. Molloy became an ensign in Captain Goldfinch's company under Colonel William G Langton.[159] Far away in a northern city, his future wife was three weeks old.

Molloy was making wise use of the finances made available through the trust fund his father had left him. 'Ensign' was the lowest ranking officer in the army but it was his first significant step towards becoming a gentleman. On 1 April 1806, Ensign Molloy was promoted to lieutenant and for six months he was based in Somerset before his company moved on to Pendennis Castle in Cornwall, where they remained for the rest of his career in the militia. Between 25 June and 24 September 1807, Molloy was paid for eighty-five days out of a possible ninety-one, with a note to say that he had taken six days of leave. He had a very particular reason for needing a week off. His twenty-first birthday was on 5 September and, just as described decades later in anecdotal stories by friends and family, he went to London and visited the office of a solicitor where he received a large sum of money. But his benefactor was not a secretive royal relative as the rumours have always suggested. He inherited the generous estate left to him by his father.

Given the ongoing success of the business and the properties owned by the trust, John's and his sister's inheritances must have been considerable. When Susannah died in 1829 she left her brother £1000, a large sum for a spinster to hold as capital. With the money from the trust fund Molloy could have bought an elegant apartment in a fashionable area of London and spent his time at the theatre and opera. He could have ordered a fine carriage and a wardrobe of silk clothes in the distinctive, flamboyant new designs of the early Regency period. Instead, on 22 December, he purchased another commission, this time a more expensive one at £450: a second lieutenancy in the regular army of the King of England and he paid in cash.[160]

* * *

Piecing together the details of a life lived long ago sometimes feels like watching a play with the scenes performed in the wrong order. When a character leaves the stage unexpectedly, the story becomes impossible to follow and the plot disconnects. These are difficult times for a researcher. All doors close, windows show blank landscapes and corridors of investigation twist into frustrating mazes that return again and again to the same point. Internet searches turn up lists of links in purple, indicating the websites have already been checked. The answers can be there in full view among the notes and bookmarked websites, but expecting to find one thing makes it hard to see anything else, even when it's right under your nose.

There were three years missing from the picture of John Molloy's life so I searched through everything again and came to the file of details for nineteenth-century military publications that included a record of his promotions. In the listing for the 95th Regiment of Foot in 1807, his name had been added in handwriting, his commission being too late in the year to be included at the time of printing. There was something written next to Molloy's name and the first word looked like 'Oxford'. This one word may be the source that prompted the assumption that he had attended Oxford University.[161]

It's remarkable how a phrase can be indecipherable even through a magnifying glass but a year later the same two words can be read easily on sight. The second word looked like 'Mil'. On the same page, next to another name, were the words 'Cambridge Mil'. I realised that John Molloy had entered the 95th Brigade of Foot directly from the Oxford Militia but I needed more proof.

The Duke of Marlborough employed the Oxford Militia to supplement the King's regular army when needed. A well-regarded military force, they were officially civilians. In late 1806, when Molloy was twenty, they were stationed in the southwest of England and in October they marched from Exeter to the village of Moretonhampstead to oversee public order during the November election.[162] The pay was not generous. Georgiana wrote to her brother George on 16 May 1836, in reply to his complaints about the financial difficulty of his new job as a surgeon's assistant in Exeter: 'Molloy desires me to tell you that he once lived in Exeter on a shilling a day.'[163]

This clue matched with the first, but the final piece of evidence was in the National Archives at Kew near London and I was on the other side of the world. Patrick Richardson-Bunbury came to the rescue with an introduction to his brother, another great-great-grandson of Georgiana and John Molloy. Andrew Bunbury kindly agreed to travel to Kew, order the records and search for a reference on militia pay lists for 1807. He methodically checked the books for each year until he found the evidence to prove that Molloy was an experienced officer in the Oxford Militia for two and a half years before entering the regular army.

* * *

The militia was a private army so, although Molloy was already an officer, he was still considered to be a civilian. When his commission

Pay record of the Oxford Militia for September 1807 showing John Molloy's leave, and move to the 95th Regiment

Crown copyright. National Archives WO 13/1712

was reported in the journal of the House of Commons alongside so many others, it would have been the very last time he was officially referred to as 'Mr Molloy'.

His final service record in the Oxford Militia, in September 1807, notes that he was 'gazetted to the 95th'.[164] Molloy had joined the 95th Regiment of Foot, the legendary corps known later as the Rifle Brigade. He was about to become the gentleman officer who would win Georgiana Kennedy's heart. The 95th was a regiment with a reputation. Many of its men were already heroes but their contribution to the battles of the Peninsular War would make them into legends.

In 1789, when Molloy was three years old, the French Revolution rocked the Western world. When the French king was executed, the monarchies of Europe formed an alliance against the new republic. A young Corsican officer in the revolutionary army began to get himself noticed and by 1796 he was commander-in-chief of the French forces in Italy. 'Napoleone Buonaparte' was confident, clever and ambitious. His power and influence grew quickly and after a series of victories across Europe, only Britain remained to be conquered.

In 1803, when midshipman Molloy was aboard the *Hindostan*, Britain declared war on France. In 1804, Napoleon made himself emperor and planned to invade Britain. But first he needed to make the coastline vulnerable, so he drew her navy away to the Mediterranean and engaged with them there. It was ships like the *Hindostan* that created a supply chain to Lord Nelson's fleet and played their own part in his victory at the Battle of Trafalgar in 1805.

The war continued on land as Napoleon extended his empire. By early 1808, when Molloy was training as a new officer in the 95th, Bonaparte had occupied Portugal. When Napoleon declared his brother to be King of Spain, France lost an ally and Britain gained one. The British army embarked for Portugal, aiming to push the French back across the Spanish border and defeat them on their home ground by invading and restoring the monarchy. Ultimately the allied forces achieved what they set out to do but the Peninsular War lasted seven years.

The first regiment armed with Baker rifles rather than muskets, the 95th were part of the 'light' division that moved across country quickly, just as Wellington required. Rifles took longer to load than muskets but they were much more accurate and had a greater range. The riflemen were trained to make good use of their sharp-shooting skills to pick off as many enemy officers as possible. They learned to travel swiftly across any kind of territory, usually moving in pairs with one man covering the other during reloading. They were the first soldiers expected to think independently, taking aim at a target and firing at will. These tactics were new in an army where men moved in battle lines or traditional formations and fired together in volleys on an officer's order, without aiming at a specific target. The riflemen also used bugles to communicate rather than drum signals, which increased their speed and mobility.

What set them apart in a more obvious way was their uniform. In a sea of bright red jackets designed to drive fear into the heart of an enemy with their boldness, the riflemen wore dark green with black facings. They could disappear from view, move unpredictably over the ground like shadows and only announce their presence when an officer was killed instantly by a well-aimed rifle shot.

The men took pride in being the first into battle and the last out. They had a key role in skirmishes, taking the lead into new territory or covering the movements of other brigades, and they were also involved in close, one-to-one fighting. These tactics meant that the 95th Brigade of Foot was considered to be the most dangerous place for a soldier in the British army. They sometimes had such severe losses in a single battle that a company was no longer viable and its remaining men were redeployed to make up the numbers in others.

Growing up in St Giles taught Molloy about human potential for both dignity and depravity, but the Peninsular campaigns showed him the extremes that people can endure to survive. There were months when life was rich and full, when fighting and marching were replaced by hunting and playing cards. But there were more times when the army pushed forward for days without sleep or food, engaging in battle as they went and enduring the ice-cold nights of Spanish winters and the battering heat of shelterless summer days.

The first week in Portugal was busy and hot, with the army landing ammunition and stores, and gathering a force of 12,000 men and eighteen cannon. The men enjoyed gifts from the local people: cartloads of oranges and figs, wine, geese and turkeys.[165] For the ordinary soldiers it felt like a feast.[166] As they headed towards Lisbon the riflemen led the way, and after three days travelling through woods and vineyards they arrived at Lyrios to face the horrific reality of war. The French had just left the town and firsthand accounts describe the evidence of violence the 95th found there. Molloy had experienced hand-to-hand fighting in his navy days so the sight of death was not new to him, but this was the first time he'd seen what an enemy force could do to civilians caught up in warfare on land. The French soldiers who had committed the atrocities were moving back towards the main strength of their army and the 2nd Battalion of the 95th Regiment followed closely on their heels for two days.

On the evening of 15 August, at the end of a long march towards the village of Obidos, the British were fired on and the war was underway. The 95th fired the first shots of the Peninsular War two days before the first significant battle at Roliça and John Molloy, almost twenty-two years old, was there.

After weeks of waiting the soldiers were over-eager and pursued the French too far. A larger force tried to cut them off and other enemy troops appeared on their flanks. Lieutenant Ralph Bunbury of the 95th Regiment was hit through the head by a musket ball. He died there, the first casualty of the war.

This was not a full-scale encounter but the new recruits were left reeling from the physical shock of the engagement. A solid wall of noise blocked all sound apart from bugle commands. The acrid black smoke that rose up each time they fired their rifles obscured the targets they were aiming at but they could see their comrades falling fast around them. Realising they were outnumbered, the riflemen took position on a hill and formed ranks three men deep, with the front rank kneeling. They held their ground without moving all night, expecting the French to advance at any moment. Finally, at daybreak, they received orders to fall back and rest. Twenty-four hours later the 95th played their part in the first full-scale battle, at Roliça. Part of a British force of 14,000 men and eighteen guns, the Riflemen distinguished themselves for their bravery and discipline.[167]

The fighting was relentless. Within weeks the 2nd Battalion had lost a quarter of their men. Molloy was wounded at Vimeiro, three weeks after arriving in Portugal. A musket ball hit him in the thigh but he refused to return home, so as 'not to alarm his mother'.[168] By the end of the year the army had crossed the border into Spain and he was once again leading men in battle, but things did not go well and the British were forced to retreat. Molloy was with the 2nd Battalion when they were picked up from the Spanish coast at Vigo, exhausted, starving, their uniforms in rags.

In 1809 he was promoted to first lieutenant, transferred into the 1st Battalion and sent to the Staff College of the Royal Military Academy in Great Marlow. His details do not appear among the listed officers' names as the documents for that period are incomplete, so the exact dates of his year in England are not on record, but the secondment meant that he was there when his mother, remarried as Mrs Merth Miler, died in May at the family home in St Giles.[169] He was back in Spain by July 1812 and earned more medal clasps at the battles of Salamanca and Vitoria.

On high ground west of Madrid, the harsh winter weather called a halt to any movement for both armies. Barracked at the small village of Gallegos, the men had time to recover from their hardships and the officers found ways to fill the time. There were walking clubs and sports events. They also enjoyed the hospitality of the local people, including the ladies. Molloy was a good-looking and charismatic man all his life, admired by men and popular with women. In his army days he was known as 'Handsome Jack' and as his regiment moved forward to the French border he left more than one 'sweetheart' behind him in Spain.[170,171]

> In the evenings, relates one of the Light Division officers, 'we got the village belles together and frequently danced through half the long winter nights; nor were our fair partners at all averse to hot punch between the boleros and fandangos. Our nights were spent in the utmost conviviality and harmony in an old barn where we messed.'[172]

By the next winter Wellington was preparing for what he hoped would be his final campaign, but his army's route into France was blocked by the snow-capped mountains of the Pyrenees. His men were about to face the most gruelling marches and relentless fighting of the war. Sometimes it rained for days on end and when it wasn't raining, an icy wind dried their uniforms hard and chilled their bones. On one occasion when the men paused to rest, they tore up the vines around them to make fires and dry themselves off.[173] Some mornings they woke to heavy snowfalls blanketing their bivouacs. Ice that melted as the sky cleared turned swollen rivers into raging torrents that carried away the army's pontoon bridges.

As they moved from the mountains and into France, Molloy fought at the battles of the Pyrenees, Nivelle, the Nive and Toulouse, adding four more clasps to his medal for the Peninsular War. At the battle of Tarbes, eleven fellow officers in the regiment were killed or wounded within half an hour and by evening the rifle battalions had lost twelve officers and eighty men.[174] That night the supplies did not arrive so everyone went hungry.[175] The next day, in rain that had not stopped all night, they waded up to their knees in mud and water to pursue the French. By 29 March 1814, the 95th were three kilometres from the city of Toulouse, where they would fight the final battle of the Peninsular War twelve days later.

After defeat at Toulouse, Napoleon was imprisoned on the island of Elba. But it wasn't the end. Less than a year later he escaped and marched triumphantly into Paris. The French king fled and Napoleon once again ruled France. When his forces arrived in Belgium in 1815, in an attempt to separate the allies who were preparing to confront him, the scene was set for the very last encounter of the Napoleonic Wars. Molloy landed in Belgium with the 1st Battalion of the 95th on 27 April. Their plan was to stop Napoleon Bonaparte for good.

Napoleon's last engagement with Wellington turned out to be 'the battle for modern Europe' but it was not a day of glory.[176] Lord Byron described it as the 'crowning carnage'.[177] On 18 June, Molloy woke before dawn in the cattle shed where he'd spent the night with the rest of his company. The night before, Lieutenant John Stilwell, known as Scamp, had commented on the danger they faced in being closed in on all sides. He said they would be caught 'like rats in a trap' if the French arrived, so the men 'setting their shoulders to the inner wall threw it down so they were free to get away as they chose'.[178] Molloy told stories in later years of how Stilwell crept up during the night and stole a biscuit from his trouser pocket. Biscuits were a rock hard, unappetising staple of army rations.

The morning brought a low mist. Molloy's company was stationed opposite the farmhouse of La Haye Sainte, under the command of Jonathan Leach, recently promoted to brevet major. They lay low in what Molloy described as a 'gravel pit near a crossroads'. The men heard the deafening noise of the battle when it began: cannon, muskets and rifles. Molloy took turns with the other officers on watch to stay outside the sandpit for a quarter of an hour at a time. At about two o'clock the French moved on the farmhouse. The riflemen took careful aim and held them back. When another French brigade pressed towards them, Molloy and his comrades had no choice but to leave their cover and fight. The 95th fought fiercely and took many prisoners but when Wellington's orders came they were unequivocal: he did not want to lose the British position at La Haye Sainte. Molloy's company returned to their positions at the sandpit and faced the full force of the French: sharpshooters, cavalry and cannon. Men and horses on both sides fell around them.

The cannon fire continued through the afternoon and they suffered more losses. At about six, the French advanced again and took the farmhouse, raining their fire on the riflemen in the sandpit from the windows above. With shooting on their flank as well and advancing columns of French ahead of them, Molloy's company were told to fall back to join the rest of their regiment. During this heavy firing, Molloy saw 'a French tirailleur very close and taking aim' at him as he 'flourished his sword'.[179] He felt the thud of pain as a musket ball entered his leg at just the point where that hard army biscuit should have been.

Hasluck described how Molloy 'lay all night on the field of battle among the slain' but this is not what happened.[180] Many years later, Molloy told his friend George Leake that when he was relieved of duty, someone called his attention to the blood running out of his boot and that was the moment when he realised how badly he'd been hurt.[181] He had been seriously wounded in the very last hours of the final battle. A military surgeon saved his life by removing the musket ball from his leg soon afterwards.

After the war, Molloy spent time in France recovering from his injury and gaining important experience as a magistrate. The Duke of Wellington appointed him Deputy Judge Advocate of the General Court Martial in Paris,[181] perhaps an indication that Georgiana's future husband was already exhibiting notable qualities of discernment and decision-making. During the next two years he was responsible for trying prisoners during the army's occupation of France. The fact that he survived the war is remarkable. With no injuries apart from two leg wounds and a powder burn that affected the sight of one eye, he was among the luckiest. He had stood side by side with men who died of starvation, drowning, exposure, accidents and mortal wounding by friendly fire. Military data indicate that more than a million and a half allied soldiers died, about 220,000 of them in the British army.[183]

* * *

The scale and range of research sources for this part of Molloy's life are a gift and a burden for a biographer. Hundreds of official letters and dispatches are public documents. Most officers kept meticulous journals giving details of every encounter and many ordinary soldiers who could write left vivid accounts of campaign life in their journals and letters. The army spent seven years in Portugal, Spain and France and I have used maps to trace Molloy's route from town to town, looking down from above using satellite images: a small wood where they spent the night, the road through a tiny village where they stopped to cook, a bend in a river where they fought for the bridge. Now I understand why the veterans of this war were so proud of simply surviving it; why they talked about it for the rest of their lives to anyone who would listen; why the comradeship of that time meant so much to them; and why they were not too humble to believe that they were heroes.

The hunt for biographical information can become addictive. The possibility of new things coming to the surface, however deeply they have remained buried for years, is enough to maintain a researcher's momentum. For someone whose internet skills have developed slowly over time through trial and error, retracing ground already covered can be exciting territory. Over a cup of coffee one morning, I repeated a search I had done many times before but more methodically. A day in the life of John Molloy suddenly emerged in colourful detail.

The 95th Rifles started the trend for what became a popular form of army entertainment during winter. They converted an old house into 'quite a presentable theatre' and the officers put on plays that were well rehearsed and with printed programs. The fame of 'the Gallegos theatricals' spread through the army and Wellington himself rode from headquarters to attend a performance. A surviving program from the 'Light Division Theatre' lists the cast of a full-length play and a short farce performed on 4 February 1813. The actors were all officers, including Lieutenant Molloy, who played the part of Catchpole the bailiff, a strikingly similar role to the one he would assume as magistrate and tax collector years later in Western Australia.[184] Molloy's old friend, Jonathan Leach, remembered how amusing it was to watch 'two young and good-looking men (dressed uncommonly well, and looking very feminine on the stage), drinking punch and smoking cigars behind the scenes at a furious rate between the acts!'[185]

The cast list is another reminder of the aristocratic company that Molloy mixed with in his army years and the pressure on him not to reveal his humble beginnings. The officer who played the part of the glamorous young lady in the play was Lieutenant Lord Charles Spencer, an ancestor of Lady Diana Spencer, late Princess of Wales, and Sir Winston Churchill. He was also a son of the fifth Duke of Marlborough, Molloy's previous employer eight years earlier in the Oxford Militia.

* * *

Molloy spent another ten years in the army but they were very different. The confrontations he faced were the uprisings of angry workers, vulnerable farmers and poor families who suffered in the aftermath of the war and the increasing momentum of industrialisation. From October 1819 to November 1820, Molloy's detachment was in Glasgow during what became known as the 'Radical War'. Cotton spinners in Carlisle and weavers in Glasgow were rising up to demand reform of their working conditions and although their actions started peacefully, the government was worried enough to call in the army. It was a difficult deployment for men used to fighting the highly trained French military force. Their opponents were poor, hungry factory workers and they walked a difficult line between keeping the peace and dealing fairly with ordinary people who were campaigning for basic rights. The 1st Battalion left Glasgow in November 1820 and went straight to Belfast in Ireland (now Northern Ireland) to deal with election riots, but Molloy was not with them initially. He made the short journey south to Carlisle in his new, temporary role: the appointment as 'Superintending Officer for Recruitment'.[186]

First Lieutenant Molloy could not afford to buy another commission so he had to earn promotion, and he succeeded. After joining his regiment in Ireland he was made a captain without purchase in 1824, but without a war to fight he was in charge of local peacekeeping once again. In 1826 he was in Ireland with the 1st Battalion, part of the British government's response to rising levels of violence aimed at landowners. In the last years of the eighteenth century, when he was a child, the rift between Catholics and Protestants was pulling families apart and influencing the emotions of young lives. He grew up hearing tales of the break his parents had made with their 'Papist' relatives and he held strong religious views for the rest of his life.[187] Molloy was leading his men against local people in the same villages where his grandparents had lived. Violence was committed on both sides but he witnessed crimes against British military forces who represented the Protestant cause as they filled what had been half-empty churches every Sunday. He must have heard reports in 1823 about the rape of a group of women travelling in County Limerick to join the 95th Brigade, the victims individually selected because their husbands were officers. Molloy never renounced his personal religious prejudices.[188]

By 1827 his days consisted of ensuring his men were ready for a battle that never came and joining in with the gentlemanly pursuits of officers in time of peace. Younger, less experienced men were advancing over his head. His old friend Lieutenant Orlando Felix had purchased a captaincy in 1824 and was destined for greater things.[189] In 1828 the brigade moved from Plymouth to Gosport, then to Portsmouth, back to Plymouth and back again to the Cambridge barracks in Portsmouth in March 1829. Molloy had had enough.

War with France was over but the crowded, hungry, downhearted years that followed Bonaparte's final defeat offered no consolation for most British families. Thousands of soldiers had come home, many of them seriously wounded, and they flooded the economy with cheap labour. Wages fell but the price of food kept increasing and with husbands back again, families were growing. For the first time it did not matter whether a man's work was in industry or agriculture, the daily struggle was for survival. Riots in cities, towns and villages were the violent outcomes of desperation. For those who could not foresee a way of changing their cheerless lives, dreams of a bright future were not on the agenda.

And then an opportunity surfaced that seemed almost too good to be true. The chance of a new life was on offer. A fresh start in a place that sounded like heaven on Earth was available for anyone willing to take a chance. Vivid descriptions of Swan River, a new colony on the southwest coast of Australia (known then as New Holland) spread quickly through gentlemen's clubs, coffee houses, taverns, markets, mills and farms. Importantly, it was to be a 'free colony', not serviced like others by the convict labour associated with shocking stories of drunkenness, crime and violence in New South Wales and Tasmania.

Although reports described emigration to the new colony as an adventure for 'men of capital', it was the kind of enterprise that offered great rewards for a relatively small investment.[190] Anyone with the price of a ship's ticket and the equivalent of three pounds to put forward in capital assets could claim forty fertile acres that would mean self-sufficiency and prosperity if they worked their land grant and made the required improvements. Men and women working as servants and agricultural labourers could get in on the scheme too by signing themselves up with settlers who would pay their way, give them a home, feed and clothe them until they had fulfilled the terms of their indentures and could become free settlers themselves. Families who could never have hoped to own a garden hooked themselves up to the dream of possessing land and perhaps eventually becoming part of 'the gentry'. Men further up the financial ladder who had always been frustratingly close to high society but blocked by low status, imagined themselves founding dynasties of their own and breaking through the glass ceiling that separated them from 'gentlemen'. Women who took in washing in the narrow alleyways of smoke-choked cities were happy to go along with their husbands and do the same work in a place where their children could play safely all year round in clean air and sunshine. For soldiers like Molloy, whose lives had become bland and uninspiring in the decade after war, the call of adventure and comradeship in a new struggle against adversity felt like a reprieve.

Captain James Stirling was appointed to administer the affairs of the new colony as lieutenant governor and, unsurprisingly, he painted a rosy picture that was hard to resist: 'a country rich and romantic'.[191] His bucolic descriptions of the area that is now Perth in Western Australia quickly reached their mark, travelling by printed page and conversation along the streets and into the boudoirs of ladies who had little to do each day apart from read and gossip. *Bell's Court and Fashionable Magazine* informed its female readers that 'in certain classes an almost unprecedented zeal for emigration prevails' and it described the Swan River as 'the main point of attraction to those who are possessed of the spirit'.[192]

The scheme needed a population of settlers as quickly as possible. Advertisements in *The Times* nearly every morning in 1829 informed the public of ships heading for Swan River, equipped with well-designed cabins, on-board surgeons, space for cargo and berths in steerage for passengers with less cash to spare. All up it was a complete package of hope, with apparently good odds and a quick return.

In November 1828 Molloy had become a Freemason. He was initiated into the Phoenix Lodge 484 in Portsmouth and gave his age as forty-one. The decision was late in the career of an officer but it was an astute one. Being part of the Brotherhood of Masons in the nineteenth century was rather like having a ticket of friendship and support that would be invaluable to a man intending to begin a new career or to travel in distant places. In May 1829, Molloy exchanged his full-time post with another officer, went onto half pay and was listed as unattached from his regiment. John Molloy had decided to change his life. He was also in love.

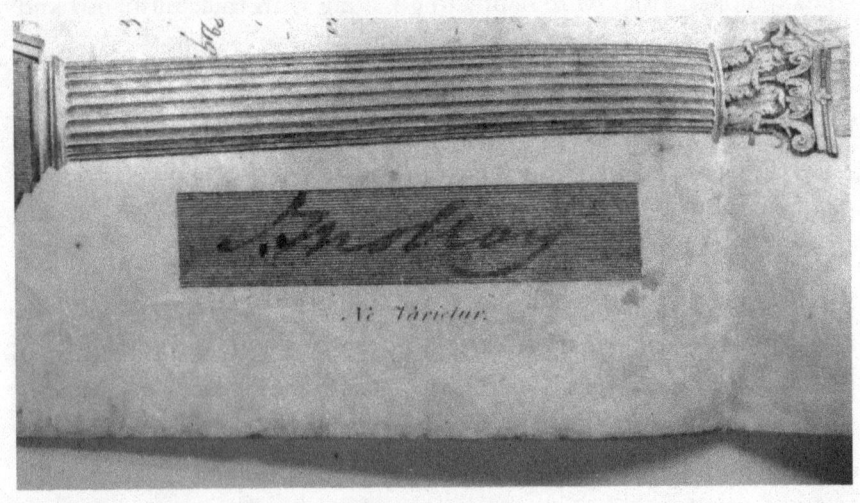

John Molloy's signature on his 1829 Freemasonry certificate

JS Battye Library SLWA ACC 4730 /A 3

SCOTLAND

Statice Armeria

May the end be blest

For the rest of his life, John Molloy remembered the moment he saw Miss Georgiana Kennedy for the first time. She was in the garden at Crosby, wearing a large bonnet, and she was fourteen years old.[193] Her father had died less than a year earlier and her mother was in deep mourning. With an attractive, unmarried elder sister, it's unlikely that Georgiana thought the handsome officer would notice her, but he did. As an old man, Molloy shared with his eldest daughter, Sabina, the vivid memory of a single moment, forty years earlier, when he arrived at the Kennedy home and saw the young woman who would become his wife.

* * *

When I began investigating Georgiana's life, I soon found that the facts about when and where she and John first met remained elusive to researchers and biographers although speculation had long suggested several potential links between the Kennedy family and Captain Molloy. Margaret Dunlop knew that Molloy had been writing to Georgiana at Keppoch House.[194] She thought they may have met when he was stationed at Carlisle Castle, because Mrs Kennedy was 'prone to flirtations' with the officers, but there is no evidence that the

Early Apples
Stubbards
Spencers pippins
Early Stagusters
2 — Quarrendons
2 Early Boxhill
2 — Brown Spice

Autumn Apples
2 — Essex
2 — Pine Apple
2 — Moxey pippins

Winter Apples
2 Royal Russetts
2 Loans pearmains
2 Nonpariel
2 ~~Winter pearmain~~
2 Royal Nonpariel
2 Ribstone pippins

A list of apple trees that George Leach sent to David Kennedy from Devon in 1811: 'fifteen kinds, two of each, properly label'd, the most approv'd sorts of fruit, rear'd by a gardener of this village who strongly recommended that the trees should be only two years old from the time of grafting'. Kennedy planted them 'on the bank' at Crosby Lodge.

Cumbria Archive Centre D KEN 4 / 13

95th were ever garrisoned there.[195] Molloy's Scottish friend Kirkman Finlay was a member of the same gentlemen's club as Alexander Dunlop, the Board of Green Cloth.[196] Any one of these connections seemed plausible, but John and Georgiana met more than 150 years ago so I thought it unlikely that the truth would ever emerge.

Visual memory sometimes works behind the scenes more efficiently than conscious, logical thought. As I scanned a list of references I had read through many times before, a name looked vaguely familiar and I stopped to try to remember why. The trail of clues from that name led me back through the pages of the Kennedy family archive on the CAC website as well as the online National Archives in Kew. By the end of the afternoon a question that has been asked for 150 years had been answered.

Georgiana's parents had an old friend whose name was George Leach. He first appeared to me as the insignificant sender of some apple trees for a new orchard at Crosby in 1811. More searching showed he was the same George Leach who was exchanging letters with Mrs Kennedy ten years later. He was a solicitor and amateur naturalist, and Mrs Kennedy often consulted him about her finances. He was the one who told her to sell Crosby Lodge and pay off her debts even though this advice was unwelcome. Transcription of Mrs Kennedy's letters eventually confirmed that George Leach was the father of John Molloy's officer friend, Jonathan Leach.

The young men joined the 2nd Battalion of the 95th Foot Brigade within two years of one another and served together in the Peninsular War. Although Leach was a more experienced soldier than Molloy, they became friends and were both transferred to the 1st Battalion. They fought side by side in Spain and France and at Waterloo. When senior officers were wounded and killed, Leach was promoted by brevet to lieutenant colonel and he commanded Molloy's company there.[197] The old comrades wrote to one another until Leach died in 1855.

The Leaches were an ancient family of 'private fortune', landed gentry with estates including the family home at Spitchwick and another on Plymouth Hoe.[198] Jonathan's brother William Elford Leach was one of the world's leading zoologists of the Regency period and his work influenced Charles Darwin.[199] A third brother, George, was a solicitor and gave Mrs Kennedy legal advice after his father died in 1823. George Leach senior's letters show that the two families had been friends for decades. In 1821, William Elford Leach suffered a mental breakdown from overwork. He was a brilliant young man and his treatment for 'mental illness' was deeply stressful for his family. It was a situation that would soon be very familiar to Mrs Kennedy.

Although Jonathan Leach was now a major, the two riflemen had been close for more than ten years when they arrived in Edinburgh on 28 September 1819 with the rest of their battalion and travelled to Glasgow on the west coast to deal with the public unrest that was causing concern on both sides of the border. Dealing with the uprisings of cotton spinners and colliers was, according to Leach, 'by no means a delectable service' but their barracks were only a day's journey from Carlisle.[200] Transcribing letters from George Leach junior to Mrs Kennedy revealed that Jonathan was taking John Molloy with him on visits to Crosby Lodge. At the time, all the Kennedy children were still living at home. Dalton and seven-year-old George were attending Walters, the school they went to before entering Rugby School. Twenty-year-old Eliza was as inclined to flirting as her mother, so the Crosby country-house parties must have been lively times for the ladies and their guests and even more exciting when attended by two handsome heroes from the legendary Rifle Brigade.

* * *

Lieutenant Molloy's visits became more frequent after he was transferred to Carlisle in early 1821 when Georgiana was fifteen.[201] Whether his new job in charge of army recruitment there was a coincidence or a request, he was living just a short ride from the Kennedy house. Letters from George Leach junior to Mrs Kennedy in March 1821, show that when his brother Jonathan travelled from Ireland to recover from an illness among the home comforts of Crosby Lodge, Molloy joined him there once again.

> It gave me great pleasure to hear that Jonathan was paying you a visit as I was sure your hospitable reception of him & the Crosby air would go a long way towards restoring his health – he had written a letter or two from Ireland of a very sombre cast arising partly from ill health and partly no doubt from the melancholy feelings excited by a consideration of our own late severe family misfortunes and I felt quite sure that he acted very wisely in exchanging his almost solitary quarters in Ireland for your fireside at Crosby.[202]

Molloy began visiting without Leach and Mrs Kennedy warmly encouraged him to stay. She was only six years older than him and he always believed that she thought his interest was in her rather than one of her daughters.[203] In the early autumn of 1820 Jonathan Leach's brother George stayed at Crosby Lodge and Molloy was there. George Leach was surprised at the level of hospitality being offered to the captain and he told Mrs Kennedy about his concerns. Soon afterwards, she went to London for a few days and while she was away, Molloy visited the house again and, quite shockingly in her absence, he stayed overnight. She mentioned the incident in her next letter to George and hinted that she thought Molloy's interests might lead to a proposal of marriage.[204] Her letter has not survived but George's reply gives an idea of its content and delivers another insight into the web of relationships that Mrs Kennedy wove around herself and her children.

> You may rely on my keeping a profound secret what you hinted at respecting Molloy, but indeed I do not wonder at it. From the kindest possible motive, a wish to pay the utmost attention to Jonathan's friend, you gave Molloy a more general invitation than I thought

prudent even when I was at Crosby. You will I am sure recollect what I said once on the subject of his sleeping at your house – I could not enlarge on it but I then thought that the least part of the evil would be the ill natured tittle tattle to which his frequent visits would give rise and I certainly did anticipate something of the kind to which you allude during your absence in London. Knowing as I did that if any attachment was found on either side or both, it must be broken off from prudential motives, I did not contemplate it with much pleasure – the question now is how is it to be put an end to? I should say by only asking Molloy now and then with other persons and by not allowing him to have the run of the house at all times & seasons – it may be difficult to break through a habit once established but it may be done by degrees. I believe Molloy to be a very honorable [*sic*] worthy fellow but at present I fancy he is wholly without fortune and it would be downright insanity for Eliza to marry him, if he were to propose it, which however I think he has too much prudence to do.

Believe me my dear Mrs Kennedy

Your sincere friend

George Leach Jr.

Without Mrs Kennedy's original letter or its draft, it is not clear whether she was suggesting that Molloy had set his sights on Eliza or whether her hints at romance led George to assume that the eldest daughter was being courted, rather than the mother. At fifteen, Georgiana was presumably not considered to be a possible attraction to the gallant officer.

Molloy's friendship with the family continued through the years but if Georgiana was already in love with him no clues have yet come to light.

While living in Rugby, she was exchanging letters with childhood friend George Troutbeck at Ennim Bank but she brought that relationship to an end without an explanation to him. She told her mother she was fond of the man but he had taken too long to propose. Troutbeck had longstanding connections with her family, as well as money and land. She wanted something more.[205]

In 1827, after Dalton had left school and spent some time in Scotland with his guardian Archibald CB Craufurd at Ardmillan House near Girvan, he purchased a commission and joined the army as an ensign. John Molloy went with him to London and introduced him to useful military contacts, then made sure he went safely on his way by ship to join the 12th Regiment of Foot in Gibraltar. Molloy wrote to Mrs Kennedy to let her know. His letter is affectionate though formal with a hint of his light-hearted humour.[206]

> My dear Mrs. Kennedy
> After making a personal inspection of every vessel at Deptford to which place we were referred ... we as a final resort had recourse to the Agent for Transports who told us the Vessel was at Woolwich and would sail on Monday next at furthest. With this information we ported up to London as fast as the tide and a pair of sculls could waft us on the bosom of old father Thames.

That first evening Captain Molloy and Dalton Kennedy went to a tavern and enjoyed a good meal.

> We found the evening had far advanced and that there hardly remained time enough to announce briefly the result of our first days sojourn in and about the big Village – we therefore sought the first receptacle for travellers and ordered a beef steak and two sheets of paper – one of which in time was used by Dalton the former we conjointly disposed of.

Molloy also sent his best wishes to the three Kennedy girls, 'all my fair friends' and assured Mrs Kennedy that he remained ever hers 'affectionately fondly & truly'.

Dalton was not close to Molloy before their visit to London in 1828.[207] He was away at school when Molloy visited Crosby and was staying in Scotland with his guardian until 1828 but he reminded his mother a few years later about the high opinion he formed of the captain once they became acquainted.[208]

> ... but as of him, this looks like affectation but it is not, G & I were generally at school, she at Kensington and I at Walters & Rugby, when she came home I had left it but I saw much of Molloy, not as a brother in law but as a brother officer & I do not believe that a more worthy upright honest fellow than Jack Molloy exists.

It is possible that Molloy was cautiously and judiciously flirting with three Kennedy women sequentially – or even at the same time. It is equally possible that he was a naturally charming person and his courtesy and attentions were misinterpreted by at least one of the ladies. At various times he was referred to as a 'dear friend' by Eliza, Georgiana and their mother. In December 1828, he was writing to Mrs Kennedy in Rugby, Georgiana in Scotland and Eliza in Wroxeter, where she was staying with Sarah Egremont, a granddaughter of the Quaker, John Mitchinson. Eliza's reply to Molloy about a cabinet he had sent her as a gift gives no indication of anything beyond a longstanding friendship. She also mentions that she and the Reverend Besley could not make their engagement public until he had a more secure financial position and tells Molloy, 'I always shall consider you one of my greatest friends'.[209]

If Mrs Kennedy had private intentions for her own relationship with Molloy, any emerging evidence that his romantic interest was directed towards Georgiana could not have come as a welcome surprise. A growing feeling of jealousy may be the source of the coldness Mrs Kennedy showed to her middle daughter during the years that followed and perhaps another clue to the reasons for the quarrelling between the sisters that led to Georgiana's departure for Scotland.

The very first entry in her diary for 1 January 1829 is a reference to the man she would marry six months later, 'Heard from Molloy'.[210] During the next few weeks she referred to him more often as 'Molloy' than 'Captain' or 'Mr Molloy' and a growing warmth became evident in her diary during spring. On 6 February she wrote, 'Heard from dear Mr Molloy' and answered his letter the same day.

The developing affection she felt was not the only thing on Georgiana's mind as the end of her first year at Keppoch House drew closer. She found it difficult to forget the strength of her feelings about the place she had escaped from. In February 1829, a year after leaving home, she wrote in her diary: 'This day last year was the last time I was at Holbrook & the last one I spent in horrid Rugby.'[211]

She loved everything about her temporary home in Scotland but did not feel as comfortable as she had when she had first arrived. As much as the Dunlop girls enjoyed her company and valued her friendship, there were some tensions with Margaret who, by the beginning of Georgiana's second spring at Keppoch, was becoming 'disagreeable'.[212] The hospitality of the rest of the family remained unchanged but 'Maggie' seemed to have taken 'prejudice'. Georgiana wrote sadly in her diary, 'How weak she shows herself to be'.[213] Local people had started gossiping about the reason for such a long stay and decided that the young guest had her eye on Alexander Dunlop himself.

> Has she a home? Why does she not return to it? It was natural that in a country neighbourhood, curiosity should be excited by the extraordinary length of her stay, and one solution of the mystery was that she intended to take possession of the house and its master and would not leave until her object was attained.[214]

Then there was the question of the wealthy, handsome and eligible neighbour. In January, James Dennistoun's younger brother, Richard, died after a short illness and Georgiana went to the funeral. A week later her favourite Dennistoun and his family called at Keppoch and she was 'depressed all day'. Not long after she left Scotland later that year, she coyly added a postscript in her letter to Helen: 'Tell me if there is not a present flirtation between Maggie and James Dennistoun.'[215]

Letters from home continued to bring sombre news. In 1828 Dalton suffered a dangerous illness during the yellow fever epidemic in Gibraltar and was lucky to survive. Around 2000 people died and it was probably the same fever that had almost claimed the young life of midshipman Molloy in 1801, such a terrifying virus that none of his navy shipmates would go near enough to care for him.

Georgiana was concerned to read that Dalton was already finding army life difficult and overspending his allowance. He complained to his mother that he did not like Gibraltar and could not manage to purchase a new horse or pay his servants. Mrs Kennedy was not pleased.[216] He was expecting to take over the Scottish estate and its income early in 1829, on his twenty-first birthday; it would have eased his financial situation. But there were serious problems. On 2 March Georgiana heard that Dalton would not become Laird of Craig and was 'deprived of his patrimony'.[217]

His uncles had brought a case against the inheritance. There were complications dating back to details about the legal arrangements his great-grandfather had made in the previous century. Dalton's serious debts meant that he needed to sell off parts of the estate to pay what he owed but the exchanges between solicitors on both sides continued for years, causing Mrs Kennedy more anguish as she watched her eldest son experience increasing difficulty in balancing his income and expenditure. Eventually Dalton did inherit the estate and there was no ill feeling with his uncles, but it was too late to save Mrs Kennedy from the growing weight of public embarrassment.

By April, in her second year at Keppoch, Georgiana knew she had to make a decision about the future, but in the short term her only option was to return to the house where her mother was staying. She wrote in her diary, 'I fear I shall soon have to exchange these beloved scenes for Rugby but all is in God's hands.'[218] Still trusting she would be rescued from the fate she dreaded, Georgiana waited for a sign, becoming increasingly anxious and unhappy. A visit to the Storys in Roseneath and a walk on the hill behind the manse could not console her.[219] In early June she was packed and ready to leave but was so distressed that Alexander Dunlop persuaded her to stay on.[220]

From the early spring, Georgiana recorded in her diary the hopes and imaginings that she kept to herself. She believed God would decide what should happen to her but faith was not enough to stop her from dreaming. As a single woman with no independent income, her choices were limited: return home, marry, or become a lady's companion. Only in her least guarded moments did she dare to imagine that a man she liked and respected might have similar feelings for her and act on them in time to save her.

John Molloy's sister was buried in St Giles on 9 January and he wrote straight away to tell Georgiana the sad news.[221,222] The money Susannah left him was delivered to the Forton barracks near Gosport where his brigade was stationed.[223] The £1000 was a substantial windfall and it may not be coincidental that he decided to leave the army and buy a passage to the Swan River. Molloy wrote to Georgiana about his plans and her diary entries during those months hint at what was on her mind. She wrote about bending to God's will but her own dreams vibrate between the lines with growing emotion as the weeks pass and her focus shifted increasingly from the pleasures of the natural world around her to 'vain imaginings' that would not go away.[224]

> 13 January: The scenery most enchanting. I was in a state of excitement & very much fatigued.
> 14 January: My imagination most busy at what it should not have been.
> 18 January: A light flashed on in my mind at dinner but this was transient. I thought of my future life & closed the day in prayer. Mary & Mr Story had mutual thoughts.

Days turned into weeks and Molloy's letters still gave no hint of any personal intentions. She was 'determined not to build castles' and on 20 January she wrote sadly, 'No letter for me'.

On 6 February she mentioned the subject again – 'I thought much of Mr Molloy's going away. He is an excellent creature' – but by the end of the month he had still said nothing about a future together. On the first anniversary of her arrival at Keppoch his letters occupied her thoughts, but it began to seem that God had no plans for her. The object of her romantic imaginings would soon be sailing away to his new life on the other side of the world and it was not just the dream of marriage that was slipping away. *The Gardener's Magazine* was typical of many other publications in the rosy picture it painted of horticultural opportunities she would be missing at Swan River.

> A gardener, who has £200 or upwards, and a healthy wife, would do well to consider the very favourable circumstances attending this settlement. A man acquainted with country matters, with 5000L, by going out there with twenty paupers, and remaining seven or ten years, would, in all probability, increase his property twenty-fold, and might then return home with the consciousness of having done good to others as well as to himself, of having promoted civilisation and happiness generally.[225]

The letters she waited for so eagerly each morning described the progress of Molloy's plans and the arrangements for his journey. His friend Captain James Stirling had been appointed governor of the new colony in January and was preparing to set off with the first group of military and settlers. While stationed in Ireland, Molloy and his fellow rifleman, Captain Francis Byrne, had met an officer of the 8th Regiment of Foot who was in Dublin receiving army training in the use of the broadsword. Marshall MacDermott had been attracted by 'the large concessions of land offered by the Government to the settlers on easy terms'. He decided to make Australia his home and Captains Molloy and Byrne decided to join him.[226]

Molloy's original plan had been to travel to the Swan River in partnership with George Cheyne, a Scottish merchant who intended to buy a Swedish ship and use it to set up a business after the voyage. Molloy pulled out of the arrangement and lost his original investment and although the Molloys and the Cheynes met again later on friendly terms, Georgiana was aware of her husband's regrets about 'his unfortunate connection with Capt. Byrne'.[227]

The early summer of 1829 was an exciting time for John Molloy as he prepared for a life of adventure, but for Georgiana it was almost unbearable. She was faced with the prospect of never seeing him again. Still waiting, she prayed that God's plan might match her own dreams and, between the end of April and the last few days of May, the increasing regularity of Molloy's letters and the nature of their content confirmed that her prayers had been answered.[228] On 26 May she received a 'particularly surprising' letter that could not be misinterpreted. It was a declaration of love.

* * *

Georgiana's writing is littered with Italian phrases that she used without pretension. John Molloy's own ease with the language was an attraction for her and a tie that bound their friendship through the nicknames they gave one another and the comfortable, multilingual richness of their private conversations as a couple. Unfortunately, Georgiana burnt all her letters one evening just before she set sail for Australia. The letter she received from Molloy on 26 May was among them but its contents have survived because of the nineteenth-century habit of keeping drafts of correspondence in 'letter books'. One afternoon in May 2005 I was at the JS Battye Library in Perth when I noticed a particular archive reference for the first time. The item was recorded simply as 'Letter of proposal'.

The librarian looked up the document's provenance and told me that the letter was 'among the belongings of the Resident Magistrate' when the old Busselton Courthouse was renovated in the 1970s. John Molloy was Magistrate at the Vasse, now Busselton, for many years. The content of the letter should have been disappointing because its signature was not that of John Molloy, but I guessed this was his own draft of the declaration of love sent to Miss Kennedy in 1829. I had to find out why he'd signed it with a completely different name. That took another year.

The letter was undated but it held clues about when it had been written. Another item in the same collection was the draft of a letter written by Molloy to James Stirling on his promotion to the role of governor and that one was signed. Stirling's original appointment was on 30 December 1828, and he set off for the Swan River a few months later. Molloy wrote, 'Allow me to felicitate you on yr. promotion & altho I may be late in the field of compliment believe me no-one feels more sincere pleasure.'[229] Allowing for the time taken for news to reach Molloy in London and his delay in writing, it is very likely that this letter draft was written around the same time as the letter that surprised Georgiana in May. Stirling arrived at the Swan River to take up his appointment in August. When the letter to Stirling is viewed in a mirror, the blotting marks made from wet ink on the facing page clearly reveal the words at the end of the love letter. This meant the two drafts were on consecutive pages in Molloy's letter book.

The mysterious signature was more of a problem. Drafts can be particularly difficult to transcribe because they are sometimes written quickly. Letter shapes that should be closed are left open, masking any distinction between the letters 'o', 'a' and 'u'. The letter 'r' written carelessly sometimes seems to disappear into the letters alongside it. Naso de Cobu? Naso de Coba? Naso de Corbo? The phrase looked either Italian or Spanish and I thought it had to be something to do with a nose. Molloy's was conspicuously sharp and downward curved, evident in a portrait from his youth and photographs in old age. But the Spanish word for nose is nariz and the Italian is naso. The last letter of the final word could be 'u' or 'a' but nothing that matched with corba, corbu or corbo.

Molloy probably learned some Spanish from local recruits to the 95th Brigade, but no Spanish word fitted the spelling. In the end the solution was embarrassingly simple. I had read those three words many times but one day I read them aloud.

Molloy's knowledge of Italian and Spanish was limited and he acquired most of the words he knew by listening to officers and local civilians rather than through reading or study. In Castilian Spanish there is a voiced consonant that sounds like a softly mouthed 'b' in spoken English. In writing, the sound is represented by the letter 'v'. When Molloy's adapted spelling is changed to what would have been correct in Spanish we discover the word he thought he had written: *corvo*. He had heard it as *corba*, a word he knew, meaning curved or, describing a nose, hooked. In Italian, the word *corvo* means crow. Trying to represent an Italian word he knew but spelling it like the Spanish word with a 'b' instead of a 'v', he simply wrote it the way it sounded. Perhaps already a familiar nickname from his time in Spain, he used it once again and declared his love as 'crow nose'. In one of the most serious letters he would ever have to write, he could not resist an injection of the subtle wit that he and Georgiana shared; it was an intellectual alliance that drew them together from the start.

* * *

John Molloy's draft of the love letter he sent to Georgiana in 1829 shows more about his feelings at the time than the final version would have revealed. The changes he made as he wrote, adding words and crossing out others, mirror his thinking: he decided to be her 'devoted victim' rather than a man 'devotedly attracted'.

My dear Lady,
            You will forgive one who unlike Hercules either in figure or disposition I never could during the bane be found spinning at the feet of a Dejanira. ~~without care~~ I more resembled Caesar who never felt the tender passion but in the reign of peace — ~~such as my~~ ~~own~~ the cares of a soldier I confess may have left some rude traces on my countenance — may have thinned my flowing locks, but my heart I'll assure you has received its first & most desperate wound. Your youth, ~~from y'r Eyes~~ discernment & penetrating glance will surely have apprised you of the conquest you have ~~achieved~~, and your tender nature will induce to commiserate & relieve the sufferings of ~~one~~ ~~undoubtedly attached to you~~ your devoted victim. One word of kindness & of hope I look for to relieve my anxiety of mind & cherish my hopes ~~of happiness~~ for the future — that withheld you will hear no more from your devoted Valentine.
                                    Naso de Cobre

John Molloy's declaration of love, 1829

JS Battye Library SLWA ACC 227A (with permission)

My dear Lady
You will forgive one who unlike Hercules either in figure or disposition. I never could during the wars be found spinning at the feet of a Dejeunira ~~in that care~~ I more resembled Ceasar [sic] who never filled the tendre papier but in the reign of peace – ~~such is my care~~ The career of a soldier I confess may have left some rude traces on my countenance, may have thinned my flowing locks, but my heart I'll assure you has received its first and most desperate wound. ^{From yr Eyes.} Your quick discernment and penetrating glance will surely have appraized you of the conquest you have achieved, and your <u>tender</u> ^{beautiful} nature will induce to commiserate & relieve the sufferings of ~~one so devotedly attracted to you~~ your devoted victim. One word of kindness or of hope I look for to relieve my anxiety of mind & cherish my hopes ~~of happiness~~ for the future – that withheld you will hear no more from your devoted victim.
Naso de Coba[230]

Georgiana waited two days before she replied and it seems she gave Molloy some encouragement because his letters continued as did his plans for emigration but, without an explicit offer of marriage, she kept on praying.[231] She knew that if a proposal was imminent, her acceptance would mean sailing for the new colony immediately. When the long-awaited letter finally arrived on 8 July, she 'believed it to be an instrument in God's hands for bringing his will to pass & the next morning was to decide'. The next day she wrote in her diary, 'I leave all to Providence. We talked & thought much of future events'. On Alexander Dunlop's advice, she decided to accept and Dalton was informed, yet she still 'scarcely knew what to do' and wrote in her diary on 18th, 'May the end be blest'.

Georgiana immediately regretted her decision. When the Storys came to stay at Keppoch they were delighted with the news but their encouragement could not calm her increasing anxiety about marrying and leaving for Australia within the next three weeks. She felt confused and shared her fears with Helen.[232] For the first time a letter from Molloy left her feeling 'miserable'. Eventually, dreading 'the finale of this affair', she asked Dunlop whether it was too late for her to change her mind. He advised her to do nothing, but receiving daily letters from Molloy left her 'quite distracted with fearful anticipations' and on 25 July she wrote to him and withdrew her acceptance, desperately hoping her letter would arrive at his lodgings before he set off for Scotland.

Immediately after sending her retraction, Georgiana went to Camis Eskan, the home of James Dennistoun, and in the evening she went straight to bed after dinner. It is likely her desperate letter was delivered too late. Her future husband may never have known how close he came to setting sail as a single man.

On 30 June an advertisement in *The Times* had caught Molloy's eye. The 600 ton ship *Warrior* was in St Katharine Docks awaiting passengers, new settlers for the Swan River Colony, and it was due to sail at the beginning of August. Captains Molloy and Byrne booked 'commodious cabins'. By early July, Molloy had applied for a marriage licence in London, but the plans changed and he quickly rearranged for the wedding to take place at Keppoch. By 26 July the date was set, and Georgiana waited for her future husband to arrive. She went to church 'perhaps for the last time as Georgiana Kennedy' and as the days passed her increasing anxiety turned to fear. She began to focus less on God's will and more on her own feelings.[233] On the outside things were the same and she was still gathering flowers, making alterations to her dresses and calling on neighbours but what she'd seen as a romantic dream had changed by 27 July to 'my unhappy fate'.

Then, the day before Molloy was due to arrive, James Dennistoun called at Keppoch and was invited to spend the night there. It could not have been a more difficult moment. His arrival may have been an innocent act of neighbourliness or a desperate attempt to provoke confrontation. Whether he had romantic intentions or not, Georgiana felt unable to talk to him about Molloy. Margaret Dunlop had to pass on the news over dinner instead. Twice in her diary entry for 30 July, as she described her nervousness about the arrival of her future husband, she managed to mention Dennistoun: 'Rather nervous. I like J. D. very much. Expected Capt. Molloy & Doe. J. Dennistoun dined here & Maggie told him.'

The next day, 31 July, Molloy's carriage came clattering up the long drive and she stood in Keppoch's grand front portico to greet him and Dalton. In the evening, the Captain and future Mrs Molloy walked together for the first time as an engaged couple but that night, the first words she wrote in her diary were, 'James Dennistoun'.

For six days Georgiana had no time to stop and think. First there was a return trip by river steamer to Glasgow to buy her wedding dress. On the next day, a Sunday, the banns were read at Cardross in spite of the 'great uncertainty' she felt in her heart. On Monday she took Molloy to Camis Eskan and James Dennistoun came back to Keppoch with them for dinner. At last, James and Georgiana 'had a long conversation after Tea'. Then there was more shopping for the wedding in Greenock and, on Tuesday, final goodbyes in Roseneath. Travelling back to Keppoch that evening on the ferry she looked back at a line of lights and shadows in the dusk, her last view of Clachan House and the manse.

On Wednesday there was a letter from her childhood friend Elizabeth Senhouse, but no time to reply. The 'Bride's cake' arrived and wedding gifts were already being delivered. Georgiana spent the whole day packing her belongings into their trunks and then, at dinner, she began to weep. Once again, James Dennistoun was there.

On Thursday, 6 August, Georgiana got up just after seven to find more letters and presents. She closed her trunks and went out to collect her wedding flowers.

* * *

In 2007, I was planning my third visit to Scotland when I saw an advertisement on the internet. Keppoch House was for sale.[234] It crossed my mind that if my husband and I contacted the realty agent as potential purchasers we could probably view the inside of the house but, just before we flew to London, a local who knew the current owners saw a reference to Keppoch House on a website about Georgiana Molloy where I had often posted information and photographs. A few emails later, Mike and I landed at Heathrow airport with a generous invitation to visit the house although it had already been sold and would be vacated within days.

Modernised and refurbished, Keppoch has changed little since the last time Georgiana saw it in 1829. The tree-lined drive sweeps up a gentle slope to the wide expanse in front of the house where carriages used to stop and now cars park beside a thick wall of rhododendron bushes. The low, stone steps that lead up to the entrance hall are elegant and inviting; the door is scaled to impress and to welcome visitors. A member of the family gave us a complete tour of the house and gardens, fed us with homemade cake and made endless cups of tea but there were times when her conversations drifted away as we moved from one room to another. I crossed the spaces between doors and windows as others did during the domestic journey of an ordinary day, 150 years before me. The drawing room and dining room on either side of the hall have tall, square-paned windows overlooking the drive and lawn. The vista they frame of the outside world – the visitors who come and go, the sky over the Roseneath peninsula – is the same as it always has been. From the room where Georgiana made lace, wrote letters and watched the snow, the windows still look out towards the Gareloch. The staircase at the back of Keppoch's large, high-ceilinged entrance hall leads to the first floor where the family bedrooms are on the front and sides of the house. Like someone caught in the act of staring at a stranger, I watched my hand fall on the carved, polished curve of the bannister rail, in the place where Georgiana placed her hand as she went upstairs on her last night as Miss Kennedy.

Until 2007, all the sources I could find stated that her marriage took place at Roseneath church on the other side of the loch, but there was conflicting evidence. She was staying at Keppoch the night before and wrote in her diary that in the morning she gathered her wedding flowers and 'put them in their rooms'. How did she transport the flowers in the little rowing boat that was the ferry and how was there time to create the floral arrangements at the manse and then get back across to Keppoch to get ready for the wedding? There's no mention of guests travelling to Roseneath for the service nor any explanation about how everyone crossed to the other side of the Gareloch. When Mike examined a document among the Kennedy family papers at the CAC, he worked out why. One small word, at the very end and hard to decipher, was the clue.

> Banns certificate and marriage certificate[235]
> These are to certify that the certificate etc having been presented to me along with a license from the Archbishop of Canterbury, I married the above mentioned parties Captain Molloy & Miss Kennedy on this day here.
> Robert Story Minister
> Keppoch House
> August 6th 1829

The Reverend Robert Story recorded that he married the couple 'here' with a note of the address, Keppoch House.[236] In keeping with common Scottish tradition of the time, the marriage took place in the home and not in the church. Mike confirmed after discussions with historians and Scottish ministers that this was usual practice and the real story of John and Georgiana's wedding day fell into place. It felt like an exciting step forward on the research trail but several years later I discovered by accident that simply checking local newspapers could have revealed at any time since 1829 that the wedding venue was Keppoch House, not Roseneath: a marriage notice appeared in the Glasgow Herald on 10 August 1829.

When the digital images of the fragile Elizabeth Senhouse diary had arrived by email from the CAC, they had shown that the two young women were regular correspondents and close friends but revealed nothing at all about the wedding. The flowers that Georgiana gathered remained an unsolved mystery. Why would a bride cut flowers from the perfect garden displays that were so carefully managed to impress visitors?[237] If Georgiana had gathered wildflowers from the hills behind Keppoch, how could she have collected enough that morning to decorate the public rooms?

The gardens that surround the house are gently informal with woodland walks under shady oak trees as well as shrubberies and lawns. We explored them all, made new pathways through a meadow of bluebells and wandered over hilly paddocks, but our own shadows were lengthening on the grass and it is possible to overstay even the warmest welcome. It was time for us to leave, but history was ready to give up one more secret.

We were walking slowly back towards the house when our host asked, almost as an afterthought, 'Would you like to see the flower garden?' She held up an ancient, rusty key. Before it slid into the lock of a small, timber-planked door, I knew where we were going and realised that Georgiana had gone there too, early on the morning of her wedding day. Like many other large country homes, Keppoch House had its own vegetable garden, orchard and flower garden. All three were positioned a few moments' walk from the house. The orchard is long gone and the kitchen garden has been sold but the flower garden has survived, a secret world.

Enclosed like an island within four high, stone walls that shelter the entire garden from wind and frost, the air is warmer, the breeze softer, the plants more luxuriant. They lean against the mossy blocks like basking beauties. The sunshine lovers sprawl and tumble across beds and paths, wind boldly around arches and statues and stretch themselves across walls, reaching up and out to the sky. Wherever there is shade — beneath the sundial, behind the greenhouse — the darker green of little-leaved plants creeps into corners and crevices.

The garden's purpose was functional, to provide the floral displays that decorated Keppoch's rooms. Well-fed beds would have been heavily layered with plants of different heights, textures and colours, varying by season but always nurtured for their prime purpose: to be cut and gathered. Many of those flowerbeds have gone and now the garden's design includes wide lawns. The rose garden, sunken to protect its buds from Scottish winters, has become a swimming pool. It is a sharp-edged thing softened just a little by the weathered age of the original stone steps that lead down to it from the path. The greenhouse is still sturdy and elegant but empty of the exotic and delicate species that once grew there.

This is where Georgiana went on all those mornings when she was busy 'in the garden'.

> 6th February 1829: Worked in the garden. Mild and fair.
> 11th February 1829: Studies. Set out the plants. Trained ivy. Worked alone in the garden. It rained very mildly.
> 28th February 1829: Planted Lilies &c.

She spent hours there, often alone, on the days when everything else in life was dark. Physical work, weeding, digging, planting, growing, clearing, pruning, feeding. Finally, gathering.

* * *

Much has changed at Keppoch but the outline of the garden, its terraces and walls, central path and the walks around its perimeter are just as they were on the morning of the wedding. The places where sunlight reached and shadows lay are the same as they have been for more than a century. The tall Scots pine opposite the gate was already a large tree when Georgiana walked through the low door and it watched her as she moved from one plant to another, from the sunken rose garden to the greenhouse to cut flowers that she herself had planted.

Georgiana marked the moment of her change in status by keeping one visiting card from her single life with one from her married life, perhaps the last and first of each. They are still in a compartment in her sewing box.

Collection: National Trust of Western Australia ACC 2008.11 Wonnerup

They decorated Keppoch's hall and the reception rooms on either side when the guests arrived. Dressed in white, Georgiana wore a veil embroidered with flowers in imitation of more expensive Honiton lace and there were white ribbons on her bonnet.[238] The next day, she wrote simply in her diary, 'I was no longer Georgiana Kennedy'.[239]

At two o'clock that afternoon the horse-drawn carriage stood ready. It was time to endure the sad, blurred ritual that would have to be repeated over and over again during the next few weeks but for the first time the Molloys said their goodbyes as a couple. Everything was different.

WESTERN AUSTRALIA

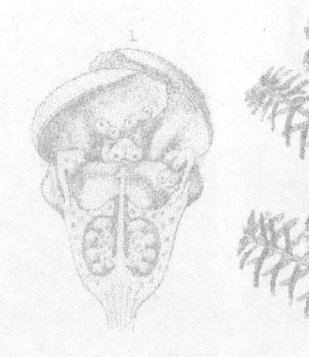

Adieu, my native land!

The Molloys spent their wedding night in Glasgow, where John had been stationed a decade earlier with the Rifle Brigade. By the next morning, some of Georgiana's fears were resolved and the ink on five exclamation marks she added carefully to her diary entry is deeply etched into the paper: 'What a night this was!!!!!'[240]

That first day of married life was the only one they would spend quietly together for more than six months; it would be a year before they had a home. The next day they travelled back down the River Clyde to Greenock, where the Dunlops had gathered to say goodbye at the dockside. Georgiana 'felt very much at leaving them' because they had 'been more than parents and sisters'.[241] It was already dark when she and Molloy boarded the steamboat and she looked back to see Maggie Dunlop's face for the last time. At nine o'clock they reached the Isle of Man and when they transferred to the boat bound for Liverpool, Georgiana was already suffering from seasickness. It kept her awake all night. Early the next morning they took a horse-drawn coach to Coventry, once again travelling on through the night. They waited there from nine in the morning until two in the afternoon, when Mrs Kennedy's coach arrived to take them on to Rugby. It was another long drive but when they arrived the bells were ringing and the whole family was there to meet them.

Mrs Kennedy had once thought that either she or Eliza would be the object of Molloy's affection. She was sure Georgiana would regret her decision to leave home and would be on her way back from Scotland within a few weeks, but things had turned out so differently and Georgiana stepped out of the carriage on the arm of her new husband, Handsome Jack Molloy. But if the daughter expected her moment in the spotlight to last, she was wrong. Mrs Kennedy did not arrange anything special to mark the occasion and once the excitement was over, the next day felt flat and disappointing. No-one visited and Georgiana spent most of the day eating wedding cake and drinking ginger beer.

Mrs Kennedy never forgave Georgiana for her forthright behaviour and even the thought of parting could not block out her irritation. She wrote to Dalton in 1828, soon after Georgiana had left home, 'I have good accounts of her but you cannot wonder after such <u>unnatural</u> Conduct to a Mother in distress so that I still feel sore whenever I think of it.'[242] She wrote in the same letter, 'It is hard work to keep in with the Caldecotts – She is so jealous & uncertain in her temper.' Georgiana's mother had no intention of creating any more scandal so she invited the Caldecotts and Butlin the banker to dinner with the newlyweds and behaved in public as a loving mother should.

On Thursday Georgiana noted how much she would miss her younger sister, 'dear Mary', and on Friday the family dined together at Holbrook for the first and last time. Ann Caldecott was not sure that Georgiana had made a wise choice and she said so to Mrs Kennedy who unkindly passed Ann's opinion on to her daughter.[243] Later that night Georgiana sat up late packing. She suddenly decided to burn all her letters. In front of Molloy, she put them into the fire and his letter of proposal was gone forever.

On Saturday morning, she said goodbye to her mother, sisters and brothers and by the moment of final parting Georgiana and Eliza had somehow managed to reconcile their differences. The coach journey to London was uncomfortable and the newlyweds arrived exhausted.

On Sunday afternoon, after a very long sleep, they went to church at Langham Place and Georgiana was struck by the poor quality of the sermon compared with what she had become used to in Scotland: 'Poor man did not comprehend what he wished to say.'[244]

She did not enjoy the three and a half weeks they spent in London, calling it 'a very strange place'.[245] Their apartment in a tall townhouse just off Oxford Street was comfortable and very central but she disliked the city and longed to be back in the tranquility of open spaces. Molloy had meeting after meeting to attend, including an appointment to sign his certificate of entry to the Brotherhood of Freemasons on 15 August. He was out every day making arrangements for the voyage, so the responsibility for buying household requirements fell completely on Georgiana's shoulders. On Monday, 17 August, the serious shopping began. It was not something that gave her any pleasure, but it was soon clear that she had the skills needed for an unusual level of household management. Her task was to buy every single domestic requirement that a family would need to last them at least a year. Molloy wrote a postscript in Georgiana's letter to Mary Dunlop and commented on his wife's capabilities: 'She is quite notable in the way of equipping herself and has accomplished the whole of her affairs in so quiet and easy a manner as if she had been a wife of ten years standing.'[246]

Georgiana had a long shopping list but when she arrived in London it was the clothes that caught her eye. On her first morning she bought silk stockings and pelerines.[247] The next day it was shoes in Regent Street and before long her shopping increased in momentum: 'Got bonnets, corsets, Blue Gown etc' (20 August); 'Got a great many things' (21 August); 'then different shops and bought green silk' (25 August). Writing to Mary Dunlop she emphasised the simple style of the clothes she was taking to Australia, but she did not mention the sweet chocolates she had treated herself to or the pink dress she had seen in a shop window and resisted for only a few days before she went back to buy it.[248]

> My gowns are all very plain without anything but hems & tucks dear Mary & my Bonnets Cottage shape with wide Ribbons so I have not given way to the vanities of this truly depressing London where I never dreamt of such dreadful vices.[249]

Georgiana wore the 'Dunstable cottage style' of bonnet, a simple shape with a low crown and deep brim that curved around the face, made of plaited straw and framed by wide ribbons tied in a bow under the chin. There were more elaborate choices available at a time when fashion was influenced by bolder trends from France and Italy and the exotic fabrics and designs from further afield in the emerging British empire. Bonnet madness was hitting British shores but she wanted nothing to do with it. Ladies' hats were getting bigger, decorated with bunches of flowers, garlands or long feathers and some women owned a whole wardrobe of bonnets for different occasions and even different times of day. Georgiana reminded her religious friend that she disapproved but she was interested enough in fashion to write in her diary that she wore her new pink dress for the first time on 3 September.

Georgiana visited the high-class shopping area around St Paul's cathedral, ordering clothes, stockings and fabric from Hitchcock & Rogers and shoes from Ridley's Ladies Shoe warehouse. Knowing that replacing worn-out clothes would be difficult in the new colony, she stocked up on plain calico for dressmaking – the same fabric made in the mills around Carlisle. By the end of the month she had everything arranged but the *Warrior*, chartered by a Mr Semphill, was not ready to sail. Georgiana was beginning to feel 'very low' again at the thought of everything she would soon be leaving behind.[250] Left alone one day, she went for a long walk from Oxford Street through Hyde Park to see her old school and call on friends, but she no longer felt comfortable in London. The city was Molloy's territory. He was out in the streets, visiting people and arranging meetings with his army friends. The couple was staying a few minutes' walk from his childhood home in St Giles, but there's no evidence that he ever

The varied environments of shore, woodland and mountains around the Gareloch where Georgiana was living in 1828–29. She walked long distances, even in snow, and collected wild flowers.

Ruins of St Modan's Parish Church, Roseneath, where Georgiana worshipped with the Story family in 1828–29. The building then was already old, damp and very cold in winter. It was bare of decoration, with an earthen floor.

Easter Garth (the white building) was a new manse on the site of the eighteenth century building where Georgiana stayed in Roseneath. John Molloy was a guest there in 1851. The bell tower of the ruined church is just visible behind the yew trees. Today's graveyard is on the site of the Reverend Story's 1828 orchard.

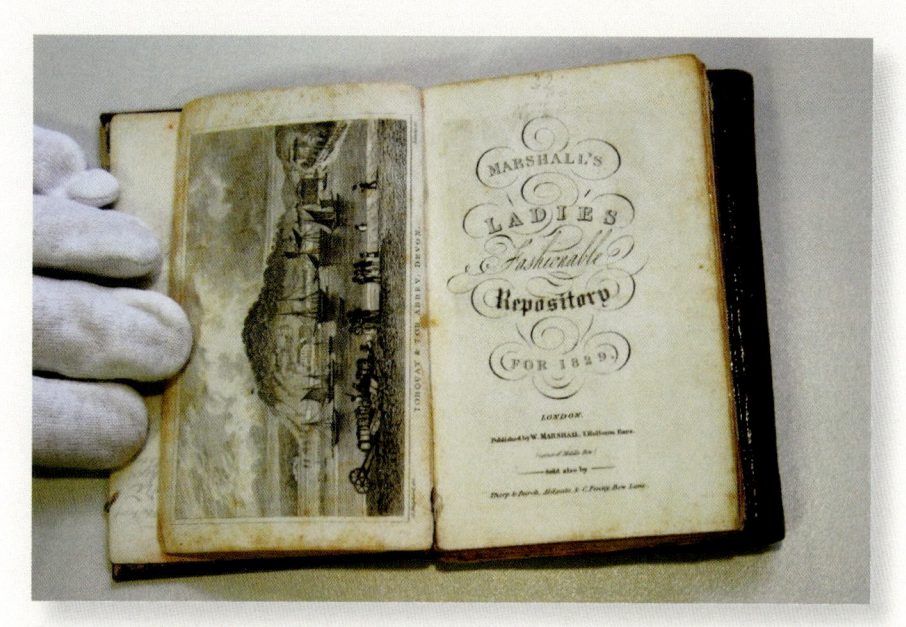

Georgiana's 1829 diary included printed pages of useful information, pictures of the latest fashions and musical scores. She used a blank space to write a shopping list for her journey to Western Australia. Her purchases included spectacles, hair pins and 'binding and tape' for the whalebone stays of her corsets.

Georgiana's 1830 diary was written in an 1828 edition so she altered each day to match the correct date. At the Swan River in March, she 'walked to Mount Eliza' and, feeling unwell, she was 'very anxious for Jack's return'. After a 'fine conversation' with Ellen Stirling she decided that the governor's wife reminded her of her childhood friend, Elizabeth Senhouse.

The anchorage of the *Emily Taylor* in 1830, off the beach in Flinders Bay, Western Australia. The shore there is rocky and exposed so the settlers used rafts to carry all their belongings over the sandbar at the mouth of the Hardy Inlet, which took several days.

A 2014 aerial photograph showing the sandbank (left) where the Blackwood River meets the Indian Ocean. The sandbank has changed but streets and boundary lines still demarcate the original outline of John Molloy's 1830 land grant behind the jetty.

Castle Bay, the setting for Georgiana's dream of a future home on the coast. She spent three days collecting plants there on the beach and in the bush along the coast. *Thysanotus* (Fringed lily), *Kennedia*, *Hibbertia* and *Hovea* were added to her last collection. When she described the cottage she would like to build there in the valley, there was a stream running all year round.

Flat Rock, Augusta, known to Georgiana as the 'granite rock', was a favourite collecting place. On one of the first family outings to collect for Mangles, she went there by boat with her husband and children.

Thomas Turner's painting of Augusta in 1830. The Molloy house is near the centre, the Turner house is on the far left with the Bussell home between the two.

Fairlawn, Busselton, 1932. The first cottage on this site was built for John Molloy in April 1836 when he began farming his land grant on the Vasse River. The house was extended later but Georgiana did not see it until May 1839 when she moved there with her children. The three-day trek was her first journey away from Augusta since the family landed there nine years earlier.

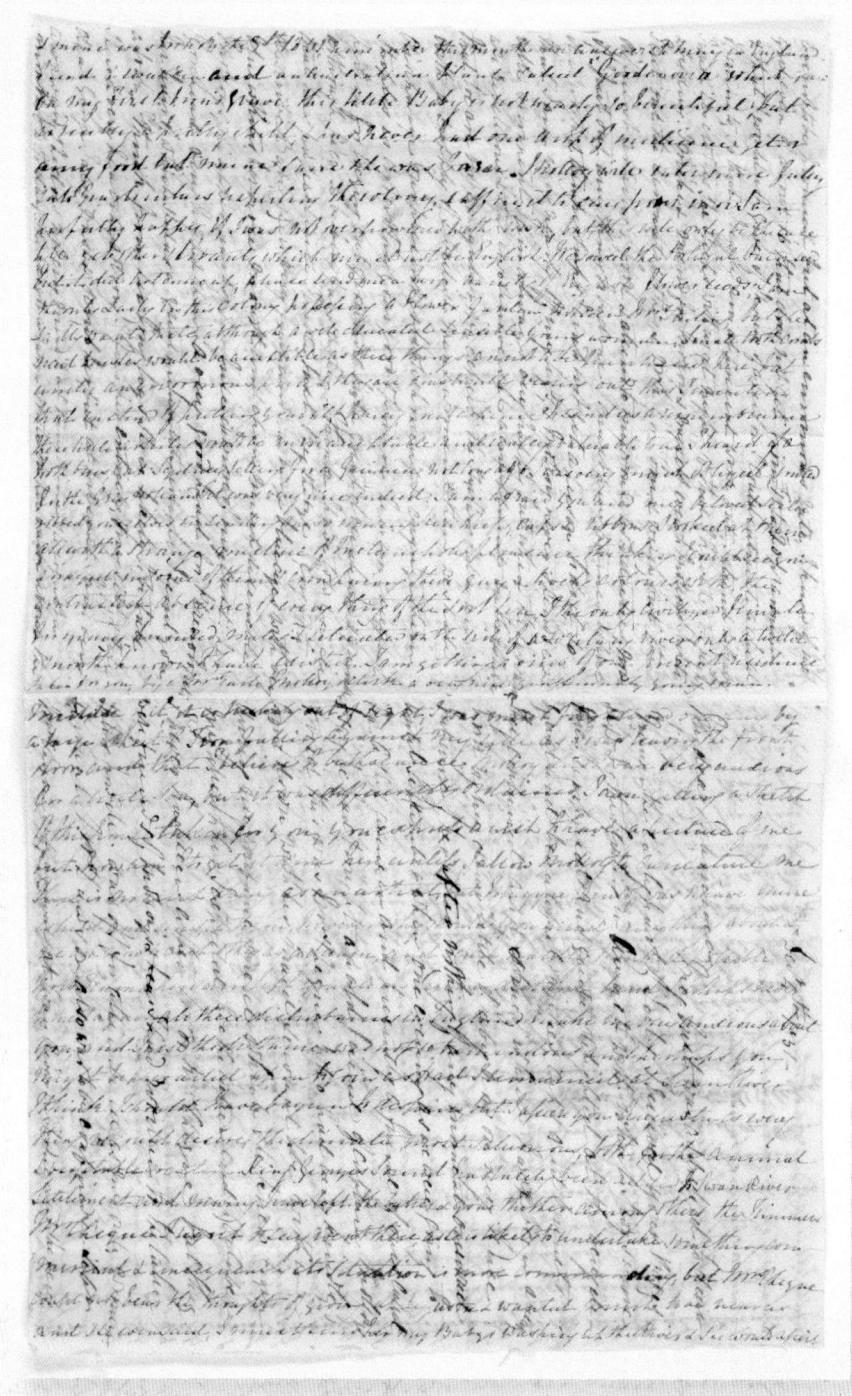

Letter from Georgiana to her mother, Mrs Kennedy, December 1831. Paper was a precious commodity in the colony; Georgiana wrote across each page in both directions to save as much paper as possible. This cross-writing often makes her letters very difficult to transcribe.

John Molloy was seriously wounded in the closing hours of the final battle in the last campaign of the Napoleonic Wars. Shown here in its carved nutshell case, this French musket ball was removed from his leg after the Battle of Waterloo in 1815.

Georgiana used scraps of old paper for her embroidery patterns. On the reverse of these drawings is a letter to John Molloy. The simple flower shapes could be repeated to create a border design along a hem or used alone on a collar.

A collection of used silk threads in Georgiana's workbox is a reminder of the way her life changed dramatically when she became a settler. Too precious and expensive to be thrown away, old sewing thread was unpicked and re-used when she made clothes for herself and her family.

took his wife there. Her diary and letters make no mention of any visit or discussion. Molloy was so close to the place he came from but unable to say goodbye to his past with the woman he had chosen to share his future.

Georgiana was impressed with the men from the Rifle Brigade and the wives who came with them for dinner, and she enjoyed the lively conversation of lieutenants Munro, Tollemache and Sullivan. The stories of these men's lives make two things apparent: first, if the officers survived the Peninsular War they went on to high-flying careers; and second, Molloy's friends were born as gentlemen. Most officers at that time came from the aristocracy, the landed gentry or rich professional families; the high price of purchasing any commission deliberately restricted appointment of officers to the 'upper classes' in the belief that they had the intelligence for command. But the wealthiest officers during the Peninsular War had not always turned out to be the wisest, and that was hard to ignore. Lord Wellington had firsthand evidence of the bravery and military expertise of men who had risen from lowly beginnings. He had also seen the loss of life when officers who had bought themselves expensive commissions showed incompetence in battle.

Things were beginning to change but not in time for Molloy to reveal to his colleagues that he was the son of a shoemaker. He was a devout Christian and would not have lied about his parentage but he may already have been subtly encouraging the intrigue that followed him through life. Until he was an old man and the social climate had shifted a little, he refused to discuss his parents. People love a mystery. They always seek a solution that fits. So it seemed obvious that Molloy, like others, had to be of illegitimate royal heritage. He was not ashamed of his father but the growing rumours about a secret past protected his honour and, most importantly, guaranteed respect for his wife. Once entered into, the charade could never end.

Molloy used the travel delay as a chance to employ an artist to paint miniature portraits of himself and Georgiana for the Dunlops.

During the two weeks of the artist's sittings, Georgiana had visits from Dalton and went to hear Edward Irving preach again. She spent a day at the Royal Botanic Gardens in Kew, with which she 'was much pleased' in spite of the thundery rain.[251] There is always something new to enjoy at Kew Gardens but there are also old paths and individual specimens that Georgiana passed by on that stormy September day. The orangery with its leafy fragrance is now a café. The ten-storey Chinese pagoda is part of the same view down the main avenue as it was in 1829, and on the south side of the lake stands an ancient sweet chestnut tree that was already about fifty years old when Georgiana was there.

In 1801 the botanist Sir Joseph Banks, for whom our own Australian 'banksia' was named, took over the management of the Royal Botanic Gardens and it was the beginning of a time of change. By 1850 the Arboretum included 2325 species of trees and shrubs. In 1853, Kew Herbarium was founded and has continued to grow,

Georgiana's botanical specimens are still stored in the simple pages of the original herbaria, including those of Professor John Lindley and his friend, the eminent botanist George Bentham. Between 1841 and 1854, Bentham acquired some of Georgiana's specimens from Lindley and they were part of the *Herbarium Benthamanum* he gave to Kew in 1854.

adding around 37,000 new specimens each year and amalgamating private collections. The personal herbaria of botanists, scientists and explorers of the past including those of Charles Darwin, George Bentham and David Livingstone, can still be studied there.

The herbarium is the central storing place for specimens used for comparison of world species, and it has a pivotal international role for research on plant and mycological biodiversity. Among the herbarium collection's seven million specimens today there are more than thirty credited to the untrained collector, G. Molloy.[252]

On 9 September the Molloys took another step closer to their new life and moved south to the coast so that John could keep a closer eye on Mr Semphill's arrangements. Things were not going smoothly and he was unimpressed with the commander's management so far. There had already been a disagreement about Semphill's first bill and Molloy was worried about the way the ship was being loaded. It was a long time since his navy days but he still knew more than most people about how to pack a ship's cargo. The waiting had already gone on for too long.

When they arrived at their lodgings in Brockhurst near Gosport, they were 'not in good spirits'.[253] Molloy had been stationed in Brockhurst the year before and lived there aboard ship and on shore during the war so it was another place he knew well. He was back at the heart of Britain's maritime world, the great port and deep anchorage where two tides meet and where his military career had begun when he was fourteen. For Georgiana, it was a difficult time.

Captains Molloy and Byrne had started on the venture together so they saw a lot of one another and it meant their wives also spent time together, but that association did not grow into friendship. Anna-Matilda Byrne was the daughter of Major General Sir Amos Norcott who commanded the 2nd Battalion of the Rifle Brigade at the Battle of Waterloo. Mrs Byrne grew up knowing only the army life and was two years younger than Georgiana but was already more wise to the ways of the world. The flirtatious behaviour she used so deliberately meant that friendship between the two women was never likely, but Georgiana rather prudishly hoped that her own ladylike ways might influence Mrs Byrne.

> I found Mrs Byrne something in manner like Mrs Abney, but much more unquiet, with a bustle, her petticoats in the air and two very pretty legs and feet protruding beyond them. However, she has much subsided and Molloy thinks when she sees more of me she will change that quick and abrupt manner for my more steady and sedate aspect. She is very good-natured and I cannot wonder that having been born and bred in the Rifle Brigade, she is fond of those Oeils so often practised in and by military persons.[254,255]

Georgiana's long, cross-written letter to Helen Story was already an attempt to save precious paper. Its content reveals the confusion she was feeling, knowing she might never see her friends again but exhilarated by the excitement of her adventure as a new wife and a pioneer. On 17 September, she and John went together to Portsmouth and met up with his army friends, but on the days when he walked to Gosport without her she was miserable and walked out to meet him on his way back. The only constant she had in a life that was changing dramatically with every day, he was already her 'dearest Molloy' and she did not know what she would do without 'so kind a creature'.[256]

When he left for four nights in London she was 'desolate without him' but made the best of the situation, filling the time with walking, reading, arranging to transport a hive of bees and, for the first time ever, selecting seeds to plant in her own garden. As the day for leaving drew closer, it was more difficult to feel light-hearted about their adventure. Week after week, Captain Molloy was paying for storage of the supplies and equipment he had purchased. The upkeep of servants he had taken on in July was draining money. And then there were the rumours. Everyone had been reading reports from the Swan River and they were not uplifting.[257] The very popular *Gentleman's Magazine* published an article describing the kind of people setting off for the colony. It must have been disheartening reading for the couple who had paid the fare and were waiting to board their ship.

> The Swan River is now the favourite settlement, and thither now repair unluckies of this country who cannot live at home, unthrifty young men who have nearly broken their parents' hearts, misanthropes, alarmists, romantics, speculators, projectors, and never-satisfieds.[258]

The new colony was a hot topic and stories were widely published about the disasters as well as the fortunes to be made. There was plenty of time to get worried: it was another seven weeks before the passengers were hoisted onto the deck by ropes attached to a chair, on a rainy morning in October. The *Warrior*'s departure was a big news item. Some passengers had paid today's equivalent of about $100,000 for a one-way trip; it was a dangerous, uncomfortable five-month voyage to a place where all that awaited them was a small military base, a few tents and an unknown wilderness. Today, a civilian emigration to a new colony on the moon would create similar levels of interest.

> Several of the passengers are persons of independent fortune who have embarked considerable property in the speculation; & two of them, named Byrne and Molloy, paid the enormous sum of 1000 pounds for the best accommodation the vessel could afford en suite. Six pianos are on board the 'Warrior' and a proportionate number of fair and accomplished vocalists and musicians of course accompany the instruments to their destinations. There are also on board fifty dogs of the choicest breed, several pens of sheep, a considerable number of swine, two milch [sic] cows and three valuable horses; but as tempestuous weather may be anticipated on the vessel reaching the Bay of Biscay, apprehensions are entertained that a proportion of the live cargo must be consigned to the ocean before the termination of the voyage.[259]

From the moment of boarding there was confusion. Mr Semphill met his obligations and the voyage ended safely but he was determined to maximise profit and made the most basic arrangements for people, provisions and livestock. The wealthiest travellers packed additional food but that ran out and the rations they had paid for were inadequate. Many animals died in cramped conditions. The Molloys had bought two of the most expensive tickets for their superior berth but they too went hungry. Passengers fell out with one another and a rift grew between people from different backgrounds. Molloy was a sociable man and on several occasions he did not get to bed until the early hours of the morning, but there were times when things got out of hand. Fights broke out and more than once his peacekeeping skills were needed to manage difficult situations.

According to Georgiana's account, the couple took on sixteen servants to travel with them, indentured for the next five years, but no complete passenger list survives to show how many of them ended up on board the *Warrior*.[260] The Molloys' own writing suggests that only nine individuals actually travelled to Australia with them.

Corporal Elijah Dawson had served with Molloy in the Rifle Brigade and was an ideal choice as a personal servant. He was strong, resourceful, trusted and recently married. His wife, Ann Dawson, was the same age as Georgiana and became her maid. Molloy's other servant, Robert Heppingstone, was also an experienced rifleman and was in Molloy's company from 1825. Emigrating to Australia must have been a last-minute decision; when Heppingstone purchased his discharge in September 1829, the Molloys were already staying on the south coast of England waiting for the *Warrior* to sail.[261] Anne Heppingstone was taken on to do household work and their three young children, Robert (Bobby), Charlotte and Elizabeth, sailed with them. Thirty-five-year-old James Staples, who once worked in the ornate gardens at Newbold Hall, signed up as gardener. He would soon have to learn quickly how to manage peas and potatoes rather than roses and tulips. Chidlow, their shepherd, was poached by another family on arrival, and stayed on in Perth.[262]

Molloy's thoroughbred mare, a beautiful huntress in foal, and his stallion, Captain, were carefully boarded along with the other animals in his party. There were thirty pigs, poultry, cows, sheep and lambs and, later, bullocks that he bought at the Cape of Good Hope. He shipped enough equipment and provisions to maintain a settler family in almost any situation: machinery and tools, rifles and ammunition, saddlery, furniture, medicine, rowing boats and, luckily as it turned out, a large seine net for fishing. Georgiana began arranging what would be their home for the months ahead, 'a very large stern Cabin, 3 windows in it, two sleeping berths apart from each other'.[263] Passengers had to furnish their cabins themselves and provide everything they needed apart from food and medicine. Contracts usually stated that the washing of clothes would not be allowed during the voyage so guides for settlers suggested taking no less than 'fifteen to twenty shirts or shifts with a proportional quantity of other garments, towels, soap, combs and utensils for eating and drinking'.[264]

In spite of the strong smell of a tarpaulin that Molloy insisted on keeping in the cabin, Georgiana felt more cheerful. The long delay had laid to rest any lingering regrets and it was a relief to set sail on 23 October. Her 'heart and spirit were lighter' than when she said goodbye to her friends in Scotland.[265] That night, as they sailed westward down the English Channel, she sat by the cabin window and wondered whether she would 'ever see England again'. In the last moments she turned not to her Bible but to her copy of Lord Byron's poetry and read his poem 'Adieu, adieu! My native shore'.[266] It seemed to describe her own situation, even down to the setting sun. She was close to tears as the ship left England's shore behind in the darkness.[267]

This was John Molloy's first long sea voyage for years but he quickly settled back into life aboard ship. His journal meticulously records the daily weather observations and details about 'divine service' on

Sundays, but there is no mention at all of his wife or her condition. Georgiana began feeling nauseous on the first morning and by evening she was violently ill. She noted in her diary that she was very seasick although the Channel was calm, and if she had not guessed it already, must have realised on the first full day at sea that she was pregnant. By 16 November she had noticed that she was 'always sick in the mornings'. She was forced to spend most of the next few months lying in her cabin on the sofa, suffering from nausea and extreme headaches. As the ship sailed south and the weather grew hotter she became weaker and at times was unable to walk unsupported.

The animals suffered too, from crowding, hunger and thirst. Molloy's stallion, stabled directly opposite another passenger's cabin, was 'stamping and knocking himself about' even before the ship set sail.[268] The mare miscarried her precious thoroughbred foal, sheep died and the Molloys had lost all their pigs by the time the ship anchored at the Cape of Good Hope.[269]

There were good days and Georgiana enjoyed taking part in the meagre but hopeful celebrations for Christmas and the New Year, 1830. When the ship crossed the equator the passengers and crew marked the moment in the traditional seafaring way, which involved throwing as much water as possible over one another. Molloy protected his wife from a good soaking with the smelly tarpaulin she had complained about. She wrote on 10 December, 'Buckets of water were thrown in every direction but Molloy threw a tarpaulin over me and I did not receive a drop, although many deluged. Mrs Byrne received 5 whole buckets which were intentionally thrown over her.' By the time Georgiana wrote to her mother four weeks later, the number of buckets deliberately poured over the unfortunate Mrs Byrne had grown to six.

One of the first entries in Georgiana's journal during the voyage recounts a conversation she had with 'the helmsman who was a negro'. He had spent time in Greenock and she enjoyed talking to him about places they both knew.[270] Striking up a conversation with a member of the crew was a surprising act for a gentleman's wife, and more so because the sailor was black and not an officer. The easy way she talked with the helmsman but not with the flirtatious Mrs Byrne could be seen as an example of her Anglican values at work or evidence of the Quaker background in her family, but whatever the reasons, her connection with any other person was one of equality. She would soon be living among other Christians who did not live by the same principles.

There was more time to spend together during the voyage than there would ever be again and Georgiana's journal records how much she enjoyed the evenings with Molloy, reading together or talking about their future. One day when she felt unwell, he hid a beautiful pink shawl in her drawer as a surprise gift, bought for her before they set sail. When her headaches grew worse, he gently cut her hair and shaved her head at the back in an attempt to ease the symptoms. They sat up late on deck at night watching the stars and playing chess. Her thoughts swung wildly from day to day, between reflecting on the past and anticipating what lay ahead. She had already taken to looking back in her diaries to things that had happened on the same date in previous years and it became a habit that never left her. On 5 November she 'examined some seeds', sowed an apricot stone and read Burns's poetry again. The next day she spent a long time sitting on deck reading botanical books and thinking about the garden she planned to create in her new home. On 30 November, as the days grew ever more tropical, she thought back on the icy Scottish winter and remembered a rare moment she had spent alone with James Dennistoun. It was not a significant incident; she met him unexpectedly during a walk along the beach road. Remembering how the icy-cold weather meant she was 'scarcely able to shake hands with Mr Dennistoun' felt important enough to merit an entry in her diaries for two consecutive years.[271]

Her journal provides a detailed picture of hardship on board the *Warrior*. One evening when everyone was going hungry, Molloy's Freemasonry connections were the source of some baked potatoes.

Other passengers kept journals too and these give glimpses of the Molloys through the eyes of their fellow travellers. James Turner, another passenger in the first-class cabins, noted the kindness of Captains Molloy and Byrne in sharing the milk from the cows they had on board.[272] Nineteen-year-old Charles Bussell, travelling in the cheaper 'steerage' accommodation, observed that he found Mrs Molloy very interesting with 'all the air of a lady well born and well bred, without having mixed much in the world'. His description of a young woman who was 'inclined to the romantic' and loved watching the night sky or talking about the beauty of poetry, matches perfectly the collection of books she took with her.[273]

On the worst days they were all hungry and thirsty, pirates came close to the ship and huge waves washed over the deck. On one occasion the captain was attacked and locked in a cabin by angry passengers. Georgiana's headaches were so unbearable that she sent for the doctor to bleed her, even though she knew it was dangerous in such hot weather. She had never felt so ill and longed to see land. Molloy knew that Captain was suffering in the badly constructed horse-stalls and he feared for the animal's life, but he had travelled the route many times as a young man and knew that life would be easier once they arrived at the Cape of Good Hope.

On 12 January 1830, the *Warrior* anchored in Table Bay. Georgiana wrote letters home while Molloy went to look for lodgings and came back with an exotic feast. She must have known by then that she was expecting a baby and badly needed fresh food. That evening their spirits were lifted as they drank port and dined on crayfish, peaches, pears, figs, roast duck and tartlets. The next morning they went ashore to meet the governor and the commandant of the garrison, Harry Smith, an old friend of Molloy's from the Rifle Brigade.

There were practical reasons for staying at the Cape, including much-needed exercise for the horses and replacing stock that had died, but for Georgiana it was the first chance she'd had to enjoy her married status in an important colonial social group. Her appearance and behaviour would be reported back to England by letter through the complex network that fuelled the ladies' gossip while they were living away from home. The *Warrior* was in port for less than a month but it was long enough to give Georgiana great hopes for the quality of life at Swan River. She enjoyed carriage rides, sampled tropical food and discovered exotic flora that were completely new to her. She stayed in a comfortable home and made friends with the most noble European ladies in the region. Lady Frances Cole was the daughter of the Earl of Malmesbury and her sister, who also lived in Cape Town, was Lady Catherine Bell.

The governor, Sir Galbraith Lowry Cole, had fought with Harry Smith and Molloy during the Peninsular War, and Molloy had known Smith's Spanish wife since the couple first met. Georgiana's world before her marriage was a small one but she did have one connection of her own in Cape Town. Frances Birkett, the daughter of her Cumberland friends, had become Lady Frances Grant when she married Sir James and she too had stayed at the governor's home. Georgiana thought of her friend as she walked the airy corridors of 'The castle', at last a house guest of lords and ladies.[274] It was the first evidence she could report to her mother to show that marriage was bringing success and influence. In her next letter she dropped in as many impressive names as she could and pointed out that she and Captain Molloy had 'certainly met with marked attention from all the Grandees'.[275] Several pages further on, she mentioned casually that she was expecting a baby.

The monotony of days at sea began again in spite of Lady Catherine's insistence that Georgiana should stay at the Cape until after the baby's birth. She was transporting bees in a wooden box perforated with holes 'with a little glass door so that I could see them at work' but soon after leaving the Cape she watched as moths got into the hive and killed them all.[276] Raspberry, gooseberry and redcurrant cuttings she had nurtured for months flowered too quickly in the heat and her Chinese roses died too.

The Molloys had bought more pigs and seed for their first crops in Australia but as they returned to the misery of poor food and a limited water allowance, Georgiana had new worries on her mind. She still had not started making baby clothes. Sewing was not work she enjoyed although, in the years ahead, it was a skill she would have to learn to endure, as her family's only dressmaker. In comparison with the previous few weeks, life seemed unbearably boring and she had nothing new to write in her journal. What she never tired of was the company of her 'beloved Molloy' but every day was the same and by 22 February she'd had enough. She wrote diagonally across the page, 'It is so stupid I shall not write any more until I arrive at Swan River.' Less than three weeks later, on 11 March 1830 the journey finally ended and a new life began.[277]

Georgiana wrote this letter to her mother soon after arriving at the Swan River in April 1830 but Mrs Kennedy did not receive it until October.

Cumbria Archive Centre D KEN 3 / 28 / 9

After months of planning her garden, nurturing seedlings and reading books on botany, her first observations were about the flora: 'Highly delighted with the country most beautifully wooded with magnificent aromatic trees and shrubs'. A pilot ship guided the *Warrior* from Rottnest Island into Fremantle and as soon as Georgiana's feet were on land she went 'instantly'[278] to examine the vegetation. It was a striking scene that she had not been expecting with trees that were fully grown, 'their branches untroubled by the storm and unpruned by man'. She also had her first glimpse of the life of the Aboriginal people of the region: 'we saw the smoke of several native fires'. The next thing she set eyes on was less appealing: a ragged tumble of settlers' mud huts and a sea of tents with flocks of cattle and sheep penned in among them. A boat took the passengers up the Swan River to Perth and they disembarked at last on the north shore.

* * *

The shoreline has changed and Perth's first pier where the settlers came ashore has disappeared, but in 1830 it stood at what was then the end of Pier Street, in the area of the Supreme Court Gardens. Today's busy jetty is just a few paces away at the end of Barrack Street, a place where boats come and go all day ferrying tourists along the river for sightseeing and taking commuters across the Swan on their daily business. On the first warm day of spring in 2011, I was in Perth, walking down Barrack Street to catch the ferry. The sun was shining and bells were pealing out across the city when, without any deliberate thought or action on my part, two loose-ended, trailing research threads suddenly met and fused to create a single strand. I remembered something I had heard on a tourist trip up the river nine years earlier.

Twelve of the bells that were ringing that morning were a gift to the people of Western Australia for the national bicentennial celebrations in 1988, and the Bell Tower was built beside the Barrack Street jetty as a symbol of the new millennium. First cast in the fourteenth century, they are the only royal bells known to have left England and they came from the church of St Martin-in-the-Fields on Trafalgar Square. They rang in the New Year over London for 275 years and were ringing as Captain James Cook set out on the voyage that ended in founding the British colony in Australia. They peal out each day over Western Australia's capital city from the place where John and Georgiana Molloy first set foot on land and they are the same bells that rang out on the rainy day in 1786 when John Molloy, the shoemaker's son, was baptised in the church of St Martin's beneath them.

The church of St Martin-in-the-Fields, Trafalgar Square, London

The Bell Tower, Perth, Western Australia

* * *

Georgiana, still optimistic, remarked on the abundant wildlife of the shoreline and the land 'beautifully wooded to the water's edge with both copse wood and magnificent old trees, large firs and bushes about 6 or 8 feet high'.[279] Then she saw the settlement she had travelled to from the other side of the world, 'many wooden & thatched mud houses scattered about, the trees only cut to make way for these buildings'. She had an idea of what to expect but it was still a shock, little more than a military camp padded out to overflowing by the tents and temporary buildings of the first wave of settlers who had arrived during the previous year. The first arrivals were lured by the promise of abundant fertile land allocated as grants of sixteen hectares for every three pounds they invested. It seemed like the opportunity of a lifetime, but by the time the Molloys arrived they were joining about 1500 other colonists and most of the best land available had already been taken. The military camp followed the usual well-organised grid arrangements with cleared areas for barracks under canvas, a hospital and a parade ground, giving Perth its first discernible street plan along the river, including what is now St Georges Terrace.[280] The independent settlers waiting for land grants or offering services and trades to the new arrivals set up wherever they could find a space and kept their livestock close by in pens. It was crowded, noisy, pungent and humid in the late summer heat that attracted sandflies and mosquitoes from freshwater lakes and nearby swamps.

Captain Molloy went back down the river to Fremantle to make sure their belongings were safely unloaded and Georgiana moved into the governor's quarters on the area between Barrack Street and St Georges Terrace today; the home that Stirling shared with his young wife, Ellen, was still a temporary arrangement with a canvas roof. When Georgiana saw Aboriginal people for the first time, she had the impression they were quiet and 'very fond of the new settlers' but Perth did not impress her and she longed to be with her husband in his tent on the beach.[281] She told her mother it was a crowded, ramshackle place 'having no resemblance to a town'. As usual, everything is described in vivid detail in her letters but disappointment hovers between the brave lines.

> Last Wednesday Molloy and I were in our boat and felt a storm coming on we were obliged to sleep on the ground. What should I have once thought of this, but for Molloy if I could I would sleep in the fire.[282]

Captain Molloy arranged to take up what his wife described as a 'small' land grant of '2500 acres' in Perth on either side of the Swan River and within a week he had decided to take the rest of his land allocation two miles outside the 'market town' of Guildford, hoping for better land and cooler weather.[283] Georgiana liked the idea of living in a more rural, agricultural community, 'a more select neighbourhood', and made a point of telling her mother that the governor would be their neighbour; he had taken a grant there the year before, naming the village site after the place in England where he had married Ellen.[284]

But the plan changed once again. It was becoming clear that the best land had already been taken. Georgiana was suffering terribly from the heat, the fleas and mosquitoes, was weakened by sickness from severe dysentery and her baby was expected to arrive within a few weeks. Governor Stirling talked enthusiastically about establishing a sub-colony in a cooler, fertile area he had seen further down the coast, and his wife strongly supported the idea. The two ladies were almost the same age and Ellen had children of her own so she may have had her new friend's comfort in mind, but she also knew that the governor's reputation relied on Perth's success and independence; the already overcrowded colony could not survive without expansion. Georgiana explained in a letter to her mother how she was persuaded, and encouraged Molloy to agree.

> Molloy & Mr Bussells and Mr Turner a builder with 30 workmen and a large family of his own agreed to try the Southern regions and under Molloy's auspices engaged an Indian Brig the Emily Taylor to convey us thence. The Governor and Mrs Stirling strongly prompted me to persuade Molloy to this end.[285]

Georgiana shopped for household things while Molloy got ready for another journey. Her list included small toothcombs, hair oil, pomade, stays, coloured stockings, Bibles and an air cushion.[286] When Molloy returned one afternoon he told her he was going to be appointed Resident Magistrate of the proposed new settlement and after the military Sunday service a few days later the news was made official, with Elijah Dawson as his clerk.[287] The two-masted *Emily Taylor* prepared to take Governor Stirling's party south, and although Georgiana was suffering badly from nausea she insisted on sailing with them. Her baby was due much sooner than she imagined.

As the settlers started the final leg of their journey to a new home, it was the livestock that came off worse yet again. No-one noticed that some women and children had got into the boat being used to load the animals and, in the confusion, all the Molloys' sheep, poultry, horses and the thirty replacement pigs they had bought at the Cape were tumbled into the river and lost. Their milk cow and the mare had strayed and when they were found they were obviously distressed. Georgiana asked her husband to leave them in Perth until they regained their strength but he refused to take her advice and both died within twenty-four hours on board.[288]

The servants had no say in whether they settled at the Swan River, as agreed when they signed up, or set off on this new venture. They had the prospect of taking up a land grant themselves in less than five years, something that would not have been possible for most of them even after a lifetime of saving in Britain. Their employers provided an income, food and a roof over their heads so, whether it was through loyalty or need, James Staples, the Dawsons and the Heppingstones followed the Molloys south.

The governor was on board, with Captain Mark Currie RN and the assistant surveyor, John Kellam, whose job it was to measure out the positions of the land grants.[289] A small detachment of sailors under the command of Richard Dawson travelled with them to support the new settlement and the *Emily Taylor* sailed from Gage Roads off Fremantle on 29 April. By a remarkable coincidence, Governor Stirling and John Molloy had both served on His Majesty's ship *Glory* as boys in the Royal Navy, just a few months apart. The two men had a strong connection from their youth to talk about during the journey but that was another memory that may have been too close to the truth for Molloy to discuss.

On Sunday, 2 May 1830, the ship anchored off Cape Leeuwin near the mouth of the Blackwood River and on Monday an expedition was sent along the coast. For the next three days the men explored the shores of the 'inlet' to discover whether there was a suitable place for a settlement. The attractions of a cooler climate than Perth, a safe harbour and river estuary were obvious and their explorations found fresh water and what looked like fertile soil. The sandbar below the surface at the mouth of the river meant they had to come ashore on the open coast on a rocky, weed-strewn beach but their sights were set on a sloping, sheltered curve in the river, protected from the autumn weather that had already set in. On 5 May, Georgiana stepped onto the quiet shore of the Blackwood River for the first time and liked it better than Perth.[290] By Thursday 6 May, the site of 'a town to be called Augusta' had been decided on and the settlers began the long process of unloading their belongings. It took five days. The Molloys' run of bad luck seemed to go on as they struggled to bring the livestock ashore in rafts that could negotiate the shallows over the sandbar. More of their precious animals drowned. Only two cows were landed and one, a particularly valuable animal, somehow managed to strangle herself soon afterwards.[291]

The logical reasons for the settlers' choice of safe haven are still evident in the landscape today, but it was not the sheltered slope of their camping place or the wind-breaking curve of the coast that first captivated Georgiana. There is something special about the sky over places that cling to the furthest western tips and edges of the land, something in the quality of light. Just before it unrolls into the Southern Ocean, the Blackwood River slides like a wide silver bangle on the wrist of the Hardy Inlet and slows as it encounters the sandbar it helped to create. Along its smooth-lipped banks, low houses and the boundaries between them still trace the lines of the first land grants marked out for each family in 1830, tucked in the river's curve and protected by the hill behind them that watched their backs. On the far bank, smoke-green trees and shrubs dip low on the East Augusta shore, looking just as they did when John Molloy and the other men first rowed upstream across the flow. It was not the safe harbour that first took hold of Georgiana's heart, but the clear, clean breathing and rolling of the river, and the light-filled sharpness of everything it touched from the green shore to the sky.

She felt as if she had come home. The softly rounded tree-covered hills, the gentle incline of the land along the edges of the water and the shining surface of the river looked so much like the Gareloch that she loved Augusta even before it had been officially named.

Cottage on the Killiter

With so little time to decide whether they were staying or not, the settlers had to explore the landscape right away. On the morning of 6 May 'the Lieutenant Governor, accompanied by several gentlemen and boats, proceeded to explore the principal river'. They went upriver for a day and a half and came back to the ship late on the Sunday evening.[292] Their overnight camping place was known for many years afterwards as the 'Governor's bivouac'.

Georgiana did not expect 'dear Molloy' back before dark and she was right. Unaware she was so close to the end of her pregnancy, she spent the next two nights alone aboard the ship and finished the book she had been reading. *Redwood* by Catharine Sedgwick was a fictional account of Shaker settlers in New England, and it depicted the everyday lives of a group very closely connected to the English Quakers.[293] Sedgwick wrote a pamphlet denouncing religious intolerance and is known today for the spirited heroines she created who did not conform to female stereotypes of their time. The main character in *Redwood* thought she was an orphan and felt different from her family until the happy ending: she discovered her true parentage and married a gentleman. Whether or not she was an inspiration, the next morning Georgiana grasped her new life by the hands and got on with what needed doing. Her first day in Augusta was spent darning the holes in her husband's stockings.[294]

She was not the only passenger expecting a baby. Ann Dawson had also been pregnant with her first child throughout the long journey and her son was born on board the *Emily Taylor* at anchor in Flinders Bay. George Dawson was the first name Captain Molloy recorded in the baptismal register at Port Augusta.[295] He was baptised on 12 May and his date of birth noted as 8 May. His was also the first name Molloy wrote in the register of burials, on 13 May.

The *Emily Taylor* sailed on to explore the coast of the bay to the east before returning to Perth but before he left, Stirling named Augusta officially, as Georgiana told her mother, 'in honour of the Duke of Sussex'.[296] Rumours still persist that John Molloy, a commoner, was asked to name the town, his choice being another 'clue' to his secret royal parentage. There is no historical evidence that such an unusual step was ever taken and plenty of evidence for the official process. It was not difficult to choose an appropriate name to pay tribute to Prince Frederick, Duke of Sussex, in the same way that the naming of Frederickstown had honoured him. His second name was Augustus and his first wife's name was Augusta. His son was Augustus and his daughter's middle name was Augusta.

Each family group made what arrangements they could and the Molloys pitched four tents on flat ground, close to a freshwater stream. On the first night there was no privacy for a lady who was used to servants appearing discreetly only when needed. The Heppingstones and Dawsons had tents just 'twelve yards' from the Molloys, and Staples was even nearer, right next to them in a 'bell tent'.[297] In the quiet of the bush, voices travel.

About sixty people disembarked from the *Emily Taylor* and they did not have much in common. Even the class structure they brought with them did not bring one family close to another. Servants had come from all over Britain, skilled workers had been drawn from a wide range of different situations and the new 'gentry' of Augusta, those with the most capital invested and the best connections, had widely different backgrounds and family histories. What linked them all was their will to survive and prosper, but the territories and expectations they marked out for each layer of humanity were soon to shift.

The largest land grants were taken up by James Woodward Turner, John Molloy and the Bussell brothers, whose town grant was between the two. These investors had the first choice. Mr and Mrs Turner brought with them a large family of children, servants, thirty skilled workers including Thomas Salkilld, a stonemason and bricklayer, and the materials needed to build a big, comfortable house as quickly as possible. 'The society here,' John Bussell wrote to his cousin, 'is confined but good. Capt. Molloy of the Rifles, and spouse, with ourselves, constitute the gentle settlers [the gentry]. Mr. Turner, a nice little Cockney tradesman with considerable financial resources' – he was a building surveyor – 'completes our stationary residents.'[298]

The criteria Bussell used for his assessment of the Augusta pecking order seems odd today. James Woodward Turner had not been born into the landed gentry but he was a very rich man and had more capital than any of the other new arrivals. His late brother, also a builder, had developed a large number of houses in central London on land belonging to Charles, Lord Southampton, and for thirty years James had been running a very prosperous building business in Marylebone. He lived in one of the best areas just off Oxford Street and his eldest son, Thomas, went to an expensive boarding school in the country. Turner's 1824 insurance policies give an idea of the successful scale of his firm.[299] He insured his workshop for £500, the tools his workmen used for £250 and his stock for £500.[300] In 1825 he and his business partner had an exciting new patent awarded for one of their latest designs. The mechanism for 'Bond and Turner's hinges' made windows weather-tight and could be adapted for sash windows and French doors. It was reported in the *Philosophical Magazine and Journal*, the Repertory of Arts Manufactures and Agriculture, the Repertory of Patent Inventions and in Newton's *London Journal of Arts and Sciences*. But in those days gentlemen were born, not self-made. If John Bussell had discovered that Molloy was the son of an Irish tradesman and learned his early lessons working in his father's shop, his assessment of the local hierarchy would have been very different.

The Bussell brothers, of all the independent settlers, were taking the biggest risk. Their father, William Marchant Bussell, an Anglican clergyman, died in 1820 leaving his wife with nine children, a small pension as her only income and very little capital. Mrs Bussell sold their last asset, a field, and scraped enough money together to buy four of her sons steerage berths on the *Warrior*. John Garrett Bussell left Trinity College, Oxford, with a Bachelor of Arts degree and was working as a tutor while waiting to be ordained.[301] John and his brothers Charles, Joseph Vernon and thirteen-year-old Alfred Pickmore were motivated by a shared determination to achieve the goal agreed by the whole family, including William, the brother who stayed behind. Their journey was extremely uncomfortable, spent in a room with a wooden ceiling that did not protect them completely from evidence of the livestock on the deck above them, and it is unlikely that the brothers had between them the sixty shirts suggested as a minimum total requirement for five months with no washing of clothes. They arrived in Augusta with very little apart from their land grants and a servant they had taken on in Perth, fourteen-year-old Edward Pearce, but their plan was to rebuild the family's fortunes after years of bad luck. They would grow their capital as quickly as possible through agriculture and then bring another brother, Lenox, their three sisters and mother to join them. Whatever it took, they had to succeed.

Other, smaller 'town' grants were taken further along the bay. The captain of the *Emily Taylor*, James McDermott, stayed intermittently in Augusta on his own land, as did surveyor John Kellam. George Chapman was the first of three brothers to arrive in Augusta, followed in 1831 by Henry and James. John Herring had been in charge of a tavern in Stepney for eighteen years and left his wife and family behind to find a better life for them in the new colony. He managed his own small grant and worked for the Bussells, but within three years he was also working as a servant for the local doctor. John Dawson, a carpenter who had arrived in the colony in 1830, left his employer and made his way to Augusta where there was plenty of work for him as an independent tradesman.[302] Although their capital investment was smaller, these and other individuals all played an important part in the success of the settlement, sharing their skills, pooling their resources and working together when times were difficult.

Molloy had transported the nineteenth-century equivalent of a kit house, a small wooden building, and on Saturday 25 May, although the rain was growing heavier, it was under construction all day 'close behind the tent' on his twelve acres by the river. That night Georgiana went to bed early but was suddenly surprised by pains she had not been expecting for a few more weeks.[303] Everything went smoothly at first and a daughter was born with no complications. Both parents had been hoping for a son.[304] Georgiana was 'laughing & talking' and, it seems, her passion for horticulture was not far from her mind even in the moments after giving birth. She said she was surprised to realise that after never liking children, her own baby seemed so engaging that it would even stop her from gardening.[305] She asked for the servants' reassurance the baby had no deformities and, a stark reminder of the marriage prospects for girls in the nineteenth century, she checked to make sure her daughter did not have thick ankles.

After nearly an hour with no sign of the afterbirth, Mrs Dawson knew enough to realise that something was wrong and 'nearly fainted with alarm'. She begged Georgiana to be still and rest. The nearest medical help was the colonial surgeon in Perth so, with no-one to ask for advice, Georgiana turned to a medical book Molloy had brought with them and the encyclopedia that was being used to prop up her makeshift bed. She had not taken much notice of the servants' opinions but what she read must have worried her. Georgiana read instructions aloud to Mrs Dawson and together they learned from the book what needed to be done. The encyclopedia was Captain Molloy's main source of information and guidance on medical, scientific and practical questions. Pages dense with text and diagrams described the normal process of childbirth and, more importantly, advised on the potential dangers.

> Should pains not recur at the distance of an hour after the birth of the infant, it becomes necessary for several reasons to introduce the hand into the womb and extract the secundines [placenta]. When any alarming circumstance happens after the birth of the infant requiring the extraction of the placenta, the practitioner is not to delay for an hour, indeed not for a minute, giving the requisite assistance.[306]

The information was very clear: if the afterbirth remained longer than an hour, it 'would soon prove fatal' and the 'mortal event' would happen either from loss of blood or more slowly from 'putrefaction'. Georgiana knew she could die if there was no physical intervention but, as strong-willed as she was, she could not bear to ask a servant to perform such an intimate invasion. Thankfully youth was on her side and nature took its course after two hours.

The baby girl was baptised by her father and named Elizabeth and Mary after her grandmothers, Georgiana's two sisters and Mary Dunlop, her other 'sister' in Scotland.[307] It was clear from the first evening that the child was unlikely to survive – she was barely able to take any nourishment and growing weaker all the time. John Molloy was no stranger to sickness and death but this was more than he could bear. His wife knew he was staying away from their tent deliberately and when he did return his eyes were always filled with tears.[308] On the twelfth day, the baby died in her mother's arms as thunder rolled on the other side of the canvas tent. Georgiana held her daughter's body tightly expecting rigor mortis to begin, and she sent for her husband. He took a long time to arrive.[309]

Elizabeth Molloy was the second child born in Augusta and when John Garrett Bussell read her funeral service on 5 June, she became 'No. 2' in the list of burials. Without telling his wife what he was going to do, John Molloy sowed rye grass and flowering clover on the grave and wove a trellis from twigs, entwining the wild, creeping plants around it to make a bower. Later, when Georgiana overcame the physical grief that gripped her for weeks, she planted pumpkins there because she knew they would quickly grow green shoots to form 'a sort of Dome' over the grave.[310]

Georgiana described the anguish of those days at length in letters to her family and close friends, telling the story of a child who was lost to hardship and misfortune like so many after her in the early years of European settlement. In November 1830, she related the long, sad story to her mother in a letter and her voice speaks as clearly today as it must have done when Mrs Kennedy broke the seal and unfolded the pages in 1831.[311]

> It rained on our faces through the tent, the wind blew about the cords, my teeth chattered in my head & my legs & thighs took the cramp with cold and wet. My dearest little child was at this moment born. I said 'Is it a Boy or Girl?'
>
> 'Oh what would you like it to be Ma'am?' said Mrs. H.[312]
>
> 'A boy,' I said.
>
> 'It is a little girl Ma'am.'
>
> I called out, 'Molloy come & look at your little daughter. I wish it had been a boy.'
>
> In a little time he came and the poor little thing was wrapped in my flannel petticoat laid outside at my feet with nothing between her little face & the sky but canvass.
>
> We had not been a fortnight landed & they could not find some string thread but used pack cord, which did it so ineffectually that the poor child lost half a pint of blood at last on the following morning, of which I was ignorant till seeing her blanket discoloured.
>
> [Molloy] seemed very fond of Baby and managed to sing to her, 'I wish I was at home again' & 'Pequeña que pasa' with the Spanish castanet song.[313] He often took her early in the morning into his

couch or bed, the only time my arms were free of her and they literally ached having her so constantly in them.

On Tuesday they thought she had caught cold or inflammation as her breathing was so short and some internal soreness seemed to make her suffer. It was scarcely possible to keep ourselves from catching colds and chills for every time it rained, which was incessantly, a cold damp used to steal over us from the wet canvass and had we been in any climate but this it would have been fatal.

Thursday morning about 2 o'clock the 3rd of June I sat up with poor Baby. She cried very much for some hours and about ½ past 5 Molloy took her on to his box lid which served as his bed and tried to keep her quiet for half an hour when I was dozing but she cried so much I took her again. He got up. I told him my fears which he said were very likely false. He went to haul the net for our subsistence being the only fresh meat we have, and before going made me a cup of chocolate.

Poor Baby very ill and dreadfully distorted her features were changed with convulsions. She shrieked and seemed in very great agony. I could scarcely hold her and Mrs. Heppingstone begged me to let her have her but I saw what was coming on and was determined not to have her out of my arms until all was over.

She seemed to sleep and Mrs. H. and I kept gazing at her for 20 or 30 minutes. She did not seem to breathe. She was so quiet that she & I exclaimed, 'Can she be dead!' After looking intently at her after her last convulsion, I had not even her eyes or mouth to close and I tried a wine glass to her nostrils to realise to myself of the awful certainty of being bereft of so pure a spirit.

When I found she was dead I sat up and held down her little legs & hands, she being already naked from the Bath. I sent for him & he was some time in coming. Mrs. Heppingstone was also absent & I cannot express to you the feeling which stole over me at that time, I sitting in a cold tent, it raining & thundering, holding my dead infant's limbs to keep them straight.

Molloy entered and approaching said, 'I never beheld so lovely and touching a sight.' With that he wept and sat down speech less [sic] at my side. The necessary preparations being made, Mrs. H. dressed & washed the corpse and cut off her hair which I send to my beloved Mother & her affectionate and kind Grandmother whom I sorely missed and longed for.

Nothing could be procured to lay her on. Mrs. H suggested Molloy's canteen but he did not seem to acquiesce & after she left the room very much hurt said, 'No my dear, little did I think my poor old canteen would be required for such a purpose. Is there nothing else?' Mrs. Heppingstone brought down her little sewing box and it being on two chairs she laid my poor dead child upon it at the foot of my bed & her fathers. There was no other place to put it and I had it before my eyes the whole of that night.

I knew not what to do. I felt inclined to rush out into the open air and charge the winds with what weighed so heavy at my bursting head.

Saturday 5th The day has arrived when I must part with what I was mysteriously possessed of. She came in sorrow. She was the source of fondest pleasure in her little life & of unutterable grief in her departure, but again I cannot wish to think of her when her hollow shrieks and cries are still sounding in my bewildered brain

The funeral was to be at 12 & the elder Mr. Bussell to read the service. Molloy chose a spot on our grant where to lay her & had the men clear it. Dawson dug the grave. Molloy made a pathway. I put her in the coffin which was common deal lined with flannel and put some little blue flowers on her body. It being winter, there were very few flowers in bloom. Mr. Bussell came. I showed him my dead child. He & Molloy went out and the servants came down to bid the cold, cold body farewell. I took the screw driver & with my own feeble hands screwed up all. No-one excepting Molloy was near or close to me for many, many thousands of miles. I was dressed in white with white ribbons by the bye, my bridal bows on my bonnet and Dearest Molloy and I followed the corpse which Dawson carried behind Mr. Bussell up to the hill.

The service being read & the grave closed up we retired but Oh what a blank was there on my return to my tent. It had happened in the short space of 13 days, now all was over forever with regard to her. You, my beloved Parent, can sympathise with me in many of these my misfortunes, but you do not know the dire extremity of not being able to either speak or write or in any way give vent to your feelings to one of your own sex, for many thousand miles & I was dubious that I had acted right. I did not know what she had died of, or anything that could console me.

It was a devastating start to the new life Georgiana had dreamed of for six months, a tragic scene in a setting of great beauty. The settlers chose their town site for its position but the most appealing factor was the lushness of its vegetation. They assumed that the tall, heavily canopied trees growing close to the river's shore indicated the soil was fertile, so they looked forward to their first harvest within a few months. Work began to create permanent homes and prepare the land for farming.

They dug wells, cleared trees and planted where they could. The Molloys had arrived without most of the livestock they had started with so every animal was precious and the building of fences began. As the settlers enclosed their stock to keep them safe and away from the crops, they also separated one land grant from another. Those first simple boundaries established the beginnings of a pattern in the landscape, still discernible today in the property boundaries and streets of Augusta. Families with money had supplies of the tools and raw materials they needed but they would have to share and help one another if anything was going to be achieved. Masters and servants felled trees and ploughed land shoulder to shoulder, behind shared oxen provided by the government. Within a few weeks, green shoots appeared in small clearings, signs of the first potato crop. Simple cottages stood where there had been tents.

Sketch of Augusta showing the Bussells' house on the left, the Turners' large house on the right and the Molloys' home between them in the distance.

JS Battye Library SLWA BA 1887 / 70

The Molloys' little house stood just behind the site of the present day memorial park on a slight rise of land close to the river.[314] Mr Turner occupied twenty acres, to a point 'about 800 yards from Captn. Molloy's S.E. limit', and between the two were the first ten acre grants of the Bussell brothers and John Herring.[315] The Turners, Bussells and Molloys were also promised the first choice to complete their entitlement as soon as the land was 'opened for general occupation'.

The landscape looked very different from the view of Albany Terrace today. The sandbar was just below the surface and there were no buildings on the high ground. The boundaries of Georgiana's first home were the riverbank and the beach. As an adult, her eldest daughter remembered that 'The Molloy garden sloped down to the beach on one side & the other was the river.'[316]

Like his neighbours, Molloy started his life as a settler with less than he had expected after losing so many animals during the journey. His seine net was put to use within a few days, hauled across the width of the Blackwood River using a small boat.[317] It was the best growing time of the year but even after weeks of clearing there was hard work ahead before the first harvest could be gathered. The families soon discovered that the trees they had admired were their greatest adversaries. The wood was hard, the trunks were thick and it was difficult to move the huge timbers, but necessity fuelled the project and they made slow progress. Three years later the view of Augusta for visitors approaching by ship showed it was still 'green and bushy' with 'dense forest'.[318]

When the roof was thatched, the Molloys moved in to their house, but for two weeks after her baby's death, Georgiana's grief made it difficult for her to do anything at all. And then, on the first rain-free day, she stopped crying and channelled her energy into an activity that was useful and healing. On 10 June, she began the work for which she would eventually be known across the world: 'I tried a great many things to divert my attention and dissipate the gloom. On Thursday 10th I gardened, for the first time dry.'

The new settlers relied closely on one another but their history is woven with the lives of many others, the men, women and children who lived near them in the bush. They could not have achieved what they did without the help of their Aboriginal neighbours. At first the colonists were of little interest to the local Noongar families, the Pibbulman and Wardandi people, and did not appear to be a threat. The people whose ancestors had been living in the area for centuries waited two weeks before they made contact, standing on the opposite bank of the river and singing to announce their arrival. They held green branches and 'a green leaf at the end of a stick', a greeting that Georgiana interpreted as a sign of peace.[319] On an unused page in her 1830 diary there are four words written in English with the corresponding Aboriginal word next to each, like a simple dictionary. In the early years when the new settlers and their Aboriginal neighbours' paths crossed in Augusta there were peaceful encounters.[320]

| Ear | Donya | Nose | Dama |
| Eye | Méal | Native | Moka |

On 28 August, HMS *Sulphur* delivered the official dispatch from Stirling confirming Molloy's appointment as Government Resident. Although unattached to his regiment and on half pay, he was still a captain in the British army with firsthand experience of a judicial role; he was the obvious candidate. Sometimes confused in autobiographical information with his other role as Resident Magistrate and Collector of Taxes, his new appointment was a quasi-ministerial job with a salary of £100 a year in which he represented the British government in the Sussex District. Molloy had diplomatic duties to perform when visitors arrived in the region, was responsible for allocation of resources, maintaining law and order and collecting custom duty. These duties meant that Georgiana was left alone for weeks at a time while Molloy was away on government business, but there were consolations: she was able to tell her mother in no uncertain terms that 'he is the highest situation except the Governor in the whole of Western Australia'.[321] On his first day in the new job, Molloy wrote to thank Stirling for the honour and put in a request for government supplies so that Captain Dance of the *Sulphur* could deliver his note quickly back to Perth: four barrels of wheat, three casks of sugar, three casks of flour and twenty gallons of rum.[322]

In their new environment, a tiny sub-colony on the other side of the world from their homes, it did not take the servants long to realise they were indispensable and in short supply. Many behaved in ways that would not have been tolerated in Britain and most left their employers as soon as possible to take their own land grants. Increasingly, Georgiana took on the hard labour of the household, made clothes for the family and servants and, with the help of James Staples, created a garden that provided fresh food for most of the year. Staples was 'idle' and had other vices but he was the only gardener available and occasional threats of dismissal came to nothing; although he wanted to leave, he could not afford to buy himself out of his indenture.[323] Clearing land to grow food was everyone's priority in the first season and Staples applied his gardening knowledge to vegetables instead of decorative flowers. But before the first year was out, Georgiana began to use his experience in the floral garden she had been planning for months, a small square area at the front of the house. While staying at Holbrook Lodge she had not visited the Caldecotts' noble neighbour, Lady Selina Skipworth, so she had only heard about the beautiful gardens at Newbold Revel but when the time came to plan her own garden, she decided to replicate its layout. Staples had seen the symmetrical flowerbeds at Newbold Revel that led down a gentle slope to the lake.[324] In 1830, on the other side of the world, he recreated their effect for his new employer on a much smaller scale, with a pattern of paths, borders and four small lawns leading the eye from the door of the Molloys' simple home towards the beach of the Indian Ocean.[325]

> Staples has laid out the Garden in a most masterly manner. The size of our Garden is about an acre & will shortly be enlarged, the model Staples says is the one at Newbold Hall. He has laid out the flower garden with great taste.

Government supplies were supposed to arrive regularly but everything else had to be planted and harvested or raised and butchered. For everyone, the days were long and exhausting. Georgiana lost weight rapidly and was often in pain from injuries and hard work. She started wearing a 'guard ring' tightly sized to prevent her wedding ring from falling off, but she got so thin that the guard ring itself flew from her hand one day and landed in the fire.

The greatest burden was not the physical stress of her daily jobs, it was loneliness. In December 1831, when she expected Molloy to be away for three weeks, Georgiana was 'very depressed' by his absence. In a rare admission of weakness, she wrote in a letter to her mother, 'I can scarcely keep from crying, my heart is so full'.[326] The overwhelming influence of class structure and the rigid power of its unwritten rules dictated the way men and women behaved. There was a straightforward role to be played with servants and a more delicate

Restored fragments from Georgiana's 1833 diary describe how her hands had become so thin that her guard ring fell into the fire while she was making a plum pudding. The torn page does not show whether she lost her wedding ring at the same time but it seems likely. She wrote: 'this makes me very unhappy'.

JS Battye Library SLWA ACC 4305A Photograph © Mike Rumble

connection to balance with the neighbours' wives, but Georgiana was the only 'lady' in Augusta and that meant social isolation whether she liked it or not.

Surrounded by other women, she was alone and living a life she could not have pictured from the dust-free, brocaded drawing room of Keppoch House. The decision to marry was acceptance of God's will, and as the months passed Georgiana knew she had made the right decision. It might be easy to assume their marriage was one of convenience: Molloy needed a wife to share his new life as a settler and Georgiana needed a husband to escape from her family. While both observations are true, their relationship was a genuine partnership from the beginning. Its starting point was not only an intense mutual attraction but also friendship and respect. Captain and Mrs Molloy actually liked one another.

Georgiana assured Helen Story that her husband was 'a dear creature' and she 'would not exchange him for 10,000 pounds per annum and a mansion in a civilized country'.[327] The feeling was mutual. Molloy added a postscript to the same letter: 'You, my dear Mr Story, spliced us so securely we have not had the least difference of opinion yet.'

The content of Georgiana's diary after her daughter's death depicts a woman coming to terms with tragedy. Her last entry for the autumn of 1830 reads, 'Baby was born', the words faint as if they have been partly erased. On 18 June she recorded the anniversary of the Battle of Waterloo and in late July she wrote a shopping list. The household was in need of a mustard pot, a cake plate, a fish steamer and three flowerpots. In August, she managed to record a day of unusually fine weather and then, in September, as spring arrived, she began to make notes once again.

Despite rain, the business of building moved quickly. A young carpenter called George Layman had won the contract to build the barracks and he took up a small grant in the settlement. Molloy reported to the governor that the accommodation for the military was almost complete and the Turners had cleared about eight acres. Georgiana's first vegetable garden was just an acre but she had plans to extend it as soon as possible to grow more flowering plants. The first seeds grew well and the family ate vegetables and salad every day.[328]

The settlement's first doctor, Colonial Surgeon Dr Charles Simmons, arrived on HMS *Sulphur* when it called in briefly at Augusta. He and James Drummond, the government naturalist, had been visiting areas along the coast to assess them for settlement. Simmons had already sent a letter of welcome to the Molloys when they arrived in Perth. A graduate of Glasgow University, he knew the area of Scotland that Georgiana loved so much and his brother George fought in the same battalion as Molloy at the Battle of Waterloo. The *Sulphur* also brought a detachment of soldiers from the 63rd Regiment under Lieutenant McLeod to replace the sailors. Augusta's future should have been looking brighter as each week passed but as the first signs of spring appeared, life became harder.[329] Domestic servants were valuable assets and there were very few looking for work, so when Mrs Dawson started refusing to do certain tasks, Georgiana had no other option but to do more around the home and in the garden. Whatever the weather, she worked alongside Staples digging potatoes, milking cows and goats, churning butter, baking bread, washing clothes, repairing mats and dressmaking. When Molloy was away, which was often, she added the weighing and allocation of supplies, record keeping and official letter writing to her long list of jobs. By the end of October she knew she was expecting another baby, but that did not prevent her from rising at dawn and working on by candlelight until every chore was completed.

One night just before Christmas when Molloy was away on an expedition with Dr Simmons, she went to bed early but was woken by terrible pain. Her agony went on through most of the night but the servants' house was forty-five metres away so she could not call for help. She did not realise what was happening until the early morning when the sad truth became obvious.[330]

Dr Simmons ordered her to spend three weeks in bed but she was at work again in January, in time for the first harvest. The house was situated on the low incline of a hill and it reminded Georgiana of the heather-topped rise behind Camis Eskan where James Dennistoun lived. She gave it the same name: the Killiter.[331] The Molloys had small fields of rye and wheat growing there but they needed more cleared land before they could be self-sufficient. Government supplies were the only lifeline until Augusta was more productive, and without a delivery from Perth since June, food was running very low. By late January, the settlers had used up most of their stores, crops withered under the hot sun and the supplies they desperately needed still had not arrived. Molloy allocated provisions carefully from the public store but it was almost empty. The social layering of the town faltered in the face of hunger and deprivation. Status and capital did not guarantee comfort when there was nothing money could buy. Molloy received his allowance as government resident in addition to an army salary but that made no difference to their circumstances. By February 1831, Georgiana knew she was pregnant for the third time.[332]

In March there was no flour left in the government depot. Molloy used his seine net and shared what he caught. Georgiana, like everyone else, found ways of making do with whatever was available. She ground wheat seeds and made griddle cakes with the dough. This was not a job she could trust the servants with when they had been living only on 'boiled fish and greens' for weeks.[333] When HMS *Sulphur* anchored in the bay in June, the supplies on board saved the settlers from starvation.

As the weather grew cooler and the rain arrived, Georgiana extended her garden and planted cuttings she had brought with her as well as seeds sent by family and friends. It was a creative combination from three different continents designed not just for visual beauty but also for fragrance. By April 1831 she had received only two letters from home since she left in 1829. She wrote a long letter to Frances

Birkett that month, narrating the long story of the voyage and her first year in the colony, with an enthusiastic description of her garden. The letter shows a growing affection for Augusta but Georgiana discloses more between the lines: the shifting of her heart between hope and regret.[334]

> I cannot say too much for this delightful spot, the climate most temperate, never oppressive, our house on the side of a hill amidst large timber trees on the banks of the Blackwood River in the middle of a Garden of nearly 2 acres beautifully laid out by an excellent gardener in our establishment, it is said to be the best garden in SW Australia excepting none, we supply our neighbours with vegetables continuously and have from every sort of British herb & root such as Cabbage carrot onion etc. Pear Apple & Peach to the orange tree & vine, Tobacco, Tamarind & different Cape trees. this is our winter & the flower garden is redolent with Mignonette which I emulated you in cutting down, and all sorts of British flowers and shrubs.
>
> ...
>
> You may think how much I like it when I have not a single companion but my own Jack Molloy. I have not seen a lady now for nearly 17 months. I attend to my house duties, mend and make for Molloy and myself yes even to Molloys caps & hats of straw, cut out the mens indispensables as we find our servants clothing, and give them each £30, 20 acres of land and a house value £30 at the end of 5 years besides paying their passage money with all this they are discontented and want to leave your service when the men can get 7/6 per day, the women 4/ and 4/6 per Dozen for washing & a guinea a week for a charwoman so let those that are fools enough to give these prices stand by the consequences, for my part I'll stand at the Wash Tub before I do it or even as Government Residents wife set the example.

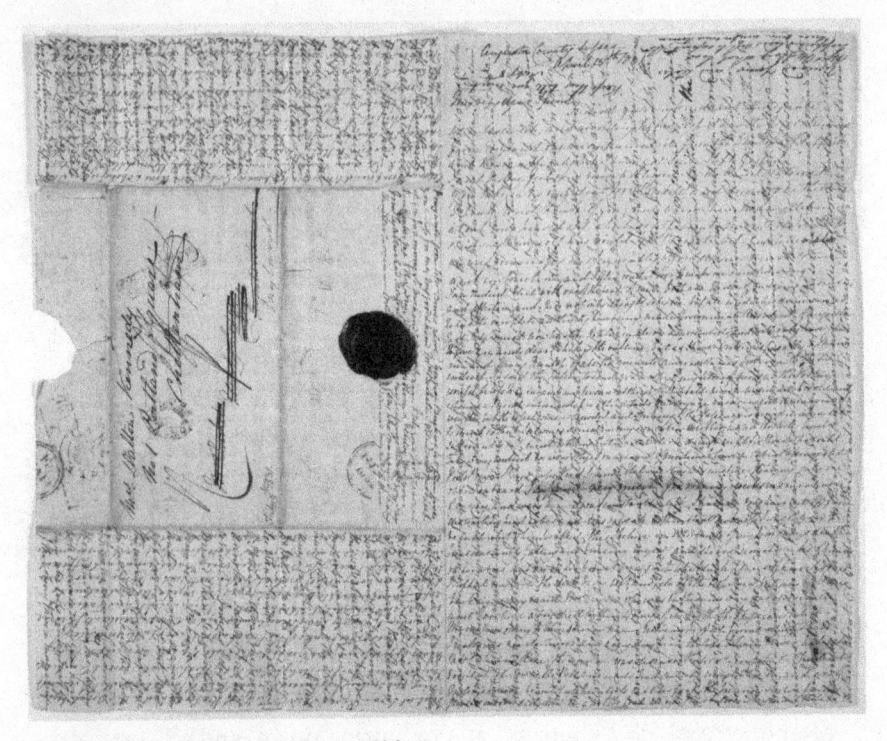

Georgiana's 1831 letter to Mrs Frances Birkett

© *Cumbria Archive Centre D KEN 3 / 28 /9*

Dearest Molloy has never thank God had one hours illness, although even he has laid on the bare ground indeed I had once the pleasure of laying on the ground when at Swan River being prevented by strong winds & a thunder storm getting upon our boat to Perth, Molloy another gentleman & myself were [*torn page*] after tossing about the whole night to give it up and I and Molloy laid rolled up in his cloak on the ground and the skies as if every now & then opening with thunder and Lightning this was about 5 weeks before my confinement & we had had nothing to eat the whole day & only had water to drink. Dr. [dear] Molloy said oh my Georgy see what I have brought you to I told him it was my own doing that I did not feel half so much in body as I did in mind when separated from him.

We have never had a quarrel or anything approaching to it but have the most perfect confidence in each other. I keep the Purse and have no means of spending it on idle occasions, his salary will increase every year he is more like Superintendent of the Colony than a Magistrate.

...

You give Burky and let him give you a kiss for me, my good and kind Mrs Birkett, I wish I could just peep at you for a moment my kind remembrance to all your good servants.

* * *

The densely packed, cross-written pages of Georgiana's honest letter to a trusted friend recount simply the main events of her first twelve months in Australia and include a harrowing description of her first baby's death. It was not until I had worked my way through all her letters in the Cumbria archive that I realised how nearly this intimate account was lost forever.

The letter was addressed to Mrs Birkett at her home near Carlisle, but when it arrived at Etterby Lodge someone else opened it, added a note and forwarded it to Georgiana's mother, asking her to explain that Mrs Birkett would not be able to reply for some time.[335] Whatever the reason for this intervention, it meant that the letter did not end up in Mrs Birkett's collection of mail, which did not survive the years. Mrs Kennedy kept most of her correspondence and her belongings were stored by a lawyer after she died. If those closely written pages had reached Georgiana's elderly friend they would have been lost, but circumstances diverted their journey and saved them. Sometimes history extends a kindness, a gift from the past to the future.

Mending and Making

HMS *Sulphur* was a welcome sight on the horizon again with six months' worth of urgently needed provisions and a new doctor, Alfred Green. Simmons was told to return to headquarters and left Augusta for good, offering the Bussells his house and his boat. Twenty-six-year-old Green, who had been a fellow passenger on the *Warrior* in 1829, became Assistant Colonial Surgeon in July 1830 as demands grew on the Perth hospital.[336] He took up a land grant, employed John Herring as his servant and settled into his new life as the local physician and surgeon. On 7 November 1831, he delivered Georgiana's baby.

Sabina Dunlop Molloy arrived at noon and her mother experienced familiar complications. Dr Green was concerned and told Georgiana she was probably suffering from a condition he frighteningly described as 'twist'. What she feared most was the procedure he would have to perform if the situation worsened. Twelve hours passed, during which Dr Green ordered extremely hot water to be applied to her stomach, gave her snuff to make her sneeze and a teaspoonful of tartar emetic, a poisonous salt compound. None of these 'remedies' worked but around midnight, while Molloy and the doctor were fast asleep, nature took its course and Dr Green announced that the delay had been caused by 'suspense and previous agitation'.[337]

Sabina was a lively child with pale blonde hair and a sense of humour that developed very early. A letter to Mrs Kennedy a few months after the birth reveals that a daughter was a joy in life Georgiana had not always anticipated.

> I am now rocking the cot for baby and singing time during her sleep. The other day as she was feeding I was looking very dull as Mrs Dawson had been annoying me. She left off and gave me such a sweet little smile that I who never cared about or wished for children thought she was sent by providence as a solace to me and another time after putting on one of the Caps you put in the Linen Box for me, I said, 'Ah! Poor grandmamma sent you that cap little Baby'. My eyes filled with tears and she instantly laughed most merrily.[338]

Sabina felt like reassurance for Georgiana, who had struggled with guilt for the first year in Augusta because she could not bend herself completely to what she believed to be God's will. Three years after the death of her first child, the events of her first weeks in the settlement were still raw in her memory when she wrote to Helen Story, who had recently lost a baby herself.

> … language refuses to utter what I experienced when mine died in my arms in this dreary land, and no one but Molloy near me. Oh! I have gone through much, and more than I would ever suffer any one to do again – I fear – I need not say fear – I know I have not made the use of those afflictions that God designed – it was so hard – I could not see it was in love and I thought I might have had one little bright object left to solace all the hardships and privations I endured, and had still to go through. It was wicked and I am now thoroughly at peace.[339]

While Georgiana was recovering from childbirth, exhausted and hungry most of the time, a letter arrived bringing the news that the man she once rejected as a suitor had married. Georgiana's next letter home reassured her 'dear Mamma' that Mr and Mrs George Troutbeck could not possibly be happier than Mr and Mrs Molloy. The letter caught her at a low time and perhaps that is why it also included a few unguarded lines about what might have been.

> Oh that I might have had but a neat cottage in sunny Cumberland or in the Highlands. My heart falls when I think of having left my native country & perhaps more from a dream I had last night about George Troutbeck and Ennim bank. I often regret I never saw him to speak to after dropping the correspondence. I could have explained more verbally than by letter. What sort of person is she? And how do they get on?[340]

After a year of clearing, ploughing and planting, it became obvious that Augusta could not provide the agricultural land needed for a completely independent colony. By July 1831, the Bussells had some flour left but no meat. They borrowed rice from Molloy, who took on their servant, Pearce, to reduce their daily outlay on food until Charles became government storekeeper.[341] When a merchant ship came in and anchored as usual outside the reef, the brothers spent their last two pounds on supplies to keep them going for another few weeks.[342] But the meat they bought and buried for safekeeping on the beach was completely hidden by sand and lost. With nothing left, they borrowed Molloy's small boat and set off to their 2000-acre grant on a promontory nineteen kilometres further up the Blackwood River.[343] They called it Adelphi, the Greek word for 'brothers', and were not sorry to move away from the embarrassment of never feeling able to return the generosity and hospitality of their neighbours.[344]

In November 1831, John Bussell's explorations north of the Adelphi reached the flatter landscape near the coast of Geographe Bay, and he recognised its potential as a future town site. It was what they had all been looking for, 'a most pleasing country and

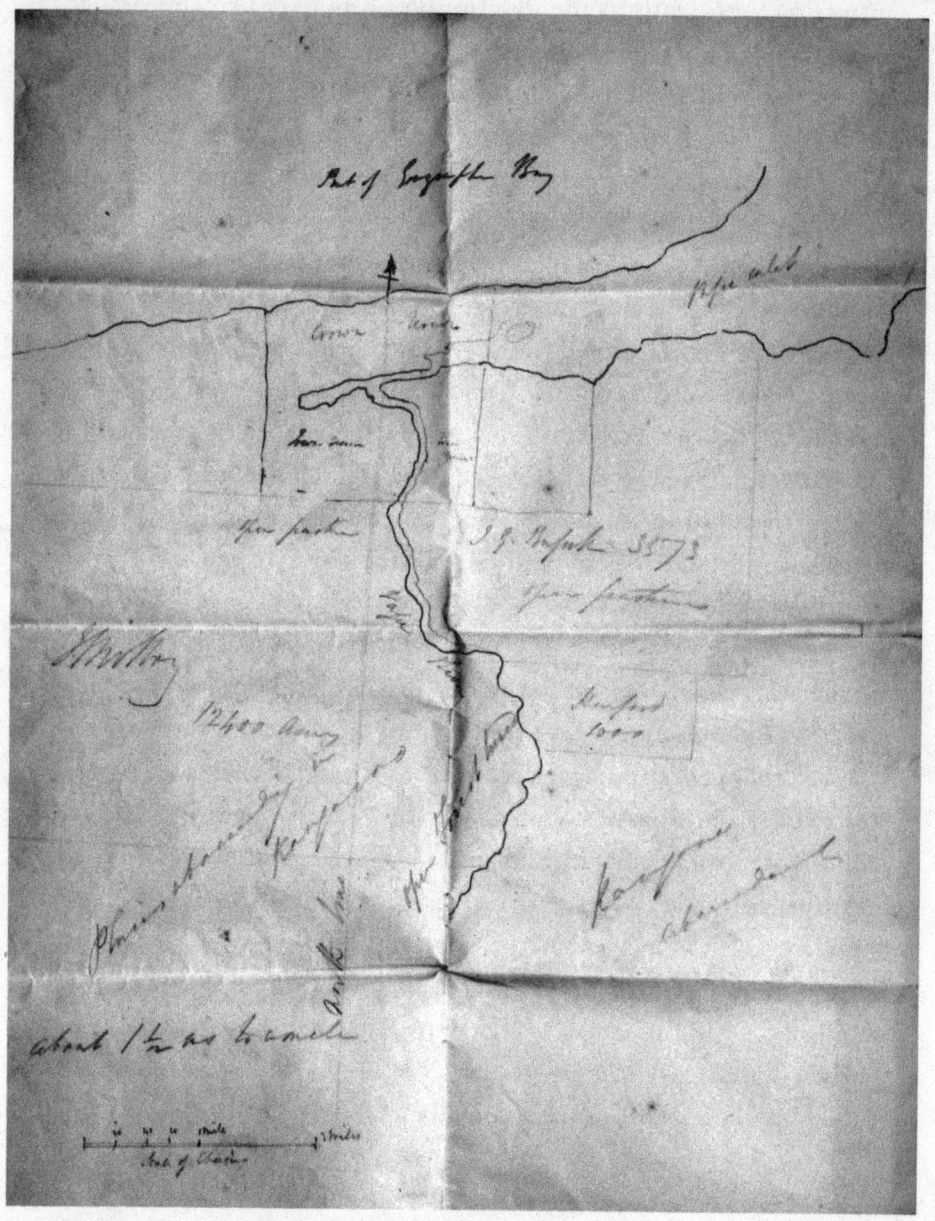

John Molloy drew and signed this sketch map of the Vasse and sent it to his mother-in-law, Mrs Kennedy, c.1832. It records 'plains abounding in kangaroos' on both sides of the river and 'open pastures'.

Cumbria Archive Centre D KEN 3 / 28 / 1 Photograph © Mike Rumble answering with truth to the description of its park-like appearance, with long waiving [sic] grass, and abounding also in kangaroos'.[345] A traditional Aboriginal hunting place and meeting area, the land had been cleared by fires for generations, but the British did not consider this as evidence of prior habitation because there were no permanent dwellings. The Bussells claimed their remaining grant of 3700 acres on the Vasse River and the location duties for Molloy's 12,400 acres there began on 13 July 1832.[346,347]

It did not escape Captain Molloy's notice that the area along the Vasse River was already occupied, and not by Europeans. He said it was, 'a populous district' with 'traces of numerous paths' and he asked for his land grant to be moved to the left bank. In October 1832, Governor Stirling approved his request to 'occupy an Island on the Blackwood River called Molloy Island' and he told the surveyor general that he would prefer it to be renamed as Dalton Island if possible, presumably in honour of his mother-in-law's family.[348] Georgiana may have been exaggerating a little when she told Mrs Kennedy the governor had given her the island as a gift, a retreat from the summer heat.[349]

The trail between Augusta and the Vasse soon became well beaten, travelled regularly by the colonists and the Noongar people connected with the settlements. By this time most of the original Augusta settlers had interests further north and were preparing for a future there, but it would be seven more years before Mrs Molloy saw the Vasse. She was not the only settler to stay on in Augusta: the Turners remained. In March 1832, Mr Turner's eldest daughter, Elizabeth Ann (Nancy), had married James McDermott, captain of the *Emily Taylor*. Georgiana had her own views about the suitability of the match.

> Mr Turner unfortunately married his first wife's sister by whom he had one child the subject of much jealousy from its mothers [sic] foolish affection and I believe had her home been happy Miss Turner would never have married one whom she had neither time nor opportunity to be attached to.[350]

Reports in Perth were still optimistic about the development of Augusta. Months later, in January 1833, a newspaper described the settlement as 'progressing in all the arts of Colonization'. Captain Molloy was 'up to his ears in business' and Mrs Molloy had managed to create space in her garden to cultivate an abundance of flowers as well as vegetables, 'all of them very fragrant, and very beautiful'.[351] The truth was less rosy. Georgiana confessed to Margaret Dunlop that the life of a settler was too much for her and for her husband. Complete exhaustion forced her to spend a few days in bed, too ill to say her prayers. Writing to Maggie at the beginning of the third year in Augusta brought back the past and created a terrible contrast with the present.

> What golden dreams we used to have about your coming to stay with me, how would you like to be nearly 3 years in a place without a female of your own rank to speak to, or be with you whatever happened.[352]

Augusta was a beautiful place to live but the reality of her life there was too far from what she had left behind, in so many ways. 'Oh! My loved sister! I cannot contain myself when I think of the past.'

In March, Lieutenant Governor Stirling went on an inspection of the sub-colonies and found that 'the settlers were contented and happy, on the most amiable footing with the natives, many of whom were employed in carrying wood and water, and performing other services for which they were regularly remunerated'.[353] His report gives a realistic summary of the settlers' reasons for planning a move to the Vasse.

> At Augusta, Garden vegetables had been produced in abundance, and grain crops, as far as they had been cultivated, yielded a very fair return, but the heavy expense of clearing the ground had confined the agricultural operations to a limited extent. The land in this

district being rich, but thickly timbered and difficult to clear. Several of the settlers contemplated removing their establishments to Port Vasse, where there are open plains of rich pasture land, as soon as they could procure flocks.

Things were beginning to change but not yet for Georgiana. Her husband was preparing to farm further north at the Vasse and staying away more often as the pressure of his job increased, and so a heavier workload fell on her shoulders. If she still had regrets, she knew it was too late; she began dreaming about George Troutbeck again, and this time her dreams included his wife.[354]

Somehow, between the many tasks that faced her each day, Georgiana managed to keep up a flow of letters to her friends and family in Britain but the news she received in return was not all good. George was expelled from Rugby School in 1830 and went to stay with a private tutor in Northamptonshire, the Reverend Barton Bouchier, but his academic performance did not improve; he seemed more interested in writing love letters to girls. Rather surprisingly he was accepted the following year as a hospital surgeon's apprentice in Cheltenham where Mrs Kennedy was living. The fact that George was entering the medical profession should have been good news, but with cholera still at epidemic levels in the area it was worrying. Meanwhile, Dalton had come up with a plan to purchase a promotion in the army and was trying to persuade his mother to find the money. He told her he would leave the army and sell his commission to pay off debts if she did not find the cash to buy him a lieutenancy, so she tried to borrow money by mortgaging the house in Abbey Street.

Mrs Kennedy's sons were the least of her problems, however. Eliza married the Reverend John Besley in November 1829 in Rugby, with Mary and Dalton as witnesses. As an assistant tutor at Balliol College, Besley's income was too low for him to take on the responsibility of keeping a wife. Marriage would be as much a financial arrangement with her parents as a love match. Towards the end of 1828 Besley was appointed sub-librarian of Oxford's world-famous Bodleian Library, so the wedding went ahead. When the 'living' in a northern parish under the patronage of Balliol College became available in 1830, Besley was chosen. A letter brought Georgiana the news that Besley was vicar of St Bartholomew in the village of Long Benton, near Newcastle in Northumberland. She was pleased for her sister, who had acquired not just a successful husband but a comfortable home and a respectable position in society as the vicar's wife.

But 'Poor Lizzy' had not left her personal difficulties behind her, and in the summer of 1832 when Mrs Kennedy and Mary visited the Besley home they found that all was not well. Before she left Long Benton, Mrs Kennedy had a difficult conversation with her son-in law and Mr Fife, the man he had taken on to look after his wife. The three agreed that Eliza was never to be left alone under any circumstances.[355]

Eliza wrote to her mother on 14 June describing her terrible sadness after the visit. Besley took her out in the carriage to explore the country lanes until dark, trying to cheer her up, but it did not help. She longed to hear music but could not bear to touch her piano. Just opening the instrument made her cry violently. She asked for secrecy about the fact that she was 'weak & very low spirited' but was pleased to say she had stopped taking medicine and had left her bedroom to go downstairs to breakfast.[356]

Not long after she arrived home from the vicarage Mrs Kennedy received 'a most alarming letter' from Eliza.[357] Things had become much worse.

> My Dearest Parent,
> Return thanks with dear Mary, on your knees, for your poor daughters Deliverance from the <u>greatest</u> calamity, to which our frail nature is subject. Start not when I name <u>madness!</u> Brought on by a foolish (tho' not unauthorized by Mr. Fife) trick, the use of the cold Shower Bath. For two Days I have been in that horrible state, doing the most foolish things, & have to be watched like a Child.[358]

The iced water shower was a cruel, dramatic treatment. Doctors used it to treat many different conditions at that time including alcoholism. Eliza's strange behaviour included picking green strawberries instead of ripe ones, sending fish by post to her mother, imagining invisible people in the room, hearing music and giving away money. Among the remedies prescribed were large oral doses of mercury, a toxic substance that blistered her mouth and left her in agony. It probably caused more hallucinations too. Her husband was on the point of sending for an 'asylum nurse' to watch over her.

Whatever demons Eliza was dealing with, people were quick to spread gossip. In May 1833, when Georgiana gave Mrs Dawson a lecture about her habit of drinking in the house, the reply was an accusation rather than an apology: 'You need not say anything to me about drinking, you may look at your own sister.'[359]

The only source of letters was by sea and when ships did not arrive there was no news. Months passed and Georgiana was anxious to hear from Eliza. She had started a long letter to her in November 1833 and before the letter was sent in May 1834, she added a few shopping requests including some picture books for Sabina, who was often called Diddy, a diminutive for 'little one'. She asked for things that would not empty 'the nearly exhausted pocket of the Poor Swan River Settlers', things with 'that enviable quality, durability'. Most of all she longed for a new teapot; the one she was using had no handle and half a spout, which meant burnt fingers every day.[360] Georgiana also mentioned some more personal news; another baby was on the way.[361]

In June she wrote to her mother in response to the latest news she received about arguments between Besley and Eliza. She could not resist pointing out that she had always been against the marriage, but another comment indicates why the cold shower bath might have been used as a therapy. She asked whether her sister's 'propensity' was the cause of the quarrel.[362] Georgiana had no way of knowing that her sister had died two months earlier. Just before Christmas, Eliza had suffered her second miscarriage. She lost triplets in the fourth month and told her mother how relieved she was that the tragedy was not caused by 'any incautious use of Spirits'.[363] After what was described as 'a short illness', Eliza Besly died on 1 March 1834 at Vicarage House and was buried in the Long Benton churchyard.[364,365] She was thirty-two.

Georgiana expressed her Christianity publicly as part of everyday life by praying, citing religious texts, attending service regularly and privately by frequently examining her own conscience, but that did not make her an unusually pious person. Like most nineteenth-century women born into a wealthy family, her beliefs were the expected norm. When she arrived in an 'unknown land' they upheld her, the only remnants of a previous life that were still recognisable and unchanged, but she was never completely bound by them or defined by them. In letters to Mary and Helen, the most evidently devout members of the Dunlop family, she usually emphasised her spiritual struggles, continuing the long conversations that began at Roseneath Manse. But there were other things that occupied her interests, and they were not always shared. 'I read only books relating to religion,' she told Helen.[366] Given her liking for Byron, Burns and botany, books that lined her own shelves, that was not the truth, but there is a noticeable thread in her writing which exposes more radical views about alcohol, 'the great vice of the colony'.[367] She was shocked to find herself surrounded by people who were regularly and publicly drunk during the day.

She saw 'the open state of regardless wickedness' around her from the moment she arrived in Perth, and before long members of the small Augusta community were also enjoying a few drinks too many when they had the chance, including her own servants. The soldiers' wives knew their government rations would be stopped if they did not attend Sunday service, so they sometimes slipped out halfway through to 'hold their inebrious orgies'. Georgiana believed that her 1830 miscarriage may have been caused by the shock of seeing one of

Mrs Turner's servants 'in a state of intoxication' and having to walk past her on a narrow path. Afraid of 'abuse', Georgiana was left 'very shaken' but tried to forget the encounter and carried on gardening.[368] The extreme nature of her feelings and her uncharacteristically timid reactions around intoxicated people are not surprising. When a parent or sibling has alcohol-related issues, the effects often reverberate through the whole family and leave deep, lasting scars.

The Bussell family's plan for emigration continued and twenty-four-year-old Lenox arrived in Fremantle on 27 January 1833 with two of his sisters and their servants, Phoebe Bower and Emma Mould. For two weeks at the end of April, Georgiana had the company of Frances Louisa junior (Fanny) and Elizabeth Capel (Bessie) Bussell. The three women must have discovered quickly that their young lives had overlapped. While Georgiana was attending the Burnetts' expensive private school in Kensington, Fanny Bussell and her other sister, Mary, were also at school about an hour's walk away. All three girls were in London for the biggest event of the year, the coronation of a new king, but their lives were very different.

From the moment their clergyman father died in 1820, the Bussell children experienced life as orphans in need of financial assistance. The brothers' planned careers in the Royal Navy and the church were no longer possible and their education depended on the generosity of the Reverend William Marchant Bussell's parishioners. A few weeks after his death, a notice appeared in the local paper requesting 'attention of the liberal and benevolent most earnestly to a case of the severest distress'.[369] Eight weeks after that, Mary and Fanny Bussell became wards of the newly opened 'Adult Orphan Institution' in St Pancras, funded by donations from wealthy people including the Princess Augusta. Places were limited and allocated by ballot to the most deserving cases where the death of a clergyman had left his family in poverty. While Georgiana was receiving the finishing educational touches she needed for a good marriage, the Misses Bussell were training to earn their living as governesses.

In the distant society of Augusta it seemed that everyone was equal with their own fair chance and wide open opportunities for success as landowners. But from the moment the two families set sail on the *Warrior* there was a chasm between the Bussells and the Molloys, a polarity that was obvious in every facet of their lives. However gracious and neighbourly Georgiana may have been, however gentlemanly, ladylike and well-educated all the Bussell siblings were, both families knew they were different. They would all be years older before that would no longer matter.

Soon after they arrived in Augusta, Bessie and Fanny talked about their family and Georgiana was surprised to learn that their mother was 'the same Miss Yates of West Indian extraction' that Mrs Kennedy had talked about in the past. As the three young women sat together in a tiny colony where news from Britain could take six months to arrive, the Abolition of Slavery Act was only weeks away from being given royal assent in London and the Quakers in Carlisle were among its strongest supporters. After decades of campaigns for the freedom of slaves throughout the British empire, the Act of Parliament would be enforced in August 1834. Bessie and Fanny's grandfather, Thomas Legall Yates senior, had owned slaves and two of their aunts still owned slaves in 1833.[370] Their uncle, Edward Rodon Huggins, had inherited land in Jamaica and the 'property' that went with it, nineteen slaves. If Georgiana also realised that the Bussell siblings were descendants of the Beckfords, the wealthiest owners of plantations run by slave labour in Jamaica, and infamous for their lives of excess, it might explain the frostiness she showed for years towards the family next door, after saying how much she liked them when they first met on board the *Warrior*. Fanny and Bessie Bussell were Georgiana's guests until May, staying in Richard Dawson's empty house before joining their brothers at the Adelphi. Fanny described the Molloys as 'extremely kind' and Sabina as 'a dear little creature'.

The great trees and hilly landscape along the Blackwood were not the only problems that contributed to the settlers' crop failures there. Familiar plants like cabbages should have been a reliable basic food source but they struggled in the warm climate and failed to seed.[371] Planting patterns from Britain did not match the weather and, in 1831, the Bussells lost an entire crop of wheat because they planted too soon after harvesting. Molloy and Turner were Londoners and the Bussells had lived in a busy town. Captain Molloy knew how to live resourcefully off the land but was more familiar with bartering with local people for bread to feed his men than planting his own fields. The settlers made an effort to employ servants with the right kinds of skills but, in the end, the group that landed in Augusta was sadly lacking in rural knowledge. The exception was Georgiana.

From the age of three she lived on a country estate and although not directly involved in the work on the farms owned by her father, the world of ploughing, sowing and harvesting was all around her. Crosby Lodge had its own stables, a grain store, an orchard of fruit trees and a kitchen garden for growing vegetables and herbs. When her mother sold the place, the auction list included 'a large quantity of wheat, oats, barley hay and straw, several ploughs, harrows, carts and a winnowing machine, several work horses, cows, sheep and pigs'. In 1834, the Molloys fared better than most with the harvest; Georgiana noticed just in time before sowing in June that their wheat contained the slightly longer, thinner seeds of 'darnel', a prolific grass that would overtake the entire crop in a few seasons if not dealt with. She also recognised the black dust that was evidence of 'smut', a destructive fungus that flourishes in ripening wheat. She knew exactly what to do and was able to adapt her knowledge to suit the limited resources available. She made sure the seed wheat was washed in salt water – an old country remedy – and then, in the absence of lime, she used wood ash, knowing that anything corrosive would pickle the fungus and kill it.[372]

VALUABLE
Stock, Crop,
HUSBANDRY UTENSILS,
AND
Household Furniture
FOR SALE.

To be Sold in Public Auction,
AT CROSBY LODGE,
In the Parish of Crosby-upon-Eden, in the County of Cumberland,
On THURSDAY, the 8th Day of NOVEMBER next;

ALL the Valuable STOCK, CROP, HUSBANDRY UTENSILS, and part of the HOUSEHOLD FURNITURE of Mrs. KENNEDY; consisting of an excellent pair of well-matched Carriage Horses, and a set of good Coach Harness, several Work Horses, Cows, Sheep and Pigs; a large Quantity of Wheat, Oats, Barley, Hay, and Straw; several Ploughs, Harrows, Carts, and a Winnowing Machine, Garden Spades and Rakes; also a quantity of Larch and other Wood fit for Posts and Railing. The Household Furniture consists of several excellent Bedsteads, one made in the year 1618 of very curious workmanship, Chairs, Tables, Trays, China, Glass, and various other Articles.

Three Months Credit will be given for all sums above 40s., upon the Purchasers entering into satisfactory Security, before they depart the Sale; all sums at and below 40s. ready Money.

ALSO TO LET,
And entered upon at CANDLEMAS next,

A neat COTTAGE HOUSE, and GARDEN adjoining, situate near Crosby Lodge aforesaid, the latter well worth the attention of a Gardener or Nursery Man; likewise a Grazing FIELD, situate in Shaddongate, near the City of Carlisle, which may be entered upon at the above time.

For Particulars apply to Mrs. KENNEDY, at Crosby Lodge aforesaid, the Owner; or at the respective Offices of Messrs MOUNSEY & SISSON, Solicitors, in Carlisle aforesaid; or of Mr. THOMAS BOUSTEAD, Tax Office, Fisher-Street, Carlisle, any of whom will receive Proposals for the above, and treat for the Letting of the same.

John Christopherson, AUCTIONEER.

Carlisle: Printed at B. Scott's Office, English-Street.

1826 advertisement of the auction of Mrs Kennedy's stock and furniture at Crosby Lodge

CAC D KEN 4 / 13 / 13 Photograph © Mike Rumble

The move to the Vasse meant more travel for her husband and Georgiana found herself with little time to call her own, but once the crops were planted she turned her attention from the growing of vegetables to the completion of her flower garden, laid out around a cross shape of intersecting paths. On 7 May 1833, Staples began digging to prepare the land and ten days later he was laying out new beds and pathways.[373] It would be weeks before there were any blooms but she could still enjoy her floral passion by working on her own dried collection of wildflowers, which dated back to 1823, in between writing letters, playing with her daughter and doing the sewing jobs that could not be avoided in her new life.[374] Georgiana was not the only parent who doted on Sabina.

> The other night she was playing in bed with Molloy and wanting to go away from him when he was retaining her, she gave him a slap on the face and said Bo way for go away
>
> ...
>
> All Baby's frocks I make like a shirt with the slit behind and confined round the waist with a red morocco or black lace belt and the beautiful Buckle you sent me. She now has for the winter two dark brown stuffs. Papa approves only of this sort and as she is his own little darling he has a right to choose. I often wish you could see them together.[375]

Sabina's childhood would have been very different if she had been growing up in the formal setting of a country house in England, living in the nursery, rarely seeing her parents and being set apart from the social life of the adults until she was much older. At the cottage in Augusta she slept in her parents' bed until she was two and spent her days as part of the community. She watched and learned from her mother's daily round of washing, sewing, gardening, making and mending, and she thrived from a life lived on the beach, by the river, in the bush. The little girl who had her father's distinctive hooked nose teased him mercilessly and called him 'Molloy'.[376,377]

The past still holds stories waiting to be told by voices not belonging to colonising Europeans. The documentary archive is considerable but nearly all the events are told from the viewpoint of white settlers. By 1832, Noongar men were helping on the Augusta farms in return for supplies from the government store. Cultural differences were already causing alarm on both sides but the arrangement seemed to have advantages for all. Problems did not erupt into conflicts but expansion of white settlements meant clearing, fencing and farming of what were once hunting grounds. The colonists enclosed or ploughed up Aboriginal food sources and indigenous animals were driven away. The ancient pattern of burning the land became a nuisance and a danger to new settlements.

The potential for human tragedy was obvious but few people spoke out. Robert Lyon Milne, who arrived in 1829, may not have been the Waterloo hero he claimed to be but his assessment of the situation in Perth was unequivocal: 'they [the Aboriginal people] were guilty of no crime but that of fighting for their country. We call their deeds murder, so might they ours'. Georgiana said he was 'the only person who has bestowed any time or labour on learning their history' and sent 'Mr Lyon's vocabulary' of Aboriginal words to her brother George.[378]

In June 1832, Lyon warned the people of Guildford, where the governor himself was a resident.

> Reflect. You have seized upon land that is not yours. Beware, and do not, as a people, add to this guilt of dipping your hands in the blood of those who you have spoiled of their country.[379]

Lieutenant Governor Stirling's own dreams of a flourishing new colony had not been realised. In 1832, the original arrangements for land grants came to an end and, after the first rush, news had reached Britain about Perth's problems; the number of new settlers had dropped dramatically and so had the input of investment they would have brought. Many agricultural servants were becoming landowners themselves, increasing the demand for labour and reducing the workforce at the same time. The colony was short of food, labour and money and the future looked bleak. In 1833, Stirling left for Britain to try to persuade the government to increase funding and to make a case for the change to a 'penal settlement' using convicts to provide a labour force. By the beginning of August he was pleading his case at the office of the Secretary of State for the Colonial Department in London. He came back a year later without all the answers he had hoped for and carried out his orders, introducing a harsher regime that meant smaller flour rations.[380] He also brought with him eighteen orphan boys and girls from the Society for Promoting Juvenile Emigration.[381]

Life in Augusta was not getting easier and food was still in short supply. Georgiana was now 'skin and bone' and Molloy ordered a hogshead of beer for her to provide extra nourishment. She told her sister that Sabina had never tasted jam or ripe fruit and lived mainly on 'hard salty meat'.[382] The settlers were arguing about damage caused by straying livestock and there were disputes about shared fences, but somehow they remained friends through all hardships. The Wardandi people were beginning to spend more time among the settlers and gave them all Aboriginal names; Alfred Bussell was 'Mundle' and the Molloys were 'King Kandarung' and 'Kymbin'.[383] Captain Molloy handed out allocations from the government supplies for 'cultivating a friendly intercourse', and sometimes an Aboriginal family spent the whole day sitting in the shade on his verandah.[384,385]

In March 1833, a Noongar man was travelling to Perth on a ship that anchored at Augusta and when it left he refused to board, saying he would stay for a while and then walk on to Perth. Galypert attached himself to the Molloy household and Georgiana welcomed him. He roasted live goanna in her kitchen and gave her his 'war spears' for safekeeping. She wrote to her mother describing details of a life that must have been difficult for Mrs Kennedy to imagine.

> The women are much to be pitied, they have all the laborious work to perform, to build the huts, which are composed of branches and barks of trees, each hut has a place for a fire before it and they are built around a circle, the women dig up roots, roast them, and mix them with clay on which the natives feast greedily as also on Frogs, all sorts of grubs and worms, lizards, and Goanas [sic]...[386]

Sharing food was accepted social behaviour in both Aboriginal and European cultures, but when the newcomers began to go hungry they were unwilling to lose what was left of their potatoes and flour. The settlements in Augusta and the Vasse were about to become the backdrop for a shocking history. One day in November 1833, a new soldier at the Augusta barracks fired a shot at some Aboriginal men who were on John Kellam's land. No-one was hurt and there are no details on record, but it was the end of trust and the beginning of change.[387]

Their impulsive behaviour with firearms was not the only reason why Captain Molloy was unimpressed with the soldiers of the 21st Fusiliers who arrived to replace the 63rd Regiment in October. When they complained about their accommodation and said the King would not be happy about his military subjects having no roof over their heads for three nights, Molloy pointed out to them that he knew what it felt like to walk all day for fourteen days in a row, sleeping rough and carrying 'a fortnight's provisions on my back'. When they decided to have an evening off because the work they were doing was so hard, Molloy wished out loud that he would 'like those men in the Peninsula for a campaign'.[388] The government resident followed regulations rigorously and the evening sermon was usually a long one but the private man was gentle and, in his wife's eyes 'the kindest of all mortals'.[389] He made her life as comfortable as he could, ensuring the windows were left closed when she slept late and making her tea and toast for breakfast.[390] But work took him away often and life was soon to become even busier for his wife. Georgiana knew what lay ahead when she realised she was expecting another baby. Exhausted and anxious, she shared her fears with her mother.

> I would give much that it should not be the case as it always costs me so much pain and Sabina is as much as I can attend to. I am not very strong and have lately had frequent bad headaches with great lassitude and the latter I cannot give way to having constantly active duties to perform.[391]

Georgiana felt 'quite depressed' for days at a time and was thinking about the past again.[392] One of her arms had been swollen and very painful for weeks and she longed for her mother and sister to take care of her, to rest on the sofa while they brought her whatever she wanted. But that life was long gone.[393] Still unable to move her arm, she worked in the garden, sowing dahlia seeds, vines, balsam and coriander. In September 1833, Captain Molloy visited their land grant at the Vasse then sailed for Perth. In the evenings Georgiana walked on the beach with Sabina and watched the horizon. When the ship returned a few weeks later they set off excitedly in the cart to meet it but 'dear Papa' was not on board.

One Sunday evening in November, a chimney fire set light to the Adelphi and the house burnt down while Fanny Bussell was in Augusta for 'divine service' on the Molloys' verandah. Dr Green set off with the soldiers but they were too late to save the home. The Bussell family had no choice but to move back to their old house in Augusta and they stored the few things that had been saved at the Molloys' home, including Bessie's piano. After four years, the instrument was a welcome reminder of old pleasures for Georgiana, a competent pianist, but when she touched the keys for the first time she suddenly realised that her daughter had never heard the sound of music. At first, Sabina was terrified and inconsolable, but by the next morning she had decided that the strange object was an animal.[394] She tied a piece of cord around one of the legs like a lead, asked if the piano was awake yet and wondered if it would like some breakfast.³⁹⁵

On 5 December, Molloy sailed once again for Perth, expecting to be away for three weeks. He and Georgiana found the separation 'agonising' but he was delayed several times and was not home until February.³⁹⁶ He missed Christmas 1833 in Augusta, the first with music for their carols and the last for the original group of settlers. An exodus began in 1834 as the Bussells moved their belongings to a new home at the Vasse, Cattle Chosen, more than ninety kilometres further north. Others moved at the same time, including Elijah Dawson, who went to work for the Bussells temporarily, and the Chapman brothers. George Layman also joined them with his wife, Mary.³⁹⁷ The Molloy and Turner families stayed by the Blackwood River, a much smaller group, and they felt vulnerable. A few soldiers were still stationed in Augusta but an advert was put in the Perth newspaper inviting applications to build a set of stocks with 'a good padlock' on the side.³⁹⁸

In February, while Molloy was in Perth hearing court proceedings, Georgiana was alone at home with Sabina. One day, about twenty Noongar men and women visited the house. She already knew them but for the first time she felt afraid. The women tried to take an embroidered urn rug from the table and she asked them to leave the house. She refused to give them the potatoes they wanted and told them again to go away, this time in their own language. Then she called for Dawson, who quickly arrived on her verandah. One of the men held his club in the air and pretended to hit Dawson with it. When Dawson held off the stick as it came down near his face, another 'took hold of Sabina's legs' and shook a spear at Georgiana. She knew it would not help to show any fear so she smiled at them and told Dawson to back off, even when the stick was whirled close to her head. When one of the men put a piece of broken glass to her cheek she said the word for 'glass' in his own language, but he 'rubbed his fore-finger in his hair until it was covered with the fat or red earth with which they rub themselves and poked it right into my face'.[399] She tried to walk past him to bring the escalating situation to an end but the group had grown to about thirty people and he dodged left and right to stop her leaving. She told Dawson to get the dogs but they just wagged their tails at everyone. It did not occur to her at any time to use the guns that were in the house. She refused again to hand over the potatoes but while Dawson was at the well drawing drinking water for the visitors, she decided to put a gun and her husband's rifle in full view on the table. Perhaps it was the unspoken message that she had guns but had no intention of using them that finally defused the moment. The group moved away to the Bussell house next door and found Bessie and Fanny alone. Two cut-glass salt cellars went missing, which were soon retrieved from two of the Aboriginal women by Dawson and Sergeant Guerin from the barracks.

Two days later, the same group came back and handed a wallaby to each of the settlers. Georgiana interpreted the gifts as a peace offering, but she admitted in a letter to Helen Story that she thought

> ... if Dawson had not been present, Mrs Dawson and I and the poor children would have been murdered or otherwise injured, for it seemed that man's full intention to prevent me leaving my own premises. It gave me a great fright.[400]

At the Vasse too, Aboriginal people were doing what they saw their white neighbours doing: taking what they needed. In April, Bessie Bussell wrote to her cousin Capel Carter and described how someone had stolen three hundredweight (152 kilos) of flour from Cattle Chosen.[401] A soldier went to Augusta to ask for Molloy's permission for John Bussell to fire at whoever was responsible. One man had dropped a little girl he was carrying as he ran away from Cattle Chosen and before long he came back with the flour and exchanged it for the child. Even so, 'John, Lenox and Charles Bussell armed themselves and went in pursuit of the other delinquents'.

In Georgiana's letter to Eliza she wrote that 'the natives are very fond of all the settlers at Augusta and we live on the most peaceful terms – but at the Swan – from the indiscretion of several persons and particularly their servants they are very hostile'. She sent Eliza a bunch of emu feathers given to her by 'Mobin, a native chief', and even after the encounter that frightened her so much, she still described relationships in Augusta as 'amicable'.

When Mary Dorothea was born on 16 June, Georgiana had the same life-threatening complications and twenty-four hours after the baby's arrival there was no option but to remove the placenta by intervention. Dr Green gave instructions to Mrs Dawson and, this time, Georgiana submitted.

She was surprised to find an unusual birthmark on the baby's lower back. Her reasoning for its cause is evidence of beliefs derived from ancient folklore, not Christianity. She was sure a birthmark was the result of either a shock or an unfulfilled desire during pregnancy. In a letter to Helen Story she mentioned that she had been expecting to see a birthmark in the shape of an Aboriginal weapon because of the fright she'd experienced in February. When she recognised the shape of a double flowering stock, *Matthiola incana*, she was quite sure it was because she had sown some seeds of that species and was hoping they would bloom as double flowers. When they opened, the flowers were double and unusually large and Georgiana was convinced of the reason for her baby's birthmark.[402]

New land grants were being taken up in Augusta even as families moved away. Molloy bought another town block for himself and another was listed in his wife's name. John Herring was appointed constable and took up another grant; John Bussell and young James Turner acquired additional 'rural and suburban' blocks.[403] No longer indentured servants, Elijah Dawson and James Staples each had one of the small 'town' grants.[404] The Bussells had high hopes for successful farming on the fertile plains of the Vasse, but their bad luck was not over. Just as they had always planned, their sister Mary

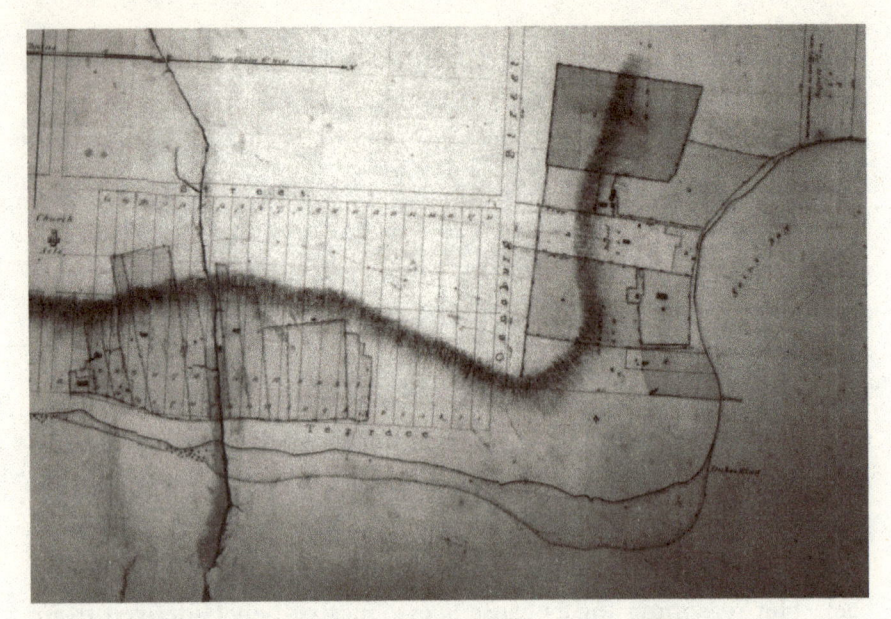

Plan of Augusta in 1834 showing new land grants and the original blocks on Seine Bay. A Hillman, Assistant Surveyor.

Augusta Historical Museum

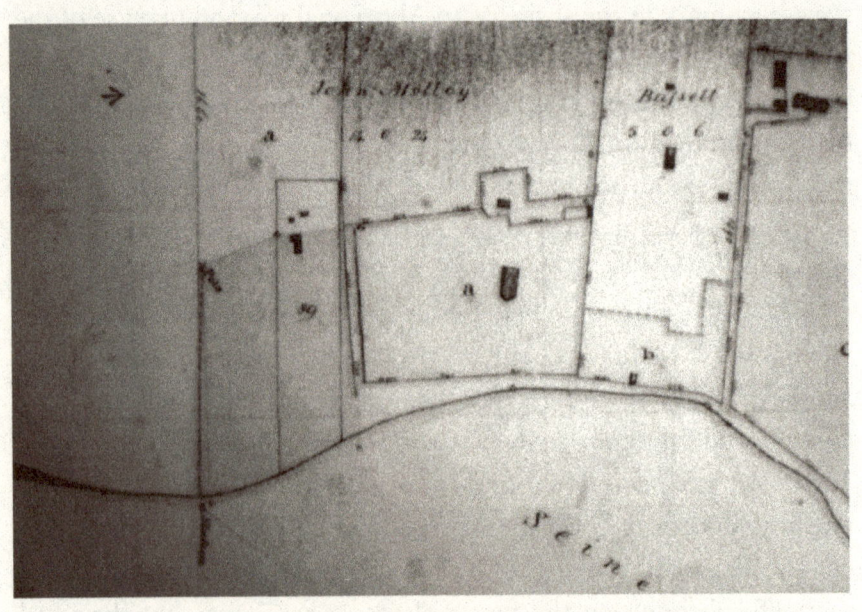

A close-up of the same plan shows the Molloy house and stockyard near the centre of the image and the relative positions of (left to right) the Bussell and Turner houses.

and their mother, Mrs Frances Louisa Bussell, arrived in the colony in August 1834. Stirling persuaded them to stay on in Perth to avoid bad weather, so they sent all eighteen tonnes of their belongings ahead on board the *Cumberland*, including the family silver. The ship sank off Fremantle and the body of her captain, James McDermott, was washed up on the beach along with some of Mrs Bussell's 'trinkets'.[405] McDermott's widow, Ann, had a young child and was about to give birth again. She refused to believe her husband was lost but eventually went home again to her father, James Turner.

For the next year, life went on in the same monotonous way. Georgiana was nursing Mary Dorothea and managing the household with only Mrs Dawson to help. In a rare moment of frankness she told Helen Story how she was feeling.

> I do not hesitate to say I am overwhelmed with too much labour, and indeed my frame bears testimony to it, as I everyday expect to see some bone peeping through its epidermis. My beloved husband much assists me, and more than many would do except such treasures as yours and mine.[406]

There were times when she thought back on the lost opportunities of her young life and the hopes she and Molloy had shared for prosperity: 'He is a perfect slave up by day break and doing the most menial work sometimes so that all the former part of our lives was all lost time.'[407]

In September 1834 the news arrived of Eliza's death and Dalton's imprisonment for debt.[408] In the case of Johnson v Kennedy, the judge had refused bail and Dalton was already a prisoner. He was publicly bankrupt, about to spend the next two years in the infamous 'Fleet', and there was more bad news to come. Mary Kennedy's engagement had come to an abrupt end, embarrassing both families who had been friends and close neighbours for generations. The Reverend John Lowry was son of the vicar of Crosby-on-Eden and would inherit land there. According to Mrs Kennedy, he had been very enthusiastic about a short engagement but suddenly backed out of the arrangement. The whole affair left Mrs Kennedy ill and in bed with various ailments including 'spasms of the heart', in her own opinion brought on by the 'mental affliction' she had suffered for more than two years from the behaviour of her children. There was a financial disagreement between the parents about the marriage settlement, but Mrs Kennedy heard that rumours were spreading about Mary's unladylike behaviour. She was determined to do her 'painful duty' and tell the young man's parents that her daughter was the innocent and injured party, so she wrote a 'pithy but ladylike' letter saying he had gone too far in the arrangement to back out.[409] The letter did not help. Lowry moved on and Mary Kennedy never forgave her mother for interfering.

In Augusta, George Layman and one of the Kellam brothers set off to walk to Perth. During the journey Layman was speared in the leg and a Perth newspaper described how an Aboriginal man had thrown the barbed spear with no incitement.[410] Readers were left to guess at the aggressor's reasons for such an outburst, and if Layman acted in any way to provoke the attack, it was not part of the story the two white travellers related. The version of events reported in writing was that of the settlers, a one-sided narrative, and that was part of a pattern that had not gone unnoticed already in other British colonies. The Quaker community in Britain had experienced the difficulty of uncovering both sides of a story during their campaigns against the slave trade, and they realised it was almost impossible to find the unbiased truth about increasingly common violent encounters: 'They are rapidly disappearing before us; and whilst we hesitate to plead their cause, they cease to exist, and we shall inquire after them in vain.'[411]

The year ended as badly as it started. In November, Sabina became dangerously ill with a fever and the usual treatments did not work. Georgiana shaved and blistered the child's head and gave her warm baths but on the thirtieth, 'Death rose – certainly hovering near her' and her heart was racing at 130 beats a minute. Sabina rambled incoherently about the baby sister she was already so fond of. Her father sat up with her all night and by morning the fever had broken. Georgiana blamed herself, feeling unable to attend to the needs of both daughters and manage the household duties as well as Molloy's work when he was away, even though she stitched her 'fingers to the bone' mending and making.[412] Sabina was a tomboy, running around outside from first daylight until suppertime, often with her hair falling loose because no-one had pinned on her cotton cap or told her to wear a bonnet. Sometimes she fell asleep during the evening meal and was left there slumped in her chair while her mother fed and bathed the baby. Georgiana believed that her 'darling child was neglected'.[413]

In January 1835, the Molloy household grew even busier when Georgiana took in Emma Mould, the Bussells' servant, who was pregnant and claimed that Charles Bussell was the father of her child. Mrs Bussell refused to believe her son was involved and the girl was made homeless when she was dismissed. Henry John was born in February and Charles admitted paternity. In March, the Molloys' servants' indentures expired and in May Georgiana had her thirtieth birthday. It was a time of privation for the few settlers still in Augusta, but shared hardships drew the little community closer. A landowner himself at last, Robert Heppingstone went fishing with his son and disappeared from the rocks while the men were separated for a few moments. His body was never found. The settlement made a collection to give his widow and 'five helpless children', and Molloy advanced her credit in supplies from the government store.

Augusta was no longer the bright young star of the Swan River Colony's future. Thomas, George and John Turner had already left and settled new land a few kilometres up the river at Turnwood. Word was spreading about the difficulties in Augusta. In August, the *Sydney Gazette* published an article written by 'A Resident' who had been travelling in the southwest. The anonymous writer described the Molloys' 'small wooden house' and 'nice garden attached' but told readers: 'I would never advise any person attempting to settle in this part of the colony'.[414]

When she wrote to her mother just before Christmas, Georgiana was still asking her to send basic items. Molloy sat in his old, grey dressing-gown by the fire each evening and his wife decided it was time for a replacement. She added two dozen woollen socks to the wish list, worsted for mending them, and some ivory and tortoiseshell side combs for her hair to replace the ones that Sabina had broken. The children's needs included both pleasure and learning: two wooden dolls and a copy of Hale's catechism, a religious book offering scriptural advice to the young and prayers for parents to say with their children. Georgiana also mentioned, almost casually, that she was expecting another 'little stranger' in April.[415]

As 1836 came into view, bringing night after night of heavy rain and thunder, she was preparing for the Christmas celebrations and the additional workload they brought with them. Without servants she was laundress, cook and housemaid, and with two cows in milk she churned for butter twice each week. When Molloy killed a pig she was 'immersed in raw Pork, hog's lard and Plum Puddings'. But the same warm weather and rain that made her daily chores so unpleasant also made her flower garden 'beautiful and fragrant', and the plants from the seeds Eliza had sent were in bloom. As the family sat down together to give thanks for their Christmas dinner, she had just one wish: 'that my own Mother could enjoy these wilds with her children & darling grandchildren & that we could once more meet never more to separate'.[416]

The Augusta–Vasse route was a cleared track by 1836. Charles Bussell was still the storekeeper in Augusta and, like John Molloy, had to travel regularly between the two settlements on official duties in both places. Elijah Dawson became constable at the Vasse and built himself a cottage on three acres at Soldier Point. Molloy started work on the new home by the Vasse River where he and Georgiana would spend the rest of their days. On Monday, 3 April, he wrote in his journal during a visit to the Vasse: 'Corporal to erect a house for me' and 'Agreed to give the corporal £12 to erect my cottage'.[417] The next day he 'fired some bush to have a clear view of my intended site on the Vasse'. This was the humble forerunner of the family home that became Fairlawn, much changed in its appearance today with few remnants of the original buildings left. The house is surrounded by the same flat paddocks that separate it from sprawling new development in Busselton.[418]

Georgiana went into labour on the night of 21 April 1836 and Molloy sent for Mrs Heppingstone as usual. After twelve hours, a son was born at 11.30 the next morning and named John.[419] Molloy spent the day ploughing, using the government oxen that would soon be sent up to the Vasse to plough for the settlers there. These seasonal tasks had to be completed without fail, even if it meant working on the day his only son was born. Captain Molloy's life had changed as much as his wife's, but in some ways that were quite different. There were weeks at a time when he enjoyed the benefits of a social life in Perth, wearing his old Rifle Brigade jacket for important events, but the contrast with his time at home must have been extreme. When he was not travelling to and fro by ship his days were spent acquiring new rural skills: trimming strawberry beds, repairing fences, mending nets and barrelling oats.[420] He now had a family of small children around him and occasionally it shows in his writing: 'Dug up some 'ta'toes'.[421]

The Molloys had three healthy children under the age of five. Sabina had a sharp mind and calm nature, Mary was still a baby but already beautiful and Johnny showed himself to be an adventurer as soon as he could walk. His mother attached a little bell to his waist so she could find him if he wandered off into the bush. They lived a simple, rural life but there were dangers around them every day that meant survival was no more certain than it had been for their father, a city child of the previous century. In July 1836, two-year-old Mary ate some small, copper caps that her father used to pack explosives for clearing trees and rocks. Her parents only discovered the potential danger after a violent episode of vomiting just before Sunday service.[422] On another day while Papa was away, Mary fell through the floor and Johnny 'nearly swallowed some shot'.[423] But there were also good times in Augusta and Captain Molloy's journal gives glimpses of a happy family.

> Mary, the Babe, walked about alone.
> This day 7 years I was married to my beloved Wife & we have won the Flitch of bacon.
> Walked on Beach with my beloved children.[424,425,426]

Things were never quiet for long. When he expected to be clearing out the pigsty or weeding melon beds, Molloy could end up restraining a drunken farmer or drawing off blood from a sick animal, but the issues he had to deal with began to take on a different nature. In early 1836 the many Aboriginal fires being set around Augusta became an ongoing worry in hot, dry weather. Mr Herring's whole crop of potatoes disappeared one night and they were not the only food being taken.[427]

Molloy regularly employed Noongar men as farm workers in Augusta and at the Vasse. Sometimes there were differences of opinion about the responsibilities that came with their roles but misunderstandings did not lead to conflict. In December, Lieutenant Henry Bunbury of the 21st Regiment arrived with a small detachment of soldiers after a four-day walk from the Murray River, to establish a military outpost at the Vasse and provide the protection the settlers had requested.

The *Champion* anchored in Flinders Bay on 14 December and two days later Captain Molloy left with John Bussell and Governor Stirling, who had been visiting the settlement. Molloy expected to be home in time for Christmas but the ship did not arrive in Perth until 23 December. The latest updates from its passengers on progress in Augusta were published on Christmas Eve in Perth. 'By the return of the colonial schooner "Champion", we have late intelligence from King George's Sound and Port Augusta and, we are happy to find, of a satisfactory nature, as relates to the capabilities of those places; but we hear, with concern, that there is not that energy and enterprise among the inhabitants, which must lead on to fortune.'[428] The contrast with a report from the Vasse was sharp: 'The Vasse settlers and at Leschenault Inlet, are represented to be in high spirits – their herds having rapidly accumulated, on the finest possible cattle runs, and every thing [sic] thriving around them.'

Georgiana managed her own homestead while weighing out weekly supplies for each Augusta household, maintaining the daily log of weather and events, gardening to put food on the table and dealing with her neighbours' problems. When Christmas arrived she waited on the beach once again with Sabina, looking for a sail on the horizon but none appeared. On Christmas Day, in 'heavy rain and violent wind' she made sure the oxen were safely tethered, fed the pigs and did her best to read a Christmas church service to the children.[429] There was no time to rest and enjoy the holidays. Strawberry the cow got into the vegetable garden and destroyed a crop of barley and broccoli, so Georgiana replanted the lot. The highlight of her festive calendar was taking the children for tea at the Turners' on New Year's Eve. As 1836 came to an end she was alone again in Augusta.

Hot, stormy weeks rolled by. She found it impossible to do everything and her placid acceptance began to crumble. One delay after another kept Molloy away from home for three months. Georgiana's strong will and sense of injustice surfaced for the first time since she had allowed herself to express feelings of anger to her mother and sister eight years earlier. There was a limit to what she could bear and that limit had been reached. She tried to maintain her husband's journal in his absence, dutifully recording the weight of rations she allocated to each person, but as she grew more and more exhausted her entries began to include the personal observations of a wife and mother.

Molloy's role came with financial advantages but also with heavy responsibilities that included being present in Perth for meetings, military occasions and official events whether or not it was convenient to his life as a husband and father. The facts that Georgiana began adding to the journal read today like a list of the difficulties she was facing alone, each one just an everyday problem but together they accumulated an unfair weight of responsibility. She struggled to free a cow that got its head caught between fence posts; she managed the changing moods of Charlotte Heppingstone, who was helping in the house; Johnny was teething. Describing herself at this time as the 'servant of all works', these are the only occasions when Georgiana directed any kind of criticism towards the man who was her 'best friend'.[430]

> Monday 16th January 1837
> I played the part I have been duly instructed in, since my séjourn [stay] in Swan River, humble to everyone & pocketed a few impalatable incivilities.
> Sunday 29th January 1837
> I am utterly wretched and shamefully left to bear the brunt of all things.[431]

Three weeks later, the life she had described privately as 'wretched' was transformed to a picture of busy domesticity in a letter to her mother. She wrote light-heartedly about her lack of private time even for the most personal moments in daily life, the result of having three small children at her feet. There are pages of details about her endless household chores, perhaps in the hope that Mrs Kennedy might just be able to grasp something of the physical exertion of such long days, but Georgiana's letter of February 1837 gives no hint of anything but happiness.

> You can form no conception of what I have to do, but I am very happy, & if I am five minutes from the children there is such a Hunt, particularly Dora, she will often stay by me when Sabina is

with Johnny on the Grass plot of which I have four in my beauteous flower garden. I have a hedge row of yuccas from those you gave us and seven of them in full flower side by side. *Entre nous* [between us] to return to Dora, I cannot even go as far as the Temple without her finding me out and, that I should not be called for, generally take up the three.[432, 433]

The same ship that had taken Molloy away returned with postal deliveries for Augusta. At some point in those exhausting, lonely weeks as another year turned, Georgiana found time to open a mysterious envelope forwarded to her by Ellen Stirling, the lieutenant governor's wife. It contained a letter that would change her life.

The letter was from Captain James Mangles, a highly regarded botanical collector in England. Specimens and seeds he had already received from the Swan River Colony were in great demand from the elite botanists, gardeners and horticulturalists of Britain, and he had written to enquire whether Mrs Molloy might be willing to collect on his behalf.

Botany by the Blackwood River

That Georgiana's interest in gardening began in childhood and lasted all her life was not unusual. The study of plants, particularly for their medicinal qualities, had been a growing science for centuries but by the beginning of the nineteenth century, ladies were becoming involved in the cultivation and care of plants for their aesthetic qualities. Traditional medicinal gardens overseen by women began to expand into multi-sensual experiments in design, colour and fragrance. As Britain's colonising arms reached further afield, explorer-botanists sent home seeds and cuttings that made their way into English gardens as flowers. Interest in new botanical discoveries created intense competition to be the first to grow and display beautiful and unusual plants. Affluent men paid large sums for the latest arrivals and hired skilled gardeners to nurture them. They grew exotic plants from seeds in the very latest heated greenhouses, and displays became available to everyone at horticultural shows and in new public gardens.

Botany was a developing science of interwoven disciplines. There was a constant flow of new plants to be studied and if they could be classified in a way that explained their derivation, some of the remaining questions about the origins of life on Earth might be answered. Growing plants was an appropriate, creative hobby for women, just a small step from the traditionally feminine arts of flower arranging, embroidering floral designs and pressing dried flowers. Books on gardening and collecting, written specifically for women, became more popular.

Horticulture was a fashionable topic for ladies and some were becoming influential on the boundaries of what had been a man's world. They were often women who had the leisure time and money to acquire expensive seeds and the expansive gardens to display them. They owned the new, heated greenhouses needed to grow exotic species in the British climate and they employed skilled, knowledgeable gardeners to take on most of the hard work. Mrs Charlotte Marryatt developed beautiful gardens on the large estate her husband bought in Wimbledon. When she suddenly became a wealthy widow in 1824, she 'consoled herself as only a true plantswoman could' by spending a fortune on the place adding shrubberies, a summer house, lakes with an island and grotto, an orangery, a conservatory, many hothouses – one just for grapes and another for tropical plants – a park, a wilderness area, groves of trees and fishponds.[434] By the 1820s women could finally take part in some of the Royal Horticultural Society's activities, by invitation, and if their husbands were fellows of the society. In 1830 the society looked again at their regulations and Mrs Marryat became the third woman to be elected a fellow of the RHS. A large-leafed Kennedia from Western Australia was first named for her, *Kennedia marryatta*, the same plant that Georgiana Molloy chose to grow trailing and rambling over her roof for its shade and brick-red flowers.[435]

The three Kennedy sisters shared an interest in plants that was expected for women who wanted to broaden their minds and prepare for marriage. *The Young Lady's Book* of 1829, 'a manual of elegant recreations, exercises and pursuits' assured its readers that botany has 'the great advantage of ameliorating the disposition, while it elevates the mind.'[436] Its chapter headings give clues about popular topics. Gardening is among them, along with some predictable hobbies:

embroidery, music, dancing, riding and painting. More surprisingly, the list includes archery, mineralogy, entomology and conchology, the study of mollusc shells. Times were changing but women who crossed the boundary from horticulture into botany on a professional basis were still bold and rare.

The prospect of a new world of plant species was something Georgiana looked forward to during the voyage to Swan River. She lent her books on botany to the Bussell brothers and borrowed others in return.[437] At the Cape of Good Hope she had been fascinated by native species she had only seen before as delicate exotics grown at Holbrook. When the early difficult weeks in Augusta were over and essential vegetables had been set, she began to plant for pleasure. Her first flower garden was a combination of European blooms and semitropical species from Cape Town, an interpretation of the familiar made even more attractive by their unfamiliar backdrop. But it was still the memories of other flower gardens that she cherished as much as the blooms themselves. The indigenous Australian plants around her did not yet have any hold on her heart because they had 'no associations' and nothing that attracted her apart from their 'lustrous colour'.[438]

She soon discovered which indigenous plants would combine most effectively with the species she already knew, preferring the natives with the most colour and fragrance. She also added to the collection of dried specimens she had started in 1821. In comparison with the showy petals and vivid stamens of European flowers, the flora of Augusta seemed at first small and inconsequential. When she wrote to Eliza in November 1832, she said she only knew of three indigenous species with any fragrance but her letter reveals that after two years she had noticed the range and beauty in the bush around her home.

> Many of the shrubs are powerfully sweet, some like May, some like bergamot. Another remarkable feature in the botany of this country, S.W. Australia, is the numerous kinds of leaves with the identical flowers, some of the Leguminous ones.

I know one purple pea flower with three different kinds of leaves, one of which is a creeper and called the blue vine, the other an erect shrub with no smell and leaves like holly, the third is also erect with leaves like the privet and in shady places the blossoms emit a scent about three in the afternoon like allspice or cloves. Another sort is yellow and straw colour of which there are five with leaves utterly distinct but I fear this last page may be somewhat tedious, as you are not likely to behold all these aborigines.[439]

For Georgiana, plants were always more than memories of home; they were a way of making physical connections with happy times in places she loved. When she opened a box of gifts from her mother in 1833, she discovered that the sturdy little specimens of *Viola tricolor* had survived the long sea journey. She wrote to tell Mrs Kennedy that she had kissed the tiny plants and watered them with tears for her distant family.[440]

Slowly, the small house by the river became more comfortable and homely. Molloy built on a stone storeroom and a nursery, with a room behind it for his wife. He added a 'sitting-room' and another bedroom, as well as a verandah where Mrs Molloy could sit in the shade and work while she watched her children playing.[441] The addition provided a framework for the climbing and rambling plants she loved so much. As Georgiana cultivated her flower garden and her family's vegetable garden with the help of James Staples, she also began collecting the seeds of native species. She realised the plants that grew so abundantly in the sheltered climate of Augusta were potential additions for the gardens of her friends and family, so she started to look more carefully and began sending seeds with her letters. Until then, she had always 'avoided the tedious operation of gathering seeds' and realised quickly that she had a lot to learn. The seeds of different species took different lengths of time to ripen. She marked the plants when they were in flower but when she returned the seeds of some were still green and others had ripened early from the summer heat or fire. There were other new difficulties to overcome and looking for plants was not as easy as it had been when she rambled along the country lanes of Warwickshire and Dunbartonshire. This time she had a baby on her hip, the bush was dense and the heat intense, but her expeditions had more than one motive and reward. Botany was an immersion in the work of the Creator. In a region without a church, isolated from any religious community, her early steps as a botanist felt like worship. She was giving thanks to God.

Georgiana lived in a world where the only topics of conversation were 'grubbing-hoes, beef, pork, potatoes, onions, anchors and anchorage, whaling and harpooning', but she persevered.[442] She began trying out different ways of packing seeds, seedlings and cuttings for transportation by ship, experimenting with the very limited resources around her. As usual, she turned her mind as well as her heart to the task in hand. In 1833 she told Eliza that, 'One very good way of packing trees or plants is by putting them in tanner's bark enclosed in an iron pot or pan well closed down'.[443] She learned from the books she had brought with her and improved her knowledge of the latest plant discoveries by ordering horticultural magazines when she could, although they were months out of date by the time she received them. She also talked ardently with anyone who shared her botanical interests, including Ellen Stirling, the lieutenant governor's wife.

Ellen Mangles was thirteen when James Stirling fell in love with her. They married on her sixteenth birthday in 1823 and at seventeen she had the first of their eleven children. The couple arrived at the Swan River less than a year before the Molloys and Ellen, too, was pregnant throughout the voyage. She was two years younger than Georgiana but by the time she welcomed the newly arrived Molloys to Government House, Ellen had been married for seven years. Georgiana liked her very much and the feeling was mutual.

Botany was a common topic of discussion in the Stirling household. At a time when stories about poor conditions and insufficiencies were beginning to filter back to Britain, the governor was keen to promote the attractions of the colony and wanted to ensure that any useful local plant species found their way into the hands of botanists and scientists who would recognise their potential. In 1831 he established a government garden and nursery and appointed James Drummond, a horticulturalist, to supervise its development. Stirling also sent seeds to Robert Mangles, one of his wife's cousins, who had made a name for himself as a collector of unusual species, growing them with great success at his home, Whitmore Lodge in Berkshire, southwest of London.

In late 1832, the lieutenant governor and his wife made an extended trip to Britain. Stirling took with him the seeds of one of the most charismatic and recognisable Western Australian plants. Newly knighted, Sir James Stirling presented them to Robert Mangles for whom the species was named, and they were propagated by Mangles' gardener, Donald Mackay. Although the slugs liked them more than any other plant, *Anigozanthos manglesii*, the red and green kangaroo paw, were flowering in the greenhouse at Whitmore Lodge by the English summer of 1834.[444]

Robert Mangles's brother was a widely travelled writer and botanical collector. Captain James Mangles RN was a fellow of the Royal Society, a member of the Royal Geographical Society and was born in the same year as John Molloy. He joined the Royal Navy a year younger, at the age of thirteen. James was a middleman, not a gardener or botanist, and he made the important connections between plant collectors in the field and the people who wanted their specimens. He used a network of contacts to acquire seeds, which he sold to a select group with the resources and knowledge to grow them, including his brother Robert. He recorded meticulously who provided him with seeds, where they were collected and where he sent each batch. Fortunately, two of his letter books survived and found their way to the JS Battye Library in Perth, Western Australia.

Captain Mangles's contacts included wealthy individuals with their own expert gardeners and commercial growers. Among them were some of the most famous names in the horticultural world including Dr John Lindley FRS [Fellow of the Royal Society] who was Professor of Botany at University College, London, and editor of *Edwards's Botanical Register*, a horticultural magazine. Another recipient was Joseph Paxton, who had moved up in the world as head gardener at Chatsworth, one of the grandest stately homes in England. Paxton had access to the most extensive and innovative horticultural resources in Britain, as well as the favour of the royal family. Mangles also sent seeds to nurserymen whose interest was on a commercial basis, including Loddiges Nursery in Hackney. George Loddiges built the largest hothouse in the world to protect the exotic species of orchids and palms for which his nursery became famous, and he moved in eminent scientific as well as horticultural circles. He was among the first nurserymen to open to the public so that the beautiful arboretum he had created in Hackney could be admired and studied by everyone. A true entrepreneur, Loddiges recognised the potential of advertising in the new wave of popularity for botany and introduced a beautifully illustrated, detailed catalogue of latest arrivals. Like a forerunner to online shopping, *The Botanical Cabinet* allowed customers to browse at home, tempted by the rare beauties available for their own gardens and greenhouses.

In 1831, James Mangles visited the Stirlings in Perth and went home with a collection of seeds from species he had never seen before, including *Trichinium alopecuroideum*, the foxtail trichinium. Robert grew the seeds into mature plants that flowered, according to Paxton, for the first time in England.[445] Mangles decided to engage the services of local collectors who could send Swan River seeds and plants to him as more indigenous species were found. He became the channel through which thousands of Western Australian seeds made their way into the greenhouses of talented gardeners and under the magnifying glasses of botanists curious to define the best means of plant identification and solve the mysteries of relationships between species.

Among those sending him seeds from Perth were his cousin Lady Stirling and his elder brother, George, who arrived with her in 1829.

Ellen was a reliable source and contributed her own ideas about the best way to pack seeds for a long voyage. James Drummond's post as government naturalist had been abolished by 1834 and he had moved out of Perth, but he was still a man of influence and reputation in the botanical world. He agreed to collect seeds and plant specimens in a business arrangement that suited them both and, in July 1835, Mangles noted that the most recent arrivals included many species that were both beautiful and new.[446] A year later, Drummond sent the seeds of a particularly intriguing and spectacular species, *Nuytsia floribunda*, commonly called the West Australian Christmas tree. Joseph Paxton wrote regularly to Mangles informing him of the duke's pleasure in the plants from Swan River that were blooming in his gardens and describing the technology being employed to protect them in the impressive new greenhouse at Chatsworth. He was delighted when he heard that *Nuytsia floribunda* seeds were on their way to him along with other 'rare & valuable desiderata'.

Mangles began to feel dissatisfied with the quality of Drummond's collections. Although the quantity of seeds had not diminished and the range was interesting, they sometimes arrived contaminated and the plants were not accurately referenced. Mangles wrote to Lady Stirling in 1836 asking if she could suggest any other collectors who might be willing to help, and 'Mrs Molloy' was one of the names she gave him. On 14 December when the *Champion* anchored off Augusta with Governor Stirling on board, it was carrying a box of seeds and the letter to Georgiana from Captain Mangles asking whether she might be willing to act for him as a botanical collector. She accepted his invitation.

The letters she exchanged with James Mangles are a remarkable legacy of her botanical work and a personal revelation of her thoughts and feelings as a settler, wife and mother. Georgiana is known today for her unique contribution to nineteenth-century botany as a collector of native Western Australian flora, and as one of the very first women to undertake the role, but she collected seeds and plant specimens on behalf of Mangles for just six and a half years. She sent him about ten letters during that period and received four in return.

Surprised and flattered to have been asked for her help, Georgiana felt unworthy. She did not know the botanical names of many native plants in Augusta. When she replied to Mangles in March 1837, she told him she loved her garden but she was not a florist, let alone a botanist, and the demands of her children and 'domestic drudgery' meant she would probably be unable to send anything worthy of repaying his generous gift of seeds.[447]

Mangles's request had arrived at the right time of year, early summer in Western Australia, but in John Molloy's absence over Christmas, work on the farm drained Georgiana's energy and used up the daylight hours. Her lonely and wretched December days passed in thinning onions, searching for straying cows, pacifying reluctant servants and weighing out rations.[448] Once again, she spent New Year's Eve with the Turners and the widowed Ann (Nancy) McDermott, but she was determined to give the children some fun.[449] On Twelfth Night she enjoyed celebrations that kept them all up until 2.30am.[450] She also made a note in her diary about the curious absence of Dr Alfred Green; in spite of the fact that he enjoyed the widow Ann McDermott's company so much, he had not been seen since Captain Molloy left for Perth.

At the beginning of 1837, Georgiana found herself doing the work of a farmhand and wistfully watching the horizon for her husband's ship. As she baled the hay sheaves and fetched corn to feed the pigs, the wind changed to the west but there were still 'no signs of a vessel'.[451] She had proved herself capable in all her roles but each time Molloy went away it seemed as if there were more problems to cope with. She was working in the garden until dark each day and dealing with complaints about stolen potatoes. On 8 February, a large fire set by the Noongar people got out of hand and burnt the fence. The house had a narrow escape. Dr Green was seen around the settlement in a state that was far from sober, so she gave him a warning and decided to hang lanterns on the trees around the house in the hope of keeping intruders away from the vegetables.[452] At last, in mid-February, Captain Molloy came home. By Sunday, 5 March, the domestic burden was being shared and there was occasionally quiet time for the family. They walked on the beach together and drank tea 'à la Romaine' on the 'Plateau verde'.[453]

By the end of March Molloy was away again, at the Vasse. He also had a 'town grant' of land at Albany, but it was the new settlement on the River Vasse that took up much of his time and energy. As government resident for the sub-colony, he had to be available to the settlers there and provide regular, detailed progress updates to Stirling. The only way to know what was going on and to ensure that government regulations were being upheld was to spend time there. Every visit meant at least four days away, with an overnight camp in each direction. His campaign days in the army meant that Molloy was used to marching very long distances in all weathers, but the year-round regularity of his journeys between Augusta and the Vasse must have been gruelling.

During the autumn and early winter Georgiana sowed the precious seeds Mangles had sent, but there was still no time for her to collect on his behalf. She had to wait for the bush to flower again, and she stayed closer to home.

On 28 April, fire destroyed George and John Turners' house near Augusta and John Molloy believed it was a deliberate attack. The loss of Turnwood was a serious setback for the family and disquieting for all the settlers but what was about to happen further north soon overshadowed this event.

The European settlement that would become Busselton was made up of the Chapman brothers, who were living on the Vasse inlet by the Sabina River, the Bussells at Cattle Chosen with the Dawsons nearby, the Laymans and a few soldiers stationed on the Layman grant at Wonnerup. It was still a very small community but it had the advantages of flat, fertile land and coastal access. Geographe Bay was frequently visited by whalers and it was an easy anchorage for ships passing between Perth and Albany. With Augusta still on record as Molloy's home address, John Garret Bussell had been appointed resident magistrate at the Vasse but when he decided to travel to England to pursue marriage plans in December 1836, his brother Lenox was appointed temporarily in his place. In 1837, according to Charles Bussell, Lenox was fulfilling the role 'big with magisterial honours'.

John Bussell had shown great interest in the Noongar languages of the region and taught himself to translate to and from English. As the eldest in the household he had a strong influence, but in his absence the remaining brothers decided how to manage the farm in their own way. When Vernon, Charles and Lenox all went away on business and twenty-one-year-old Alfred was left to oversee the property, the Noongar cow-herds failed to turn up for work. Some damper disappeared and Alfred dismissed the suspects the next day. In June, the Chapmans' heifer was speared. On the 27th, a party including George and Henry Chapman, Dr Alfred Green, Elijah Dawson, Lenox and Alfred Bussell set out with soldiers from the 21st Fusiliers to find Gaywal, Kenny and four other men they thought were the culprits, with eyewitness accounts from the three Aboriginal men – Injangoot, Nugundung and Bobbingoot – who had originally been accused as evidence. The party of settlers soon found the men they were searching for.[454] Their reports state they met with 'hostility' and were outnumbered. As one man raised his spear, Elijah Dawson fired at him and in the shooting that followed, Aboriginal men were killed or severely wounded. Gaywal and Kenny escaped. In his letters to the government resident and the colonial secretary, Lenox reported three deaths. Bessie Bussell wrote in her diary that nine Aboriginal people were killed and two were wounded.[455]

Afraid of reprisals, Lenox Bussell wrote to Molloy asking for more military support. Two soldiers arrived from the Augusta barracks and brought with them Molloy's request for formal evidence statements from witnesses. On 13 July, while Dawson was talking with several

Aboriginal men he knew, Gaywal threw a spear at him through an open window of his house at Wonnerup.[456] Another glass-tipped spear grazed Mrs Dawson and hit the wall. Elijah Dawson broke off the spear in his arm and ran outside with his gun. When he aimed at the men but did not fire, they ran away. Contemporary accounts of this incident vary considerably. The number of Aboriginal people present was variously described as between nine and twenty. The only evidence that Gaywal speared Dawson's cow was circumstantial. The settlers had been expecting a revenge killing, a concept they recognised, so they set out to apply their law and punish the guilty. Since Dawson was seen to shoot the first Aboriginal man, Gaywal was doing the same thing. The Dawsons abandoned Wonnerup and moved into some huts close to Cattle Chosen. The Vasse colonists were soon unsettled even more when they heard rumours about large groups of Aboriginal people gathering near the deserted farm. They were 'shouting and yelling' and 'by no means intimidated by what had already occurred', so Lenox sent out a party to 'dislodge them' and three Aboriginal people were killed: a man, a woman and a boy. When the next search party went after Gaywal again in August with strict instructions not to fire at anyone, 'a few shots were fired' and a wounded man dropped his child as he ran away across the river.[457]

The words chosen by each writer to describe what happened next carry the full weight of personal viewpoint with them and illustrate how different accounts can subtly shift the central elements of a story that becomes fixed in history. Lenox's report recounted how the child was left 'drowning' and a 'compassionate person rescued him'. He assured the colonial secretary that he had sent messages to the parents to say that the child would be returned 'on application being made for it'.[458] The account of another eyewitness, George Layman, told how they 'took a child prisoner about fourteen months old'. He added, 'I expect before long the natives will resent this.'[459]

The boy was taken to Cattle Chosen and put in the care of Fanny Bussell. Her feelings towards him were gentle and affectionate but her diary entries suggest that her opinion of Aboriginal people was very different from Georgiana's. She saw him as 'a beautiful little creature' and was more interested in choosing clothes for him than the fact that he was desperately trying to call out to his parents using the 'coo-ee' call he knew they would recognise.[460] Phoebe Bower, the Bussell sisters' maid, asked to look after the child and begged that she might be allowed to call him 'Reuben'.

The relationship between the British and Aboriginal people was changing and colonial law was deployed as a control mechanism. White settlers badly needed local knowledge and enjoyed the benefits of cheap labour provided by Wardandi people who were willing to work on their farms but most could not accommodate marked cultural differences when they affected their own households. Aboriginal people knew what it was to be hungry when food sources were limited by climate or region, so they freely shared what they had in times of plenty. When the settlers had what seemed like an excess of stored food, their Noongar neighbours could not understand the imported logic of not sharing the surplus. The crime of 'stealing' in these circumstances was a foreign concept to the traditional owners of the land, but it was deeply ingrained in British law. Enforcing the Christian seventh holy commandment became increasingly central to the colonial justice system as Aboriginal people began to take what they needed or wanted with greater confidence. In May an Anglican missionary, Dr Louis Giustiniani, protested publicly against a sentence of seven years' imprisonment given to an Aboriginal man in Perth for 'stealing' a bunch of grapes growing on what had been his own country. There were many who disagreed with Giustiniani's views that the traditional owners of the region should be compensated for their loss: 'I think that the act of settling the country and introducing the Christian religion, even through such agents as the Doctor, is some remuneration for the use of their land'.[461]

In July, at the House of Commons in London, a parliamentary select committee was debating whether Aboriginal people should have the right to appear in court, whether they should be provided with an interpreter and whether district magistrates like Molloy and Bussell should be able to issue punishments. The committee's view was that 'the observation of our laws would be absurd and to punish their non-observance of them by severe penalties would be palpably unjust', but this was not reflected in the recommendations they listed in their report.[462] The civil and criminal colonial laws of the British government would apply to everyone alike, with no exceptions that recognised Aboriginal customary laws and practices, values or culture. British law was administered as before in Western Australia but in the October quarter sessions in Perth, the judge addressed the jury to point out one thing that had changed: 'The present Session might be said to present a remarkable era in the Criminal Annals of the Colony, as the Calendar, for the first time since the establishment of the Settlement, did not contain the name of a single European or white prisoner'. The only prisoners for trial were 'Aborigines of this country, who were charged with separate commissions of the crime of theft'.

There were other tensions closer to home. In September 1837, Mary Bussell married Patrick Taylor, a Scot who had travelled to Western Australia on the same ship. Georgiana first met him in Scotland in 1829 while she was staying at Keppoch House, and her early impressions were good ones.[463] He was a devout, austere man and contributed a great deal to the community in Albany where he and Mary settled, but Georgiana had misgivings that grew each time the couple visited. Taylor's father was a slave broker in the West Indies with other children who were born there before he married; their mother was a slave. The slave trade had made him a rich man and the Jamaican branch of the Taylor family was very well known so Georgiana may have wondered about the sources of money used to purchase the Scottish estates that gave Patrick a privileged youth. Mary Dunlop also knew Taylor from Scotland and advised Georgiana to try to 'break thro' the imaginary barriers and be friends with them ... letting love cover all faults & overcoming evil with good'.[464]

In late October, Molloy recorded his concern about Alfred Green's episodes of shaking. The doctor seemed to recover but then he was delirious again. This was the man responsible for everyone's health, including Molloy's children and his wife, who was soon to be expecting another child. Dr Green's patients knew that his habits meant he was sometimes 'absent from duty' when needed.[465] As an adult, Sabina remembered the night when an intoxicated Green arrived after everyone had gone to bed, demanding to borrow Molloy's boat so he could drown himself. Molloy agreed to lend the boat, knowing that the doctor would not be capable of walking as far as the river but Georgiana was dismayed and begged her husband not to help. Green did not make it any further than the house that night and in the morning Molloy put him safely in the barracks under guard until he was sober.[466]

As the days warmed, Georgiana's life grew easier with the company and support of her husband. After months of frustration she was finally able to start the enormous task she had accepted nearly a year earlier. It was time to begin finding, collecting and preparing her first botanical collection, and she had a lot to learn. On Wednesday, 4 October 1837, John Molloy recorded for the very first time an expedition to gather flowers for Captain Mangles. The excitement of a new venture, in a new season, extended to the whole family as they set off in Molloy's boat to the 'Granite Rock'.

From that day, Georgiana had a purpose beyond the thatched house, the settlement and even the colony. She was the government resident's wife and a mother, but for the first time in eight years she was an individual of intellectual worth and potential not limited by her humble surroundings and the 'odious drudgery' of her life.[467]

For the family's first botanical expedition on behalf of Mangles she chose a perfect hunting ground, and she visited many times to search for flowers and seeds during the next two and a half years.

The place where Molloy must have landed their little boat is still evident on a flat point beneath gnarled, twisted saltwater paperbarks where the rock reaches into the Hardy Inlet and no trees grow. Known today as Flat Rock, the granite outcrop is unchanged. A bare dome of brown hues from amber to ochre, it stretches out like a sleeping giant. Low bush still scratches its perimeter and twenty-first-century botanists go there to find granite-loving orchids.

They were happy days. But five weeks later, after three visits to Granite Rock with the children, Georgiana's life was torn apart again. As always, even in his grief, John Molloy wrote in the journal.

> I have the melancholy task of recording the loss of my dear little infant son in his nineteenth month by an accident, he was missing for a few minutes about the hour of ten this morning and Alas! After searching for him in different directions Charlotte [Heppingstone] went to the well where he was found drowned. We tried to restore animation for about five hours – without success – the Lord had taken his spirit from him, it hath pleased him to bereave us of him – May we bear this affliction at his hand as we ought & bow to his holy will.[468]

The next day Molloy officially recorded 'John Molloy, 1yr & 10mths, drowned, infant', the seventh name in the parish burial list, but the entry in his journal uses the words of a father, not a government official: 'Committed the mortal remains of my little one to the earth.'

The tragedy should not have happened. Georgiana felt sure her son was still alive for several minutes after they pulled him from the well, but Dr Green was at the Vasse and there was no-one to ask for advice. Once again, with a child dying in her arms, she did not know what to do.

Johnny had been alone for just a few moments. Charlotte quickly noticed his absence and went to look for him. The well was only 'a stone's cast' from Georgiana's window.[469] It was not deep and the flow was slower than it would have been in winter, but the dark cavity and the sound of gurgling water were too fascinating for the toddler to ignore. Although Captain Molloy had a new cover made the day after the funeral, Johnny was not the last inquisitive boy to fall into the well.

In the late 1940s, a five-year-old boy was camping nearby with his parents. The riverside and the beach looked much the same then as they had in 1838. He remembers trees like the ones described by Georgiana, and the fun of spending days by the ocean. But most of all he remembers the day he fell into the old well, intrigued by the shadowy view through its slatted cover. He was saved by a wooden trapdoor that fell onto his arm and stopped him from falling further until rescuers came to pull him out. Although the well wasn't deep, he was not tall enough to touch the bottom with his feet.

Today, all traces of the well are hidden from view but, beneath a drain cover in the road, the spring still gurgles loudly as it runs downhill into the river.

* * *

There are many approaches to research and they do not just involve the finding and interpretation of facts. Sometimes it is only by combining imagination and empathy with knowledge and secure sources that the past begins to appear. Questions that ask, 'What would I have done in the same situation?' and 'What did that mean for the way these people lived their days, hour by hour?' can sometimes flick open the closed door of time.

The Molloy journal in the JS Battye Library covers a period of five years and ends with diary entries for early 1841, after the family had moved north to the Vasse. Written at the back are stock management records to 1842 and John Molloy's gardening notes for the crops around the house. His rough plan of the layout of the garden records the dates of sowing and ploughing and brings to light the full range of fruits and vegetables he harvested, including vines. From 2008, when I first saw it, his careful sketch helped me follow the timetable

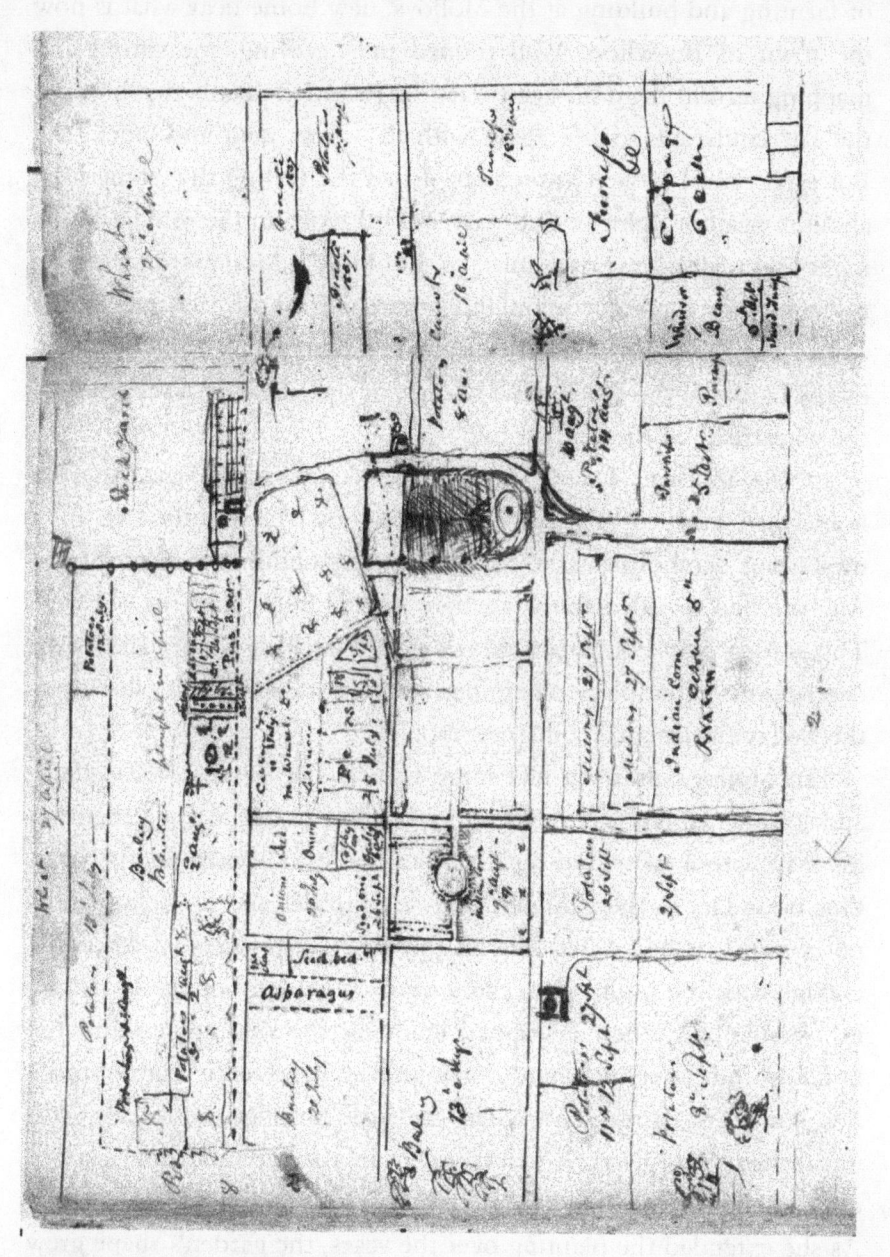

John Molloy's gardening plan c. 1837

JS Battye Library SLWA ACC 6927A/2 (with permission)

of farming and building at the Molloys' new home near what is now the town of Busselton. Well trained in surveying, measuring and mapping terrain from his army days, he recorded details that brought the flat landscape to life again with its wheat field and stockyard. But each time I looked at the plan, I had the feeling that something about it was not right. In February 2013, I woke in the middle of the night and realised my own mistake. Looking at Molloy's drawing on my computer screen at midnight, I watched a little thatched house appear for the first time, surrounded by intensive planting bordered by the banks of the Blackwood River, not the Vasse, and sheltered by the wheatfield on the Killiter hill.

In the moment I realised that the sketch shows the Augusta homestead and not Fairlawn, I understood the significance of a mysterious symbol near the house. A man's childhood memories of Augusta had revealed roughly where he had fallen into the old well. The garden plan confirmed its position, matching Georgiana's own description of the place where her son drowned. John Molloy drew the well with the correct map symbol.

But Molloy's drawing had more to tell. The graves of Elizabeth and Johnny Molloy were easy to find. Their father marked them on his map with a cross, but their mother marked them in another way. One boundary in the garden had always puzzled me: an oblique line, not vertical or horizontal like all the other edges created when the cottage was first built, when there were no garden borders to dictate its orientation. When I stopped studying the outlines around the building and thought about the woman who lived there, I understood. For ten years, from 1830 when the little wooden house was still unfinished, Georgiana walked every day in a direct line from her front door to the place where her children were buried. It was a diagonal. As she extended the planting over the years, the garden's shape grew around her sad pathway.

* * *

Georgiana was gripped by 'a dangerous illness'.[470] She withdrew from life completely for six weeks but was determined to fulfil the promise she had made to Mangles before another year's flowering passed by. On 28 December the family went out to collect the seeds from the plants they had marked the previous summer. With them went Dr Green, pursued by disaster as he always seemed to be. He lit his pipe and accidentally set fire to the whole area, and they were 'obliged to flee before the smoke & flames'. The next day when they all went out again 'to collect for the Manglesian box', Green borrowed Molloy's boat and forgot to bring back the anchor.

Georgiana began exploring the bush with a new incentive for close observation. As she realised just how many different species grew in Augusta she also began to recognise the huge practical demands of the task she had taken on. The collecting was difficult, especially on the hottest days. When she found a new plant in flower, she marked it so it would be easier to find it later in the season. She had to select the most vigorously growing, perfect examples of each species, ideally bearing leaves, flowers, buds and seeds, then lay them flat in a basket that allowed each plant to be separated from others with the most delicate on the top so the petals were not crushed. Seeds from each plant had to be wrapped separately so they did not get mixed up or lost; cutting out and sewing the little muslin bags she needed was yet another task for her.

In the evenings she wrote up her notes, giving each specimen an identification number and recording its details, including where and when it was collected, and its botanical name if she knew it. For an untrained botanist, the job of identifying differences between similar plants was complex, requiring careful comparison of small details. Then came the job of drying and preparing. She laid each specimen between two thick sheets of absorbent paper, and very carefully positioned the leaves and petals so there was no overlap. She pressed them gently under weights for a few hours at a time over several days, checked them to shift their positions slightly to a fresh part of the paper if necessary, and gradually increased the pressure by adding more weight, until the specimens had dried out and were flat.

The next part of the process was to group and order the specimens for mounting onto individual pages of the *hortus siccus* ['dry garden'] that Mangles had sent her. This was a large, purpose-made book to store the specimens flat and keep them dry, and a wooden box to hold it that would also accommodate the bags of seeds, layered for travel in sections or drawers. The book was designed to have each page attached separately by 'tying in', but Georgiana decided to leave the pages loose so that Mangles himself could decide how best to organise them botanically. She probably added a little camphor to the glue to repel any tiny insects still remaining on the sample; it was a common technique. She had noticed a difference between seeds bought in Britain and those of the native plants in the bush:

> In this uncultivated land and temperate climate, insects and reptiles have unrestrained license – and the seeds of each plant afford sustenance to some of the animal creation. Consequently, the seed vessels of each are generally inhabited by some worm or grub. This is particularly the case with those contained in a silique.[471]

Georgiana decided to create a second, duplicate collection for herself with the same numbering system, so she could learn more about each plant from Mangles and discuss them with him by letter. She had faced many challenges since her arrival but the enormity of this project was different. It was the meticulous, intellectual work of a lady and she was determined to succeed.

By the end of January 1838, with the help of John Molloy and Sabina, she had collected so many specimens that she used her own box to pack them because it was larger than the one Mangles had sent. She wrote to him again, planning to put the letter inside the box and dispatch it on one of the ships expected to arrive in Flinders Bay within a few weeks. First, she unburdened her heart and told him about the death of her son. Mangles was a stranger to her and she asked his forgiveness for writing in the 'minute detail that friendship warrants'.

Georgiana already knew enough to understand that native plants the settlers thought of as weeds were potentially the most interesting for the collectors who would eventually receive what she had gathered for Mangles.

> I have sent you every flower we have worth sending and many I fear you will consider worthless/esteem unworthy, but having obeyed the 'Golden Rule' I have ventured to introduce some literal Weeds. Often in hearing of foreign countries, I have wished to be acquainted with the most common plants, having more curiosity to see its weeds than the finer productions. The latter were too important to pass observation, the former too humble to be worth removing.[472]

She thanked him for being the reason why she had started to take a more intense interest in the native flora of Augusta, and explained why the task had brought her pleasure even though it meant that her other work had to take second place for the first time.

> Often has Molloy looked at a buttonless shirt, and exclaimed with a woebegone Visage, 'When will Captn. Mangles's seeds be sown?' and recently he has laid aside all his own operations and accompanied the children and me by Land and Water, for a day's search in quest of seeds and Flowers. We have had three or four Gypsy parties on your account, with which Sabina and Mary were much delighted. Indeed, my dear Sir, I have been more frequently from my house this year in making up your collection than for the whole of the nearly 8 years we have lived at Augusta.

Even as she described the pleasure she had found in collecting, she could not help devoting a few lines to thoughts of gardening in her homeland once again.

> I have no hesitation in declaring that, were I to accompany the box of seeds to England, knowing as I do their situation, time of flowering, soil and degree of moisture required with the fresh powers of fructification they each possess, I should have a very extensive conservatory or conservatories, of none but plants from Augusta. I do not say this vauntingly, but to inspire you with that ardour and interest with which the collection leaves me, and cordially thank you for being the cause of my more immediate acquaintance with the nature and variety of those plants that we have exchanged for the productions of our own country and which also benefits my children – as from necessary avocations, but for your request, I should never have bestowed on the flowers of this Wilderness any other idea than that of only passing admiration.

Georgiana's letter reveals the botanical skills she was acquiring as she became engrossed in the practical tasks of collecting. She described how she had dealt with the most delicate flowers that began to curl when glued and she had learned that the loss of colour from drying was not as critical as the right way of laying the specimen for viewing. She was particularly anxious about infestation and told Mangles that Molloy was trying to find a tin box in Perth so she could use it to line the wooden box. A small crack in the timber could be disastrous to the large *hortus siccus* during such a long voyage.

Not surprisingly, given the time she had devoted to Mangles's request, Georgiana felt able to list a few requests of her own, making clear that everything would be paid for in full. She wanted sweet peas, hibiscus and seeds of creeping and climbing plants for their decorative effect, but her list also included medicinal species and plants that would literally add longed-for flavour to family life: rhubarb for tarts, tansy for puddings, lemon thyme, lavender, sage, sorrel and borage. In adding more to her already long letter she lightened the tone by directing her playful wit in his direction.

West Australian Christmas tree (*Nuytsia floribunda*). In 1842, growers and botanists in Britain were still trying to raise these successfully from seed but their hemiparasitic nature, the need to obtain nourishment from the roots of a host plant, made this difficult. Georgiana was frustrated in her final attempts to collect the seeds for Mangles in 1843 because she was unable to walk in the months before she died.

West Australian Christmas tree (*Nuytsia floribunda*)

Kingia australis grove on Molloy Island. These slow-growing plants, abundant in the southwest, were still among the most desirable items for wealthy British gardeners when Georgiana was collecting for Mangles. The seeds of *Kingia australis* were among the very last 'small, small harvest' she managed to send him.

Georgiana's collections included seeds, fruits, leaves and flowers from tiny plants to large trees. The creamy white profusion of Marri flowers is still a familiar sight today but the specimens she sent to Mangles were originally recorded as *Eucalyptus calophylla* and not as *Corymbia calophylla*, the botanical name since the new genus Corymbia was created.

Dwarf burchardia (*Burchardia multiflora*). The specimens Georgiana prepared still reveal the botanical and artistic skills that made her collections so special. With no professional training, she combined attention to detail and precision with a creative talent that displayed each plant perfectly.

Dwarf burchardia (*Burchardia multiflora*)

The plant commonly known as the *Augusta kennedia* only grows naturally today in the Augusta-Cape Leeuwin region. Its botanical name has changed three times since Georgiana first used it as a vigorous climber over her verandah: *Kennedia marryattae, Kennedia macrophylla, Kennedia lateritia*. Nineteenth-century botanical illustrations captured something of the plant's appeal and Georgiana's own dried specimen (below, from 1841) reveals its structure, but the living plant conveys the flower colour and twining habit which first attracted her.

This specimen of *Kennedia marryattae*, collected by Georgiana, is located in the Herbarium of the Royal Botanic Gardens, Kew.

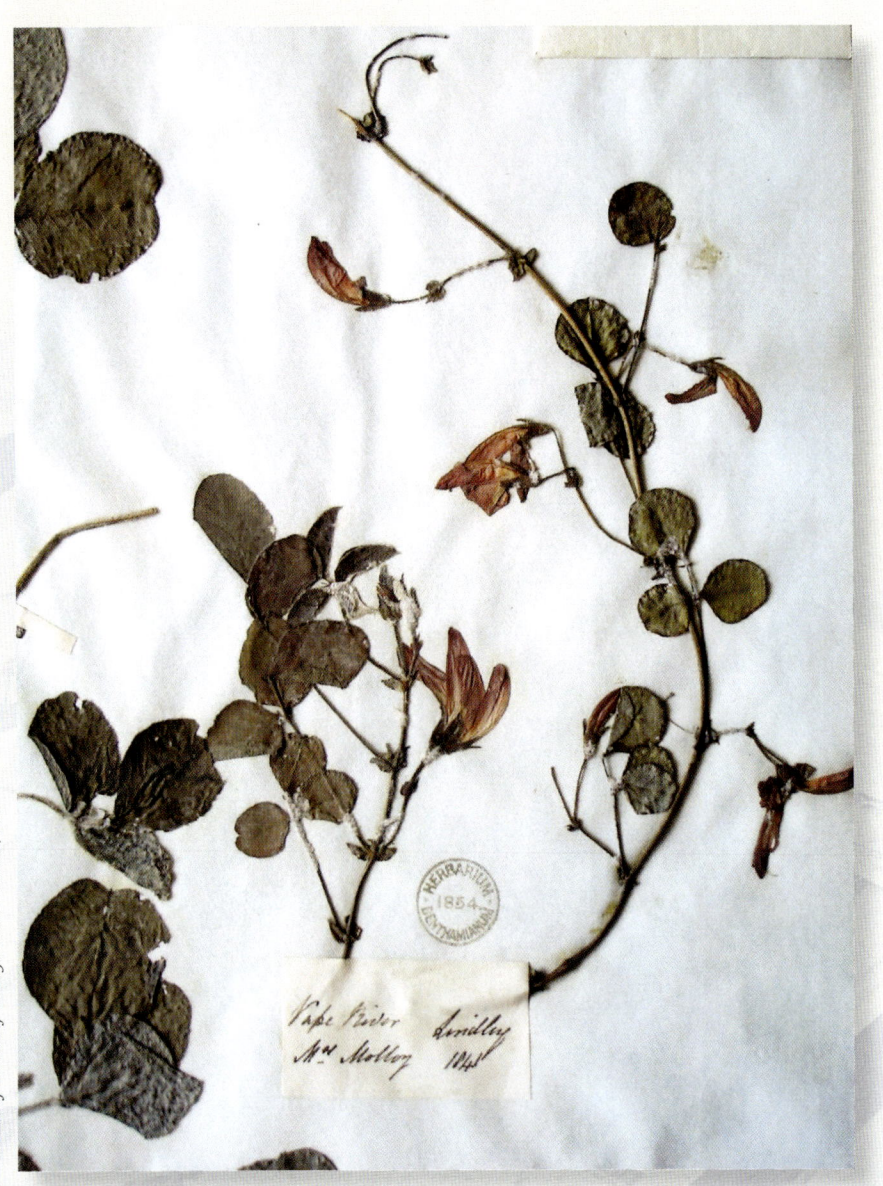

From *Maund's Botanist*, circa 1837: " '*Kennedya Marryattiana* [sic] – Mrs Marryatt's Kennedya' ... first raised in the year 1836, by Mr Robert Mangles, and in the gardens of Mrs Marryat, from seeds sent home by Sir James Stirling."

Augusta Kennedia (*Kennedia lateritia*) growing in the author's garden.

Cowslip orchid (*Caladenia flava*)

The petals of a Cowslip orchid vary from pale buttery lemon to deep rich yellow, often striped with dark red.

Cowslip orchid *(Caladenia flava)*

It is more than 175 years since Georgiana collected these specimens, dried them and prepared them for shipping to Britain yet here they still retain some of their original colour.

In the summer of 1841, Georgiana had her first holiday in eleven years and spent three days collecting specimens with her husband at Castle Rock Bay. Her collection included several species of *Thysanotus* (Fringed lily). Sometimes she was unable to give the botanical name of each species she sent to Mangles, but it is likely that her specimens included *T. arenarius* and *T. sparteus*, shown above.

Georgiana's 'Castle Rock' collection lists simply a 'Fringed lily' with no detail about the species. With more than 40 growing in Western Australia, identification still requires careful observation. This illustration of another Fringed lily, the 'many-flowered Thysanotus', *T. proliferus* (*T. multiflorus*) appeared in Sir Joseph Paxton's *Magazine of Botany and Register of Flowering Plants* in 1840.

You, I doubt not, have often heard of the inexhaustible properties of a Lady's pen; and as you have brought this infliction from an unknown person on yourself, I shall have less compunction in visiting you, although etiquette would demand the reverse.

No ship came to convey Georgiana's 'voluminous epistle' and her botanical collection. Months passed and the arrival of another baby weighed heavily on her mind; she knew what to expect and that her doctor might not be sober. In the first week of May, while Captain Molloy was away at the Vasse, Georgiana asked Green to call in to see Sabina, who was unwell, but after three requests his valet told her he was 'in a high state of intoxication'. She waited twenty-four hours then went to his house to collect him but the smell of rum on his breath was still strong. In a remote community where salted pork was often the main source of protein for months on end and the antidote to a lack of fresh fruit was a ration of wine or rum with every meal, the doctor certainly was not alone in his weakness for alcohol. But as the settlement's surgeon and physician, its effects on his daily life had become very public.

Knowing that her life and that of her unborn child would very soon be in his hands was not reassuring. The entries in Molloy's journal that week are in Georgiana's handwriting.[473]

> Thursday, 3rd May 1838
> La Donna mending mats and very depressed at what had & what was going to occur.
> Friday, 11th May 1838
> Busy preparing & arranging what may be my death bed.

Just after eight o'clock in the evening on 1 June, another daughter, Amelia Georgiana, was born during 'violent gales with thunder & lightening [sic] almost without interruption'.[474] 'La Senhora' suffered a haemorrhage after her confinement. Two weeks later she was recovering but could still only sit up in bed.

The rain was still falling heavily on 24 June when Molloy, recently returned from the Vasse, received news about 'a rupture with the natives, two of whom were shot'. His entry in the journal deflects blame from any perpetrator and he avoids detail that could be seen as judgemental. He had presided too many times in the courts martial of Paris, more than twenty years earlier, to commit to any kind of comment until he knew the facts. He was concerned about the rising tide of violence and unauthorised reprisals by men armed with guns. He baptised the baby two days later and set off again immediately for the Vasse.

Georgiana continued to work on the flower garden and weeded the vines with Charlotte Heppingstone. Her life had become no easier after eight years in the colony and with fewer neighbours for support things were difficult, but there were compensations. A purple creeping plant mingled with a pink flowering climber over one side of her verandah, darkening her sitting room but framing its view up the Blackwood River like a painting.

> The receding points give it almost the appearance of a lake. In the background is the boundless and evergreen Forest. On the other side of the Verandah – which is Molloy's work of rustic branches – grows the nasturtium, which is of deeper orange than it ever attains in Britain. It is not at all afflicted by the winter months, and as it has been sown since 1833, and has formed an almost impervious and cool shade of almost incredible beauty from its profusion of brilliant blossoms and gay light green foliage.[475]

There were visitors, including the Turner ladies, so her days were long and active but there was little sleep at night; she lay awake with a dreadful toothache. And there was something else on her mind; no ships had arrived in Flinders Bay since the year before. The seeds she had packed so carefully and her long letter were still unsent.

Georgiana was unaware that while her letter waited to begin its journey, Swan River fever was gripping the gardeners and botanists of Britain more firmly than ever. The indigenous plants outside her window were the same rare prizes and novelties being bought and sold for high prices among the glitterati of the horticultural world. They were the floral treasures being coaxed into life in heated greenhouses; seedlings that were better fed than most of the population of England. There was intense interest in their potential for economic and medical use. Most of all, they offered a completely fresh field of investigation for European scientists and botanists searching for new evidence about the ways living things originated and diversified.

On 17 August 1838, Mangles received a letter from James Gowen, head gardener to the Earl of Carnarvon, informing him that Dr Lindley had decided to write an account of the botany 'of that interesting region' the Swan River, and wanted Mangles to send him any new species.[476] An additional incentive was mentioned: '& if there be a good new plant in it he will erect a new genus "Manglesia" in honour of yourself as the donor.'[477]

The plants whose seeds had been packed since the previous summer began to bloom again in the Augusta bush. Georgiana had completely filled her own large *hortus siccus* as well as the smaller one Mangles sent her in 1836, so there were now two boxes waiting for shipment. There had been no letter from him since the first nearly two years earlier and it seemed that however well she had managed her task it would come to nothing. She had no professional botanical training but she knew that any chance of success was slipping away with each day the seeds stayed in their boxes. The frustration of imminent failure was almost unbearable: 'I have scarcely patience to look at the box as it stands and know that every hour renders the intent more precarious.'[478]

She had been careful but there was always the possibility of disease or contamination by pests whose eggs hatched inside the containers. And there was another worry: there were other collectors living nearer to Perth, men with experience in the field and with easier access to the shipping routes. In September, Georgiana added more to her January letter and apologised for the delay. She also added a bank cheque to cover all the items she had asked for and one or two requests including 'a garden rake fit for a lady's use': 'I am obliged to borrow one of Captn. Molloy's with the most formidable teeth, spreading destruction and next to annihilation where ever it is applied.'[479]

With no-one left to help her look after the children she had to take her daughters with her when she went out collecting, and they grew up copying their mother and learning skills from observation she had acquired from books and experience. She told Mangles the little girls had been very useful to her in finding tiny plants she could not see because their eyes were so much closer to the ground.

> For in our impervious Bush it is really difficult to find what you are in quest of ... Indeed, Sabina I shortly found to be infinitely more au fait at discovering and remembering the abode of differently described plants than I was myself. I have known her unexhausted patience to go three and five times a week to watch numbers 83 and 74, lest the seeds should be opened and shed. She is six years old! and such a pursuit is highly delightful to her young Mind, besides the pleasing accompaniments of a distant Walk. Here the children are bereft of most of the amusements of a highly civilised country. Sabina has already imitated me in forming a collection of dried flowers, fastened by ligatures and Mary who is also very serviceable in discovering and collecting, to say nothing of 'pulling flowers for Captain Mangles', has made up several of the most strange parcels for your acceptance. Ever since your box arrived in 1837, you do not know the ridiculous articles presented to me for you. Every time her hair was cut a portion would be enclosed for the box.[480]

In the first cold, stormy week of September, Georgiana stayed indoors reading to her 'little family and instructing them'. When her 'dearest Molloy' came back overland from the Vasse, he brought letters from her mother and William Phillips with more bad news. Her youngest brother, George, who had married Amelia Agg from Cheltenham three years earlier, had died on 13 March 1838 at the house his mother was renting. He was twenty-four. A few weeks later, John Molloy went north again taking more of their belongings and most of their cattle with him. Georgiana bottled vinegar, made cream cheese and cleared out the stored barley. She had inspected it and noticed it heating up from inside, due to 'a quantity of green matter'. It was a time of imminent change and her husband was not unaware that she was beginning to dread leaving their home. He wrote to her even when he was away for just a few days and sometimes his letters included a plant cutting from the Vasse, dried and pressed ready for her to use.[481]

The time for leaving Augusta was getting close. There was no longer any doubt that the settlers' future was on the Vasse plains, where farming could feed them and provide an income. The Molloys had held on to the Augusta dream for as long as they could but the government resident could not sustain the demands of his job from so far away with the increasing size of what was already becoming known as 'Busselton', and Fairlawn was ready to receive its family. The *Lady Stirling* anchored in Flinders Bay early on the morning of 16 November and Molloy used the chance to dispatch more of his family's belongings to the Vasse. The next day he worked out how to transport the shipment, including timbers from George Layman's old house in Augusta. Molloy built a raft and hired Mr Turner's boat to have it towed out across the sandbar to the ship. Whether the wind was too strong or the raft wasn't seaworthy, the day did not end well. The raft broke apart and sank. Mangles' two precious boxes, the fruits of Mrs Molloy's dedication for more than a year, nearly ended up at the bottom of the ocean but were finally handed over to the ship's captain.[482]

Georgiana quickly wrote another note to Mangles expressing her 'readiness to serve'. At the very last moment, she added pepper to her collection as a preservative and on 22 November, the ship set sail with Molloy and Dr Green on board, heading for the Vasse to offload the household goods and on to Perth. The ship took Georgiana's letters separately from the freight and on 30 November, Ellen Stirling wrote from Perth to her cousin Mangles to tell him she had received a letter from Georgiana saying he would pay the cost.[483] Mrs Molloy's first botanical collection was on its way.

Two days before Molloy succeeded in loading Georgiana's precious boxes on a stormy day in Australia, Dr Lindley sat down on a summer morning in leafy west London and wrote directly to Captain Mangles: 'I am anxious to get material as I am bent upon publishing "A View of the Botany of the Swan River Colony".'[484]

A brand new source of specimens from a meticulous, reliable collector would enhance Mangles's reputation even further and provide Lindley with the raw material for a very popular publication. Nothing could have been further from Georgiana's mind as the intensive preparation around her went on. With each ship that passed through on its journey to Geographe Bay, more of her belongings were taken away to a house she had not seen. While Captain Molloy was planting vegetables and building a stockyard further north, she was gardening in Augusta and doing what mothers do.

* * *

There are rich historical sources stored in libraries, museums and private collections but, if reading goes deeper, the most human stories are often found in simple domestic documents. In collecting material for this book I have read some texts many times over the years and then, because I am thinking differently, I suddenly realise they have more to tell.

The Molloy journal was the government resident's own record of weather conditions, paid employment and significant events in the community. One regular daily task was the care of the government oxen, the only heavy labour the settlers had, so each day's entry names the person responsible for them. In the spring of 1838 this person was

1838 November

Tuesday 23rd Fine NW. Busy at saw trestle. Jacky as herdsman
Wednesday 24th W. Called on Mrs Turner. Jacky do
Thursday 25th R. Mrs Bryan to church, all the Children at Mr Bryan's
                                                                               Jack

Friday 26th D. Welsh brought home the new Mattrass cost 4/ Mr Turner
         Bussels Mr McDermot called.   Jack

Saturday 27th R. Mr Turner Bussels to tea by Jack.

Sunday 28th R. Read Morning and Evening Service Charlotte destroy
      -ed her self. 2 natives secured. Mr Turner dined Mr Bryan Jack

Monday 29 R. Corporal came at nine & left off about 5. hoeing Potatoes
      Indian Corn. Mr Thomas Turner returned from survey
      Lieut Helesporale Molloy's soldering brass   Jack
      Cobbets Gardener. 2 Bullet thanks to Turner. Bussels.

Tuesday 30th R.
      Welsh Thomas cutting firewood. Turner Bussels & Mr McDermot
      rode to Conical hill & did not return till the following
      day Natives about   Jack

Wednesday 31st R.
      Welsh from Breakfast time to 2 o'clock burning fire
      cutting Wood. Received some Cash to keep for Master Welsh. Jack

November
Thursday 1st R.
      Mr Turner to tea Wrote to dearest Molloy & Cap.t Mangles
      Corporal returned soldering Irons Turner Bussels the mouth
                                                               Jack

Friday 2nd. Dull & showery Turner departed for Vasse.

Saturday 3rd R. Took a stroll with the Children   Jack

Sunday 4th R. Read Divine Service   Jack.

Extract of a page from the Molloy journal, November 1838

JS Battye SLWA ACC 6927A / 2 (with permission)

usually 'Jack', and I guessed he might be one of the Wardandi men employed to help with livestock and crops. I had loaded the online images of the journal so many times before and never stopped to notice the difference in handwriting on one of the pages.[485]

On the last Sunday in November, someone new took over the writing of that single word. Someone who pressed very hard with the quill pen and wrote very carefully. It was a childish hand. Georgiana had gone against her mother's wishes that the children should be sent away to school and was educating them herself. For the first time, Sabina was allowed to practise her handwriting in Papa's official journal.

***

Accounts of hardship and tragedy thread their way through almost a decade in the fledgling colony. The last few weeks in Augusta were dismal for Georgiana, but that did not stop her from remembering life in Augusta as a happy time.

> I have a little organie as it is called, or a sort of instrument like an Organ and Piano united. It is like a Work table in appearance and being a wind instrument has the advantage of not getting out of tune. This the children often dance to, and at dear Augusta, I used to take it on the grass plot and play till late by Moonlight, the beautiful broad water of the Blackwood gliding by, the roar of the Bar, and ever and anon the wild scream of a flight of Swans going over to the Fresh Water Lakes. The air perfectly redolent with the powerful scent of Vergillia, Stocks, and *Oenothera biennis*, Clove Pinks and never fading Mignonette. We used always to have Tea outside, and for our amusement and interest I had sown the *Oenothera tetraptera* and *Oenothera biennis* profusely in the Borders adjoining this plot, so that we might watch their expanding blossoms.[486]

It was not a good time to be moving house. Mary had such a fever that Georgiana had to send an urgent note to Captain Molloy at the Vasse and he came home straight away with Dr Green, only to be confined to bed himself for the next ten days. 'Dear Papa' recovered enough to finish packing for the journey and to dig up the crop of potatoes. Letters from Perth arrived with news that the soldiers were being removed from Augusta and sent to Albany and also of Molloy being charged with misappropriation of government resources by 'applying an escort to private purposes'.[487] The end was not what they had hoped for in the early days when Molloy wrote to his mother-in-law in 1832 and told her their prospects were 'brightening' and he looked forward to seeing 'a good large city rise on the Bay'.[488]

The dream of a prosperous future in an idyllic situation had been fought for but it was time to move on. Captain Cole's whaler was anchored in Flinders Bay and he offered to take the family upriver in one of his rowing boats, while the rest of their belongings travelled overland to meet them further upstream. The night before they left, Georgiana said her final farewells to the Turner family.[489] She walked the path at the side of the house for the last time, up the Killiter hill, and planted red roses on the children's graves. Then she pulled her favourite plants and wrapped them carefully to keep them damp, packed into a straw basket that could be attached to her saddle. Sabina was seven when her family closed the door on their home by the Blackwood for the last time, but she always remembered, as children do, the shock of witnessing her mother's distress. 'I remember my mother's grief at leaving Augusta, she stood at the door for a long time taking a last look at it all till Papa took her hand and led her away.'[490]

Georgiana stayed behind when Molloy went travelling and she had rarely been more than a kilometre from the homestead in ten years. The prospect of a camp under the stars with her family and the anticipation of seeing their new home for the first time were antidotes to sadness. A few days later she found words to describe the extremes of emotion she felt.

It was very pleasant and the commencement of a grand undertaking. Dear Molloy removed every offending bush with his foot, first the one side and then on the other, carried Baby, Amelia and though grieving at leaving Augusta where I had spent so many eventful years the time was so interesting and the scenes so pleasant, it was the most perfect commixture of pain and pleasure I have ever endured.[491]

A Garden in Busselton

The trek from Augusta to the Vasse was a temporary escape, a taste of freedom between the domestic responsibilities of one home and the next. For three days on the river and in the bush, Georgiana had everything she had hoped for when she boarded the *Warrior* a decade earlier. The first night at the Governor's Bivouac, cooking over the fire and sleeping under canvas was something she had longed for. The next day, 8 May, the group crossed the Chapman River. She and Molloy walked with the children and Charlotte Heppingstone rode one of the donkeys. Dr Green was leading the packhorses overland from Augusta. A night of heavy rain at the 'Black Snake creek' camp did not dampen the family's fun: 'Bunker the other donkey carried the baggage. At one camping place the tent was blown over and Bunker got in & ate the bread.'[492]

On Friday, 10 May 1839, early in the afternoon, the small party crossed the flat plains of the Vasse. Its park-like landscape, 'abounding with kangaroo' bore no resemblance to the wooded softness of Augusta and, for Georgiana, it was 'a terrible change'.[493,494] A few months later she wrote to Mangles, 'My mountain-loving eye looks in vain for a rise or hill'.[495] The river, at the beginning of autumn, was a narrow, understated cousin to the majestic Blackwood. Molloy had done everything he could to make the house ready for his family.

There were vegetables growing and crops in the paddocks. They had fruit, meat, cereals, milk, cheese and butter, but there was one thing still missing. A flower garden was not an essential for survival, and Molloy had no time to spare for growing ornamentals when there was building and ploughing and reaping to be done. But he had thought ahead and the space between the house and the river was allocated for his wife's garden. That first evening, after dinner, Georgiana unwrapped the plants she had unearthed so carefully four days earlier in Augusta and planted them at Fairlawn.

> My poor plants – torn from their native soil – they seemed to participate in the feelings of their mistress and had evidently met with some terrible reverse.[496]

On Saturday, 11 May, Georgiana began unpacking and wrote in her diary that she found everything at Fairlawn 'wonderfully comfortable' but the next three words are revealing: 'considering all things'. Clearly, a woman's touch was needed around the house.

Life returned to normal the next day; she did the washing. Five days later, Captain Molloy set out for Perth so, once again, Georgiana took on full responsibility for all his official duties, the home, the children and the farm. She churned milk, made butter and baked, drew off wine, weighed out groceries and dealt with escaped bullocks.[497] Little had changed for her, apart from the view.

Just across the Vasse River at Cattle Chosen, John Bussell had recently returned from England as a married man. On 24 June, he and his new wife, Charlotte, and her three children from a previous marriage, 'the Cookworthys', were invited to tea with Mrs Molloy who had still not found a moment to begin laying out the flower garden. Georgiana sent a boat across the river to collect her neighbours and waited on the bank to greet them with the baby, Amelia, in her arms. Like so many others, the new Mrs John Bussell was struck by her ladylike behaviour.

... her complexion was very fair, and she had a quantity of fair hair, she was dressed in a dark blue print, very plainly made. We walked up to the house together. In the parlour was a bright fire. Tea was ready and on the table was a beautiful bunch of wild flowers – for her garden was not in order, and she could not bear to be without flowers in her room. The little girls were seated on each side of the fire on low seats, there was a small piano in the room on which Mrs. Molloy played when tea was over, and we spent a pleasant evening.[498]

Two months later, on 9 July after a fine washing day, Georgiana began gardening for the first time at Fairlawn. She had so little time to herself that the journal pages stayed empty for weeks and John Molloy could only manage to record that he read Divine Service each Sunday. On 30 September, he set out for Augusta. As he walked away down the track, a carpenter called Bletchington was building Georgiana's verandah; a place for her to sit in the shade during the coming summer. She was about to begin collecting again and would soon discover a profusion of native plants she had never seen before as spring bloomed along the Vasse.

Molloy had just returned to Fairlawn when Tom and George Turner arrived from Augusta with news that Richard West, one of their father's men, had killed a Noongar man called Dundap. The incident had started in the same way as so many others over the previous nine years: potatoes were taken from Mr Turner's garden. Aboriginal guides helped locate the suspects, who denied the accusations. They said others were responsible, but Dundap and the two other men were identified as having been in Augusta on the right day. Richard West, John Herring, James Turner and John Salkilld held the men in Turner's house and took turns to guard them.[499] All three prisoners tried to escape several times despite the fact they had been warned they would be fired on if they tried to get away. As they ran off yet again, West fired his gun. Dundap's companions caught him as he fell and died.

It was an exhausting time. Molloy was coming and going almost weekly between the Vasse, Augusta and Perth while the prisoners were detained at Fairlawn for several weeks and the Molloys expected a visit from John Hutt, the new governor. Georgiana and the children were unwell but she was planning her botanical project until, on 12 October, there was 'surprising news' from a visiting soldier: her sister Mary had arrived in Western Australia on the *Shepherd* on 18 September.[500]

On 25 October the two remaining prisoners were taken to the Vasse gaol, a small stone building in the grounds of Fairlawn, for trial.[501] Molloy and John Bussell recorded evidence given by Herring the constable, West and Salkilld. Captain Molloy sent their depositions to the colonial secretary with his conclusions after cross-examining the prisoners and considering the evidence available. His verdict was that the accused were innocent, deliberately implicated by statements from the guilty men. He told the colonial secretary there was 'nothing cast up to throw further light on the affair'.[502]

Then he went straight to Leschenault to find news of Mary and a few days later, when Governor Hutt called at Fairlawn on 9 November, he brought with him the letter from Mrs Kennedy that told Georgiana too late that Mary was on her way. Stress is a modern concept, but Georgiana was under daily pressure that her counterparts making lace in the drawing rooms of English country mansions could not have imagined. Her new home did not have a bed for her sister to sleep in. She carried on churning butter and doing the washing. When she hurt her leg, Molloy took over the cooking. There was hardly any time to prepare for their guest's arrival and the future was on Georgiana's mind for another reason. She was expecting a baby.

Mrs Kennedy's letter was written in Scotland, where she was staying with Dalton on the Craig estate although he still was not the legal landowner. Without taking advice, Dalton had gone for a quick-fix financial arrangement to clear his latest debts. In 1839 Georgiana was the only one of the Kennedy children who had not brought public shame into her mother's life, but time and distance had not softened Mrs Kennedy's heart. Dalton and Mary were both living on money their mother sent them and neither had a home of their own. Mrs Kennedy's letter claimed that she was 'desolate and deserted', and its message was loud and clear.

As always, she expected Georgiana to manage as an independent adult with a husband who, in her mother's opinion, should have ensured her financial comfort. Mrs Kennedy's personal letter to John Molloy gushingly expressed her affection for him but between the lines there was a sharpness. Her real opinions rise closer to the surface with each line and the sting is in the tail. She made sure it was quite clear to him: if he had married the mother and not the daughter, he would have been a wealthy man and his wife would not be churning butter.

> My dear Son[503]
> Your letter followed me here and I hasten to answer it – It would have afforded me the greatest <u>happiness</u> I now can feel could I have been any use to you. (I use the word Happiness because it is a strong term and to show you the inclination is not wanting)
> ...
> Mrs John Forsters [sic] House in castle Street was sold the other day for £5,500 – it is not as good a house as mine so that if you are as fortunate, it will leave a <u>very</u> handsome sum after the debt which is upon it is paid – I feel your kindness in wishing me to be near you, but I am too much worn out not with age but with afflictions to be able to undertake such a voyage – could I ever anticipate the pleasure of beholding you both and my dear grandchildren in England I then might be made a happy Grandmama, but as to my coming to you it is out of the question – What do you intend to do about the education of your children – will you not be sending them to school – I am exceedingly uneasy about dear Georgy's bad recovery after her last accouchement, and must desire if you have not written already that

you will lose no time in doing so for she is never out of my mind – I wish you had called the little one Elizabeth Dalton Molloy – you have not paid me the compliment of naming any after me[504] – I cannot make an apology to Philips for you not writing, because <u>such a letter</u> would admit of no apology and excuse me for saying seems not only rude but most slighting on your part.

...

I am now left alone in this world, with none but strangers to close my eyes, it is a desolate state to be in after all the children I have brought into the world, but I leave my blessing with you and yours and pray for you daily – Continue then to believe me
Your affectionate Mother
E. Kennedy

P.S. as to wanting a servant to churn butter – that is easily put right – your dear wife will now be sufficiently acquainted with that act so as to be able to teach the most expert.

I should indeed be thankful to accept your kind offer of a home with you desolate and deserted as I now feel, but it is not at all likely. –

Tell Georgy her bad eyesight is owing to her nursing her children too long, it always affects the sight.

In May, 1836, Mrs Kennedy had moved in with her son George and his wife in Exeter, Devon. Still in need of money, she had remortgaged Crosby for £200 that June.[505] After years of being rented and receiving only the most basic maintenance, the house was in a 'ruinous state, with more rats than any of her tenants could bear and cows grazing in the garden because the fences had collapsed.'[506] Prospective tenants were asking for repairs before they would sign a lease. She was still employing William Morley as her land agent but it was becoming a charade; she did not have enough money to pay for maintenance. She was renting a house herself and wrote to her landlord asking him to give her more time to pay what was due.

Left with no other options, she instructed Morley to put Crosby and its estate up for sale, hoping to sell for £9000. George Saul, a local landowner and solicitor, negotiated a much lower price for a client and, in March 1837, Thomas Irwin, a merchant from Liverpool, became the new owner. Mrs Kennedy's tenant moved out, her last few pieces of furniture and some paintings of very little value were carted off and sold, and Morley pointed out that she no longer had any work for him to do.[507] After 300 years, her family connection with Crosby was over. In her youth she was described as an heiress and four of her children held expectations throughout their lives, but it was a struggle for her to meet their financial demands. Years later, when Mary was a married woman herself, she was still asking for handouts and complaining: 'When I look back to Crosby Lodge days I wonder where all the money can be gone for ever since we left it we have never lived in any thing [sic] like style.'[508]

The last two properties that Mrs Kennedy owned were tucked into a corner of a desirable neighbourhood at the quiet end of Abbey Street and, in 1838, she was receiving rent for the mansion house from Eleanor Carlyle, the main beneficiary in the will of Mrs Lodge, who had rented the house before her.[509,510] She badly needed the money so her letter to John Molloy about the building's value seems more like financial boasting than a genuine concern for Georgiana's inheritance. It is also a reminder that Mrs Kennedy's maternal concern remained focused on her other children, whatever their behaviour. Georgiana's sin was her emotional independence, and it was never forgiven.

There was not much time to create a room suitable for a spoilt young lady from Cheltenham, one of the most fashionable and up-market towns in England. A building boom there in the 1830s resulted in stylish new houses, elegant streets and shops selling the latest expensive designer items. At Fairlawn, the carpenter made shutters as extra protection for the calico stretched over glassless windows and he built a floor in the guest bedroom. Working as quickly as possible, he made a bedstead, then a dressing table and washstand.

In the middle of all the commotion, little grey-eyed Amelia began talking for the first time.

Mary made the long voyage 'in the care of Captain Jardine' then travelled south from Perth on the government ship, the *Champion*, and arrived in Geographe Bay on 9 December.[511] She was not the only visitor for Christmas. On 14 December 'Mr Price the naturalist' arrived, keen for company on flora walks in the area.[512] Johann Ludwig Preiss was a botanist and zoologist who created a collection of 200,000 Western Australian plant specimens, often paying high prices for them. He stayed at Fairlawn for a month, enjoyed being guided to the best local places to find specimens and borrowed Jack the pony to go collecting further afield. Sabina thought he was 'a queer old fellow' and she could not understand why he was so obsessed with plants that she and the other children thought of as weeds.[513] He made kind promises to Georgiana, saying he would send her seeds and information, but left the colony without contacting her again.

When Molloy set out on an overnight kangaroo hunt on the twenty-sixth, adapting the British habit of fox hunting on Boxing Day, the management of the household, its guests and Christmas festivities fell on Georgiana's shoulders. Mary Kennedy was not much help and made a fuss about the weakness of her right arm, which was smaller than the left.[514] Despite this, Georgiana generously exaggerated her sister's contributions in a letter to their mother ten months later as Mary was packing her bags: 'She has saved me a female servant and has done all the ironing and for the greater part of her stay here the washing, besides taking my place in the Dining room'.[515] Sabina's descriptions of her aunt are revealing, her memories those of a clever child who overheard adult conversations.

> [Aunt Mary Kennedy] had been spoilt. She disliked the life & was little help to us, she could not even nurse the baby as her arm was weak, the result of a fall when a child from the arms of her nurse, which resulted in a slight curvature of the spine & a stiff arm.[516]

When the *Champion* arrived in Geographe Bay it also carried something that Georgiana had been longing for: a reply from Captain Mangles. As well as sending more *horti sicci* and the botanical materials she would need for her work, he had responded thoughtfully to all her requests and read between the lines as well, sending food for the mind and the imagination to enrich his correspondent and her children, too. There was a box of 'useful, beautiful and handsome' gifts, including some well-chosen books and a more personalised present, an inscribed copy of his published book of travels.[517] Three years had passed since his previous letter arrived and almost a year since her first collection of specimens had been dispatched.

It was the end of January before Georgiana found time to write and thank him. Her gratitude for his presents was enthusiastic. 'Words fail me,' she wrote, but she was probably unaware how much he would benefit financially and professionally from the treasures she had sent him. Her list of requests was growing more specific as she grew in botanical expertise, and she felt more confident about asking for the materials that would help her do the work he had requested. She wanted 'seed papers folded and ready' like the ones that had arrived with Mangles's first box, and 'little Paper Bags' to save her some time in searching for precious paper and folding it. She also suggested that he might send different coloured paper to 'increase the effects of some Plants if in the next *Hortus Siccus* ... especially for Grasses, leaves, and White flowers'.

> The children have had a Week's holiday and so have I, although I have necessarily been very assiduous, always working from after Breakfast till 12, and ½ after 12 at night. This seems incredible, but I had first to fix the specimens, to arrange, then paste on labels to that forbidding old Log Book, – which looks anything but neat and clean; then write attempts on character and make the Bags and cases ...[518]

Dr Lindley had requested the seeds of a specific species growing in Augusta and Georgiana told Mangles that Charlotte Heppingstone had collected them. Charlotte had become interested in plants from growing up as a servant in the Molloy home and had 'imbibed a taste and some information respecting them'. She helped with the 1837 collection for Mangles and knew all the names. Georgiana was sad to miss the chance of a ride down to Augusta, but household duties kept her at Fairlawn.

> I would with all my heart have rode over myself for them, and really have liked nothing better, as being in the Bush is to me one of the most delightful states of existence, free from every household care, my husband and children, all I possess on Earth, about me.

The Western Australian bush had taken hold of Georgiana. After the rugged coast of Cumberland, the lush riverbanks of Warwickshire and heathered mountains of Scotland, each different and unique, she had found a place that transformed itself from one landscape into another within the space of a few paces. On a summer day under white-hot sky she could turn the corner of a kangaroo path through shoulder-high melaleuca thicket ticking with cicadas, and find herself instantly cool in shady peppermint woodland noisy with birdsong. After a summer storm, dry brown skirts of grass trees were transfigured and drenched with diamond drops, parched air was suddenly weighted with sharp eucalyptus perfume and trunks of jarrah trees steamed on one side where the sun hit them. Searches took her from profusion, the vivid bee-loud drops of red-gum flowers, to the secret perfection of tiny, rare orchids. Whether she went on foot or on horseback, each expedition was an addictive blend of familiar and unexpected pleasures, a sensory indulgence that sometimes left her breathless with delight.

> ... we came on an open plain of many acres in extent, scarcely a tree on it, and those that grew, large and fine. I discovered a plant I have

been almost panting for. A very small, neat, white blossom, on a furze looking bush, we found a great quantity of it.[519]

Georgiana found the words to convey her feelings about the professional intimacy she felt with Mangles, a man she would never meet. The few letters he wrote to her have not survived, but they must have given her good reason to believe that they shared a mutual passion for plants and flowers. The distance between them was yet another frustration she had to bear. Surprisingly, she thought of it not as God's will but the work of a playful Fate, preventing her from meeting Mangles while at the same time connecting her with someone 'so instrumental in bestowing kindness and gratification at so remote a part of the Globe'.

> Our Acquaintance is both singular and tantalizing, and somewhat melancholy to me, my dear Sir, to reflect on. We shall never meet in this life. We may mutually smooth and cheer the rugged path of this World's Existence, even in its brightest condition, by strewing Flowers in our Way, but we never can converse with each other, and I am sincere when I say, I never met with any one [sic] who so perfectly called forth and could sympathize with me in my prevailing passion for Flowers. I doubt not you are an admirer of Scenery, for I generally find the two sentiments inseparable.

As quickly as possible, and trying not to disrupt the hospitality her guests expected, Georgiana collected as many specimens as she could from the varieties that were new to her at the Vasse and added them to the plants from Augusta. At the end of January, Captain Cole's whaling ship, the *America*, had been in Geographe Bay for more than a week and was due to sail for New England. It was too good a chance for her to miss and she frantically gathered the last few items for the *hortus siccus*. On 2 February, she and John Molloy went out to collect the Isopogon seeds Mangles had asked for but their horses bolted and by the time they were found it was too late. Georgiana treated Mangles to her sense of humour again.

> Last Thursday the America, Captn. Cole, arrived in the Bay, having (to use a technical term) 'filled up'!!! She proceeds instantly to America, and I am anxious to send what I have been able of Plants and seeds to obtain for you.

She wrote quickly, 'I must concentrate my subjects, as I have much to say and a short space to write in.'[520] If the box could be forwarded from New York to London, it could arrive sooner than if she waited for a direct shipment from Fremantle. Molloy had sold Captain Cole a steer and Cole was pleased enough to agree to the plan. On 4 February, Georgiana's second collection began its long journey to London via the Atlantic Ocean. It contained her long letter to Mangles and 106 specimens, each numbered and matched to her own collection so she could communicate easily with him about individual items. Her notes show that she believed forty of them to be new species. Among them was the *Acacia extensa*, the Wiry wattle she had gathered in her first spring at Fairlawn. It grows only in the southwest of Western Australia.

***

In 2005, Dr Alexander George from the Western Australian Herbarium was the botanical liaison officer at the Herbarium of the Royal Botanic Gardens in Kew and he kindly arranged for us to see some of Georgiana's specimens. Kew undertakes world-class scientific research but many of the old collections are housed in a building that has changed little since 1877. The original ornate handrails decorate galleries that run around all four walls on two storeys and old wooden cabinets stand row upon row, each one containing simple manila folders of dried specimens.

Acacia extensa, **Herbarium of the Royal Botanic Gardens, Kew**

Collector: Mrs Molloy; Specimen: K000356617 Photograph © Mike Rumble

The first folder he showed us contained the same acacia that Georgiana had finally sent to Mangles in the Australian summer of 1840. She had picked a stem and flower of the brightly blooming yellow wattle on the Vasse plains in spring then dried, mounted and shipped it a few weeks later. The specimen's journey has been far longer than the ocean voyage, and its story goes on through the decades after Mangles received it. He sent it with many others to Professor Lindley at University College in London and it became part of Lindley's own large herbarium. Lindley's close friend, the botanist George Bentham, was deeply interested in the flora of Australia and he acquired many of Lindley's specimens. Georgiana's *Acacia extensa*, along with others she had sent Mangles from Augusta and the Vasse, became part of the collection George Bentham took with him when he agreed to work at Kew Herbarium in 1854.

The flowers had faded to a pale, dusty orange and the leaves had dried to dull grey but the acacia was still as perfectly arranged and complete as when Mangles received it. Mike suddenly decided to be bold and asked whether I might be allowed to touch the specimen. As the camera lens clicked I placed my hand gently where Georgiana's hand must have held the same delicate stem when she positioned the leaves and flowers for best effect.[521]

* * *

There were always visitors at Fairlawn and through the summer of 1840 Georgiana provided afternoon tea for neighbours or dinner and an overnight bed for visiting whaleboat captains. In spite of the heat and her advancing pregnancy, she collected for Mangles and filled two *horti sicci*. She had designed a large box herself with sliding lids to store and separate specimens that were too big to fit into the pages of a *hortus siccus* and she had it made to what she thought would be the best dimensions, about 910mm by 200mm and 150mm deep. It would be an expensive package to ship and even though Mangles had told her he was not concerned about cost, she was determined to make the contents of the box worth their weight in botanical value. When there was a moment of peace, she sat in the shade of her verandah and read the expensive books he had sent her. Although they were full of new gardening ideas and information about the European and Australian plants she was growing there was a stark contrast between the expectations of lady gardeners in England and her own situation. The precious books included titles she had been longing to read, including *The Greenhouse*, but many of the techniques and resources that British gardening books described were beyond her reach and her finances. She had learned to be resourceful and used perforated raisin trays to sow seeds and planted decorative flowers in any available container, including a broken teapot. Her new purchases had to be as practical as possible and although she had the space and inclination for a greenhouse at Fairlawn, glass certainly was not an affordable option.

> The Greenhouse
> For cottage or villa residence, no species of greenhouse, so far as convenience is concerned, has more advantages than a structure in the verandah fashion, that is, a covered projection, having a glazed front, and the roof wholly or in part of the same material.[522]

As Georgiana increased the momentum of her collecting in Australia, her first collection from 'Port Augusta', shipped in late 1838, was causing a stir among the botanists, collectors and gardeners in Mangles's wide, influential circle. His brother Robert wrote to say that Queen Victoria had politely declined his offer of plants from the Swan River 'having made a rule not to receive presents', but others were eager to get their hands on the latest arrivals.[523] In July 1839, Captain Mangles listed the names of the lucky few who received the seeds: Joseph Paxton at Chatsworth, the famous Baumann brothers of Bollwiller in France ('one of the finest nursery collections on the continent'), Loddiges ('a perfect set'), the Royal Horticultural Society, Knights of Chelsea, Brown of Slough, Hastings of Regents Park in London, Charlotte Marryatt of Wimbledon, and Mr Long the head gardener at the Zoological Society.[524] Lindley was one of the first to send his thanks.

> Your friend Mrs Molloy is really the most charming personage in all South Australia & you the most fortunate man to have such a correspondent.
> That many of her plants are beautiful you can see for yourself & I am delighted to add that many of the best are quite new. I have marked many with a X.[525]

By 1839, Joseph Paxton had been promoted from head gardener and was manager to all Her Royal Highness's estates. He grew on his share of the Augusta seeds at Chatsworth where he was creating one of the finest landscaped gardens of the nineteenth century. Paxton's praise for Georgiana's first offering was fulsome. Her collection was 'collectively, the best and contains more good things than I have before received from that interesting part of the world'. He commented on the unusually high quality of Georgiana's 'important collection of seeds', which were 'far superior to any we have received at Chatsworth', and he mentioned the 'splendid things in the *hortus siccus*' including many new specimens of 'Hovea, Chorizema, Daviesia, Boronia, Epacris and Kennedya' and other new plants. He also pointed out that they should be grateful to Mrs Molloy's small helper. The 'Floral Gem' that the 'infant botanist Sabina Molloy' had watched over and collected was growing well, a 'very beautiful' species of Drosera, a carnivorous sundew. Marked No. 109 in his list, it was a new plant that Mangles was keen to name after its young collector.[526]

Lindley wasted no time in publishing the information he had gathered, first in 1840 as an appendix to *Edwards's Botanical Register*, a highly regarded, illustrated magazine with a wide audience. His *Sketch of the Vegetation of the Swan River Colony* quickly became a reference source in Britain for people wanting to acquire plants from such a 'remarkable country', offering detailed descriptions of new species that European gardeners could select for their visual appeal. The plants that Lindley recommended most enthusiastically and the words he used to convey their attractions give an interesting insight into nineteenth-century views about what was, and was not, considered aesthetically pleasing in the world of horticulture.[527]

Lindley's document drew mainly on plants and seeds sent by James Drummond and Georgiana Molloy, but her name was not included in his main list of acknowledgements: James and Robert Mangles, Drummond, Andrew Toward (gardener to Her Royal Highness the Duchess of Gloucester) and Nathaniel Ward, a doctor and collector who invented a small portable greenhouse that was used widely for transporting plants on long sea journeys.[528]

A new botanical name that first appeared in Lindley's *Sketch* was *Adenanthos barbiger*, the hairy jugflower, and in his own herbarium there are two specimens presented together, one from James Drummond and one from 'Mrs Capt. Molloy, 1839'. John Molloy never worked at botany as tirelessly and enthusiastically as his wife, but he did collect what became a type specimen, the original example on which the description of a new species is based, and Drummond recorded the evidence. When Molloy returned to Augusta from the Vasse after an expedition in 1837 he brought the plant with him, one of the heaths that grow there today. Georgiana sent what would be named *Adenanthos barbiger* to Mangles in 1838 and he forwarded it to Lindley, where it joined a thousand other specimens in the personal herbarium the professor used for research.

When Georgiana wrote her next letter to Mangles, her husband was collecting for her and knew enough about what was special or interesting to recognise anything new. In early March 1840, Molloy brought back from Augusta a selection of specimens to go into the *hortus siccus* including one 'magnificent' plant that Georgiana had never seen before. He noticed the *Xylomelum occidentale*, now commonly called Woody pear, during the walk down to Augusta and learned its Noongar name, Danja. He put a cutting under a stone to dry it out and collected it on the walk back to Fairlawn. Georgiana also told Mangles about riding out with her 'excellent husband' to collect Isopogon seeds. They gathered a full bag on 12 February 1840, dated by Mangles in the 'Vasse collection'. Whether it was John Molloy's passion to collect new floral specimens or to make his wife happy, or both, his contributions were sometimes significant.

As the weather cooled Georgiana began another letter to Mangles. Her writing reflects the pleasure she was finding in discovering so many native plants that were new to her at the Vasse, and the flat, park-like landscape made it much easier for her to travel further from home when she went out collecting on foot or on horseback. It was as if she hardly knew where to look first.

> March 14th and April 15th
> I found in bloom a bright red species of 'Verticordia' with such rich tufts of flowers. These I carefully affixed for you, a pretty yellow plant of the same class, I imagine, and several others for which I await Mr Preiss's judgement. These were in a swamp.
>
> Molloy has just brought me in such a beautiful yellow pea flower. I long to send you a twig. It is the first flower I have seen for three months.[529]

She was still mixing native plants with the introduced species that Mangles sent her and had started using planting as a central theme to the changes she made at Fairlawn:

> Are there any other Maurandias than the Barclayana? Will you send me some seed of the 'Nemophila insignis'? I am anxious for creeping plants, as I have just had a small cottage built for myself and I shall make the verandah into a sort of conservatory.

Lindley's 1839 *Sketch* included a description and illustration of the beautiful and mysterious *Nuytsia floribunda* and his notes show that he, at least, already knew that this species had parasitic qualities. It needed the roots of a host plant to survive but that was not widely known; the gardeners of Britain were trying unsuccessfully to grow a specimen from seed and matters were made more difficult by the fact that the seeds were very difficult to obtain. Mangles listed *Nuytsia floribunda* and the stately *Kingia australis* as his two 'desiderata' from Swan River in his *Floral Calendar* of 1839. *Kingia australis* was 'a subtle plant indeed' according to Paxton, and a treasure that the Duke of Devonshire was keen to have on display in his great conservatory. 'His Grace was most anxious to know more of the Kingia than I could inform him, if you happen to know much about it', he wrote to Mangles.[530]

Since Christmas Georgiana had been watching and marking the flowering Nuytsia trees, glowing orange-yellow like burning beacons on the Vasse plains. In March the new season's elusive offerings were ready to gather.

> The seeds of Kingia and Nuytsia you shall have. This is their precise time of ripening and the last named grows here in great abundance, and splendid it is. It looks so rich among all the sombre Eucalyptus of the present season.
>
> It presents to my mind the rich and luxurious trees which adorn paradise.[531]

But her baby was due in a few weeks and the physical exertion of daily treks to protect, check and gather the seeds at the hottest time of year was beyond her. Perhaps her yearning for the botanical pleasures she was missing is reflected in the name of the daughter, Flora Elizabeth, who was born on 8 May 1840 with blue eyes the colour of violets.[532] At first it seemed Georgiana would get over the usual complication, but in the first week of June her condition deteriorated after a haemorrhage and she was confined to bed. Mary Kennedy and Fanny Bussell tried to make her comfortable and cool her fever but they all recognised a serious, life-threatening infection. This time her recovery took much longer than ever before. As Georgiana lay helpless during her 'dangerous illness', she knew that rain was returning and the bush was flowering again. Her distress was so great that she sometimes cried out, longing to get back to her collection for Mangles. Two weeks later, when she was able to sit up, she wrote to him: 'In all my illness and real suffering I did not forget you. As Spring approached I lamented not being able to gather the flowers as they came out.'[533]

By the middle of June and still not well enough to go out collecting at a critical time of year, she gave six-year-old Mary and two-year-old Amelia the task of bringing home the early flowers they found during their rambles. The little girls did well and came home with

> a very dwarf species of Drosera just like No. 110 only white instead of orange and a powerful scent resembling the snow drop positively no delusion no association but *bona fide* resembling Britain's earliest tribute of Spring.

John Molloy helped too, and returned from a kangaroo hunt with 'a bouquet of beautiful scarlet flowers'. Georgiana decided that she would go out to mark them for seed collection and send the dried flowers but only, she told Mangles, 'please God if I ever get about again'. Another full recovery was not something she could assume, especially in a climate she did not think 'as healthy as Augusta', but she was optimistic that plenty of kangaroo soup, wine and porter (dark beer) would help. Another letter from Mangles arrived with perfect timing on 20 June, followed later by boxes of useful, thoughtful gifts.

Although one of the boxes was badly damaged by sea water from being landed during a heavy storm, most of its contents were still intact and Georgiana set about drying them and cleaning off the sand. Mangles had sent cuttings of plants and fruit trees, packets of seeds and botanical items for Georgiana, a mouth organ for the children and a telescope for Molloy. There were also books and periodicals, including a Shakespeare anthology. These were precious things that were difficult and expensive for Georgiana to acquire but there was one book that held a very personal surprise: a copy of *Edwards's Botanical Register* for 1839, containing Lindley's 'Sketch of the Vegetation of the Swan River Colony', and she read it immediately. In the notices of new plants, she was named three times as a collector.

Mrs Molloy, described by Lindley as 'a lady enthusiastically attached to the Botany of this remote region' and 'a lady enthusiastically fond of flowers' was cited as the collector of *Pultanaea brachytropis*, a 'pretty little greenhouse shrub from Port Augusta'; *Euthales macrophylla*, 'a greenhouse perennial of the easiest culture'; and *Eucalyptus calophylla*, 'a beautiful plant'. More significantly, the professor wrote that her 'zeal in the pursuit of Botany has brought us acquainted with many of the plants of that little known part of the world'. When she read that he considered himself and his readers 'indebted' to her for so many acquisitions, she was overwhelmed. But she was not the only collector celebrating at Fairlawn that day; 'Mr Molloy' was recognised for his own contribution, *Boronia dichotoma*, a tall pink boronia with a strong fragrance, found on the banks of a 'beautiful turn of the River Vasse'.

Two days after the book arrived, Georgiana added more to her letter to Mangles.

> 8th July 1840
> The notices of the Swan River 'Floral Botanical Register' has quite inflamed my ardour; and instigated me to greater exertion, to think how small an aid I have lent to your cause.[534]

When she packed the first collection in 1838 her objective was only to do the job as well as she could and to be of service, but her expertise and attention to detail had gone far beyond that and it was not long before her name was appearing in other botanical publications. That same year, Mrs Molloy's *Babingtonia camphorosmae*, *Eucalyptus calophylla*, and *Pultenaea brachytropis* appeared in *The Floriculture Magazine and Miscellany of Gardening*.[535] In 1841, her *Euthales macrophylla* was described in the 'new and rare plants' section of *The Floricultural Cabinet and Florists' Magazine*.[536] These were books and magazines that were read by gardeners, horticulturalists, landowners, dukes and duchesses as well as some of the most eminent men in the scientific world – and probably by her mother too. Georgiana started out as an amateur botanist in the original meaning of that word, a 'lover' of her topic, but from her very first endeavours she was receiving recognition for her work and knew that her name was recorded in the world of botany.

She had a natural ability in using words to convey her most extreme emotions, choosing and placing phrases with a powerful simplicity that still draws readers to her letters. Although she was only collecting for Mangles during seven years of her life, her writing sharply reflects the relationship she felt with the bush, the place where she always felt most at peace and most at home.

> We have but very few flowers until Spring. September and October are most delightful months. The purple creeper begins to bloom in July, the red in August, but in those two months the Wilderness indeed 'begins to blossom as a Rose'. The stiff and inelegant grass plant even is decked in borrowed colours, from the purple and red creepers, and white Clematis (or Kennedia, I believe) the former appellation I gave it in ignorance of the proper one where the bush has receded and left an even surface of grass and weeds appears the 'enamelled carpet' of which we so often read.[537]

Her writing consistently reveals her as a woman who was strikingly ahead of her time, yet also as a woman archetypical *of* her time. Georgiana's intense personal, intellectual and sometimes spiritual relationship with the natural environment chimes in perfect harmony with the 'still, sad music of humanity' heard clearly by the poets of the Romantic Movement in the presence of nature and described so vividly by William Wordsworth in one of his most well-known poems.

> The Clouds that gather round the setting sun
> Do take a sober colouring from the eye
> That hath kept watch o'er man's mortality;
> Another race hath been, and other palms are won.
> Thanks to the human heart by which we live,
> Thanks to its tenderness, its joys, and fears,
> To me the meanest flower that blows can give
> Thoughts that do often lie too deep for tears.
>
> 'Ode: Intimations of Immortality' 1804[538]

By the end of July Georgiana had received another letter from Mangles and her new collection was ready, packed in a box made to her order by John Molloy, but there was no way of sending it. The bush was in bloom and she had time to walk or ride out with her children to collect for Mangles, even though it was still a physical challenge for her. She suffered headaches from stooping and she restricted her seed-hunting to the afternoons, binding her temples to relieve the 'excruciating' pain from such 'necessary exertion of mind and body'. Writing to Mangles again between August and October as her sister Mary was making plans to leave the colony, Georgiana recounted details of many 'excursions', riding with Molloy across swollen streams on her horse, Kate, exploring further and further afield on foot with Aboriginal helpers and often walking with her daughters. On 29 September she found an *Acacia incurva* and collected a specimen. That same low shrub was captured for history in the pages of the *London Journal of Botany* in 1842: '357 *Acacia incurva*. The Vasse River WA, Mrs Molloy. Field label attached, presumably written by Mrs Molloy, dated 29 Sept 1840.'

Although her husband and sister laughed gently at her 'all engrossing theme' Georgiana was writing with new confidence. She referred to Dr Lindley's request for more seeds as if a direct appeal from one of the most famous botanists of the time was no longer daunting, and the correct botanical names for plants flowed from her pen with almost musical assurance. She had been changed physically by the hunger and hard labour of the early years in the colony, but there was another change. For a few years at Fairlawn her mind and spirit found the balance she had dreamed of.

> Today I have been employed in your service. After breakfast the children and I went in search of flowers: it has been a beautiful day and I have not been for so long a walk for months.
>
> We went on a very nice ride a few days back in a South Easterly direction following a small tributary stream to the Vasse, the banks were thickly studded with Banksia acacia and She-oak, the ground was adorned with crimson flowers of Kennedia, but not so profusely as it will be in a week or two hence.[539]

The seeds of *Nuytsia floribunda* and *Kingia australis* were on her mind, and late one afternoon on her way home from exploring an area that was new to her, she found exactly what she was looking for.

> As the shades of night were commencing we reluctantly turned homewards when other 'Agréments' met my eye — what! But a grove of Nuytsia floribunda. I thought myself really blessed that these desiderata should place themselves before me. You will think I am romancing when I tell you that, out of the Nuytsia Swamps, we came upon one as thickly and universally covered with 'Kingia'. If I understand rightly what Kingia is — the grass plant with many short heads branching out. Whereas the 'Xanthorrea hostile' are very tall and upright. These four things had occupied my mind many a long day, and I was quite exhilarated at finding these treasures so unexpectedly. Before I was working blindfold.

Noongar men and women who worked at Fairlawn often helped Georgiana with her collecting. She knew there were cultural differences between European and Aboriginal views about flowers and was appreciative of the concessions made on her behalf around the home and on expeditions into the bush. Still not fully recovered from her illness, she received a surprise, a small bunch of wildflowers 'from a Native who was aware of my floral passion'.[540] Georgiana knew that traditional views meant her Noongar companions felt differently about the ways the settlers used cut flowers. There were never problems when Aboriginal women walked out with her to gather plants or collected them on her behalf, but the new settlement at the Vasse was not becoming known for good relationships between the European inhabitants and the traditional owners of the land. In May 1840 the *Perth Gazette* had reported an incident that was the beginning of a shocking series of events in the region.

Henry Campbell was one of the 'orphan emigrants' sent to provide household labour for the colony and the boy had been working as a servant at Port Leschenault, now Bunbury. Accounts of what happened vary and include stories of rape and revenge but whatever the details were, Campbell committed an act that broke Aboriginal law and was speared in May 1840. Henry Bull, the Government Resident of Leschenault, and a party of soldiers quickly caught the three men they suspected of killing Campbell. One was Nugundung, a son-in-law of Gaywal, who had been a suspect in the spearing of Chapman's heifer in 1837 and accused of throwing a spear at Elijah Dawson. On the orders of the governor, Bull punished them 'offhand, in some way' hoping to avoid an even more serious situation, but some people felt that British law had not been properly enforced.[541]

Governor Hutt had different views from Stirling about the best way to ensure peaceful relations between settlers and Aboriginal people. His new policy promoted education and protection of individual rights, and at the same time he began gradually withdrawing detachments of soldiers from small settlements. Farmers like those at the Vasse lost not only military protection but also extra pairs of hands at harvest time. There was a growing view in some homes that those responsible for implementing colonial law were not doing their job properly and the settlers would have to take matters into their own hands if they felt endangered.

At the end of September, a whaling ship arrived from Augusta heading for Perth and then for the Cape of Good Hope and America. A year after arriving at Fairlawn, Mary Kennedy had had more than enough of colonial life and she set sail, but was so seasick that she needed a woman to travel with her and the ship quickly returned to Geographe Bay. On 27 October, with Charlotte Heppingstone as her servant, Mary finally left Australia but she had one other companion on board. As an adult, Sabina remembered the story of her Aunt Mary's scandalous departure.

> Mr Burt [sic] who had come out with Mr. and Mrs. J. Bussell in the *Montreal* wanted to marry her. My parents did not approve he was a weak sort of man apparently incapable of doing much to keep himself much less a wife – so I suppose partly on this account they urged Aunt M's return to England sending Charlotte Heppingstone as her companion. Charlotte married the 1st mate and settled in Honolulu. Mr Burt took his passage in the same ship unknown to my father & Mother.[542]

William Baker, Commander of the *Mentor*, performed the wedding service on board his ship 'off the coast of New Holland' on 14 November. As if in defiance of the Molloys' wishes but presumably to fulfil legal requirements in each port, the couple married again on 18 January 1841 while ashore at the Cape of Good Hope and for a third time on 13 April 1841 in New York.[543,544] William Henry Birt was the son of the Reverend John Birt DD, the vicar of Faversham, and it was Georgiana herself who introduced Henry to her sister. Birt was one of eight siblings and had gone to sea as a youth after his mother left the family and his father fell into despair.[545] He was twenty-one and Mary was thirty-four when they boarded the ship. The young sailor had no savings or regular income; she paid for his ticket back to Britain and told her mother later that she received no money at all from him to keep her after they arrived. It was a marriage destined for failure. Birt went to sea again as quickly as possible and Mary, with nothing to live on but money her mother sent her, lived in one room of a boarding house run by a lady that her husband 'admired'. Her letters to Mrs Kennedy during the following year make miserable reading.

Summer arrived again at the Vasse. In December, John Bussell recognised Nugundung outside Picton Barracks. He issued an arrest warrant and took the prisoner home with him to Cattle Chosen but he had acted in an area under the jurisdiction of George Eliot, the new government resident there, apparently without informing him. Eliot, who was Governor Stirling's nephew, was not pleased. There was an enquiry but Bussell remained adamant that he had behaved correctly and for the best. At the end of December, a judge sent Nugundung to the Aboriginal prison on Rottnest Island for a year.

Occasionally a prisoner was granted leniency for good behaviour but, convicted of the murder of Henry Campbell and the attack on the Dawsons in 1837, Nugundung's chances were slim. Gaywal's understanding was that his son-in-law had already been punished and British law had been satisfied, so unwarranted banishment from country and imprisonment on Wadjemup, a forbidden place, seemed like the ultimate cruelty. Stories soon began to circulate that a white man would be speared if Nugundung was not returned to his home. No change in the sentence was granted.

Georgiana's latest collection and her letter to Mangles were finally sent in December when the government schooner *Champion* arrived again. As 1841 arrived the time drew close again for *Nuytsia floribunda* and *Kingia australis* seeds to set and she was free of house guests for what was left of the summer. The plains, riverbanks and swamps of the Vasse were hers to explore from Fairlawn to Marybrook, the Molloys' estate on the coast, as well as the 'half-mile strip' they owned giving access between the two. She was working on something she felt valued for beyond the kitchen and the dairy. When she was involved in her botanical work, whether collecting in the bush or collating specimens at home, she remembered who she really was.

> When I sally forth either on foot or Horseback, I feel quite elastic in mind and step; I feel I am quite at my own work, the real cause that enticed me out to Swan River.[546]

What Georgiana did not know was that she was collecting in a region that is unique in its geological formation, an 'old, climatically buffered, infertile landscape' (OCBIL) that acted as a refuge for plant diversity during periods of climate change. She had the good fortune to be searching for plants in what today is recognised as the Southwest Australian Biodiversity Hotspot.[547] The remarkable range of species she found was a source of fascination and the tiny delicacy of the native flowers no longer seemed like a drawback to their beauty. As she became more knowledgeable, the search for new indigenous varieties was an obsession and a delight, but her sense of home was not fulfilled at Fairlawn. Its narrow river was never more than 'a very small, sluggish stream' in the dry season and the park-like views were too flat.[548] Her senses called out for the ocean breezes, wooded hills and open water of Augusta, Roseneath and Cumberland.

In January 1841, James Drummond, no longer the government naturalist but still a prolific collector, received news from Sir William Hooker of Kew Gardens. The seeds that Drummond had sent him from Western Australia had been well received in Britain and the huge success of the colony's 'many valuable specimens' was reported in the newspapers. The commercial and botanical value of the wild plants around Fairlawn was soaring, but Georgiana's mind was on something else.

The American captain of a whaler on its way west along the coast invited the Molloys to join him on the *Napoleon* for the journey as far as Meelup. Captain William Plaskett anchored in Castle Bay and his guests spent three days there. They walked the bush, climbed the steep, craggy valley and watched night fall over the Indian ocean. Georgiana gathered plants and seeds in the bush that grew right down to the beach, including 'White kennedia (No. 3, Castle Rock)' and realised that she'd found the place where she wanted to spend the rest of her days.[549] When she heard that Mangles also had a high opinion of the bay, she decided to share her secret with him: 'I am now about to tell you what is known to none but Molloy, Captain Plaskett, the Governor & myself'.

> All the American captains, 5 in number, concurred in declaring its valuable situation, not only in wood and water, but the position, of this I understand nothing, but the beautiful congenial scenery to me is exquisite and so enjoyable in this part of the world, and so pleased was I with this enchanted valley, a ravine of about 100 acres in extent with a rapid stream in winter – then (the first in the new year) dried up that I conjured Molloy, nothing 'en publique' but to apply for it. It would have given us first choice of all supplies, the 1st intelligence [news] and as the vessels proceeded to Geographe Bay, time and leisure to answer all letters, all vessels pass it for the Swan and Leschenault whether or not they put in at the Tub.[550]
>
> The banks of the richest black mould rise abruptly from the ravine, now studded with your choicest greenhouse shrubs, Hoveas, Kennedias, Helichrysum, Macracantha, Thysanotis, White Kennedya, and the tall handsome Blackboy, or grass plant of Augusta. This in the face of the boundless ocean, for in the Bay you cannot perceive anything of Cape Naturaliste.
>
> This dell is confined by high granite rocks, just as it were poised ready to fall, very high and extending up the valley, gradually rising from the beach, until they attain a height of much above 400 feet.

> What a view for a breakfast room! a cottage with a circular verandah entwined in this sheltered spot with choicest fruit.[551]

The Molloys left the whaler at the bay and travelled home on foot, exploring the coastal part of their grant, crossing Toby's Inlet and sleeping in tents for two more nights. Then it was back to business as usual at Fairlawn.[552] The potato crop was ready for harvesting and there was time, at last, to start work on the flower gardens. In her letter to Mangles in February 1841, Georgiana described her next project, a summer garden leading gently down to the riverbank at the back of the house and a carpet of asters planted beneath the peppermints 'according to the Chinese mode', so she could see them from her windows. Before long, her husband was busy laying out flowerbeds 'with geometrical precision', but conditionality was the subtext in all the future plans she shared with Mangles that summer; everything depended on her survival if there was another baby.

She was collecting regularly once a week and had marked the *Nuytsia floribunda* trees when they flowered so she would be ready at just the right moment. When the time was close, she laid cloths underneath them and wrapped the flowers in small bags to catch the seeds as they were ejected, but fires set by Aboriginal people in the area made them ripen more quickly and the task was almost impossible. She was determined not to fail but the trees had to be checked every day and, when she was unable to get away from her work at home, three trusted Noongar helpers went for her, 'much greater auxiliaries than white people in flower and seed hunting'. But there were also unexpected, 'murderous circumstances' that kept Georgiana close to the house that summer.[553]

On 22 February, Gaywal and George Layman had a serious argument at Wonnerup, Layman's home. There are different accounts of the reasons for the fatal encounter and the only written reports to survive are those of the colonists, but whatever first sparked their mutual anger, at some point Layman insulted the Noongar elder publicly and gravely by tugging at his beard. Gaywal speared him and Layman died within a few moments. Others threw spears, in front of many witnesses and a party of settlers, and soldiers set out immediately from Cattle Chosen to arrest Gaywal for murder. This time, John Molloy was with them.

When they found the men they were looking for in a larger group they decided to capture everyone, and in the shooting that followed, the Europeans killed five Wardandi men. The suspects, Gaywal and his sons Woberdung, Kenny and Mungo escaped, but on 6 March a group of colonists and farm workers set out again. John, Alfred and Charles Bussell and Molloy witnessed the death of Gaywal, who was shot by a servant named Kelly while running away.[554]

Rumours spread quickly from one settler household to another at the Vasse. Georgiana wrote to tell her mother that Aboriginal men in the region were threatening to 'kill all the whites' with 'the 3 Bussells named as their first'.[555] Alone in the house with the children, she never went 'from Dining room to kitchen without a pistol'. Georgiana's sister, Mary, had recently returned from Australia and when Mrs Kennedy wrote to her about these events, the new Mrs Birt was already living alone in one room, begging her mother for money and afraid that she had miscarried her first child. Mrs Kennedy wrote bluntly to Mary: 'If you have not miscarried, Mrs Pocklington will be able to lend you patterns & put you in a way to make your own baby cloathes, [sic] much cheaper' and then continued with a comment on the latest news from Georgiana: 'She certainly possesses more energy than any woman I know of'.[556,557] This is the only surviving evidence of any admiration their mother expressed for Georgiana but its timing was thoughtless at the very least.

Captain Molloy had to find a way to catch the remaining suspects, and he needed to do it without more innocent bystanders being killed in the name of British justice. He wanted a solution that would not involve angry settlers carrying guns. By 9 March he had come up with a plan and sent a note to Captain Plaskett, whose ship was still anchored in Geographe Bay.

Brunswick Terrace
Tuesday Morn / July 8
day 31

My dear Mother /

This moment my dear Husband has come in to Breakt & tell me the "sails are bent" & Oh what a hearing for me, he will now leave me in a few days I think it right to let you know this, he has not a moments time since he join'd, from six to six hard at work scarcely breathing let alone eating time when he does come in to breakfast at 8 dine at one & tea at six I am almost worn out with thoughts & preparation I think I shall stay here that that a journey down died for me & to come on ere I reach London in the Mail way Carriage I was jolted to pieces much too fagged to go down

The letters that Georgiana and her sister, Mary, wrote to their mother are very different in both content and appearance.

Letter from Mary Birt née Kennedy to Mrs Kennedy 1841 © Cumbria Archive Centre D KEN 3 / 56 / 61

The next day, Plaskett invited Woberdung, Kenny, Mungo and their companions on board for dinner, saying he would return them to land later to hunt some duck. As Molloy predicted, Gaywal's sons did not suspect that Plaskett knew they were fugitives. They accepted the captain's offer of a meal and by the end of the afternoon all three were prisoners on board the *Napoleon*.

Nine months later, in February 1842, Charles Bussell shot and killed an Aboriginal man who had been seen running away from the flour store. The verdict was 'justifiable homicide'. In March a seven-year-old girl, Cumangoot, was brought to Cattle Chosen by two Noongar men who said they had caught her with a bag of flour. Her tiny feet matched the small footprints left on the floor of the Bussells' flour store but she denied being involved. When an Aboriginal man used 'intimidation' she admitted her guilt but denied that she had had accomplices. Bussell took her into the kitchen and, according to his lawyer, noticed that fear had made her tell the truth. He tried to frighten her into revealing names by aiming a gun at her, clicking the lock a few times, but he thought she had noticed that there was no cap on the gun so he added a cap and fired it. The lead shot passed through her arm and body and she died soon afterwards. John Bussell's wife and daughter were sitting in the room at the time.

During his trial in Perth for manslaughter, Bussell told the jury he had believed the gun was empty of ammunition and did not know his brother Alfred had reloaded it. The court was 'satisfied that it was an accidental occurrence' but felt that it must 'remark on the illegality of attempting to extort confession by intimidation of any sort, which was wholly against the spirit of British law'.[558] The court felt that Charles Bussell's own thoughts when he reflected on 'the fatal outcome of his indiscretion' would be punishment enough and they fined him one shilling.[559]

People were talking about the Vasse and debating how closely the law in action was upholding the justice decreed by the government. They were not the only ones asking questions about the number of innocent people who had been killed while running away from pursuers. The government had had enough of people taking the law into their own hands and claiming self-defence. The Vasse settlers were quick to come to the Bussells' support, but the names of John and Georgiana Molloy are noticeably absent from the long list of signatories to the very public letter in the *Perth Gazette* in May 1842 expressing thanks for 'the liberal, spirited, and persevering manner' with which the Bussells had 'constantly met the aggressions of the natives upon the lives and property of the settlers'.

News about violent conflicts in Australian colonies found its way to Britain, but it was always European voices that conveyed the information and some groups, including the Quakers, recognised the potential for biased viewpoints. In their 1841 'counsel and caution to emigrants to newly-settled colonies' the Religious Society of Friends offered ten 'hints' that could lead to the 'temporal and eternal welfare' of immigrants and the indigenous people. They included the following advice:

> Be very careful that … the natives have the full benefit of equal laws and equal rights with yourselves. Let not this principle be a dead letter, but an operative rule of conduct in all the acts and relations of life.
>
> Let not any say in their hearts, 'I know not these things. I suppose the Government has done all that is right. I cannot search out these matters.' Remember that he who wilfully shuts his eyes, is responsible for what he might see.

So far from the ocean and blocked from a view of the sunsets by its flat terrain and trees, Fairlawn would never replace the little house in Augusta but by the end of 1841 it was a home festooned with flowers, matched or contrasted deliberately by colour, shape and habit. Georgiana had outgrown her desire for an ordered garden in the style of a great house. She designed the plot at Fairlawn to mingle indigenous species with introduced plants for the best effect, and she used them all in an architectural way that would not seem unusual to garden designers today. The planting looked natural and unplanned, but the way the creeping and climbing species tumbled over the ever-growing buildings had been worked out meticulously. Her sitting room off the verandah was almost hidden beneath climbing roses and there was a summerhouse in the middle of the garden, its walls and roof smothered in the *Maurandya barclayana* she was so fond of. The building was still there many years later when the Molloy grandchildren played and enjoyed its shade, picking the lilac, bell-shaped flowers to adorn their hair as their own mothers had done.[560] Georgiana's flower garden was her view from the house to the banks of the river, where she created a safe bathing place with a row of purple fig trees for shade and a lawn of wild thyme that released its delicious fragrance when the family walked over it with wet feet after a swim. There were 'nooks of greenery', shady places under boughs overhanging the river and 'islets of rock' with more plantings on them. A granddaughter's description of her own memories of visits to Fairlawn must also mirror the childhood of Sabina, Mary, Amelia and Flora Molloy: 'In the cool of the evening & sometimes by moonlight we had bathes' and 'We used sometimes to take the little children with us & float them about on wide planks'.[561]

But Georgiana was not going to forget the ocean breeze, hills and open horizon of the place she had set her heart on in the coastal valley at Castle Bay. When she wrote again, she told Mangles they would not be at Fairlawn much longer because its position was far from ideal, and if she had seen it beforehand they would never have built in that place. 'It is so hot in summer, all the labours of Winter in the garden are burnt up.'[562] But the weeks turned into months and what had become the usual way of life continued. The scenes of daily life at Fairlawn would have been nothing less than shocking for the children's grandmother; the Molloy girls went barefoot like the Noongar children who lived among them.[563] Without a household servant or cook, Georgiana and ten-year-old Sabina prepared meals for the family and any guests, served them in the dining room with its bare clay floor and glassless windows, then carried the dirty dishes from the house outside to the kitchen and washed them. It was very unlikely that Mrs Kennedy had ever served a meal to the table or washed a dish in her life. She wrote to Mary and Sabina in January and told them how much she loved them but included a few hard-edged pieces of information obviously intended for their mother. Grandmamma mentioned that she had heard from Captain Mangles who 'seemed displeased that he had never received a Box but one from Australia'. This very old news was designed to unsettle Georgiana and the letter ended with a complaint to make sure it reached its emotional mark, telling the children, 'You ought to write more frequently'.[564] Additionally, the postscript showed Mrs Kennedy's usual lack of tact: 'My own health is wonderful were it not for the troubles of my mind'.

In February 1842, the Reverend John Ramsden Wollaston was a guest at Fairlawn.[565] He had bought land at nearby Picton and was building a small wooden church. The *Nuytsia floribunda* were in flower again and Georgiana could not let any help go to waste, so for a few days he became her riding companion and together they marked the flowering trees in another bid to collect seeds for Captain Mangles. On 11 April she wrote for the last time, disappointed that she had been able to gather so little seed: 'I send you the small, small harvest.'[566] There was other news, too. She was expecting a baby.

As Georgiana prepared herself for what she knew must lay ahead, the Earl of Orkney's gardeners were growing on her seeds in the impressive greenhouses at Taplow House and readers in London were enjoying the January 1842 edition of *The Gardeners' Chronicle*, a 'stamped newspaper of rural economy and general news'. In the notices of new plants, on page 223, they read Mrs Molloy's description of the camphor myrtle, *Camphorwort babingtonia*, she had collected in swampy land at the Vasse River. The lady to whom they were 'indebted for many seeds from the Vasse River' told them that it grew to seven or eight feet in height and in summer formed 'a delightful shade to the traveller crossing the swamps'.

In June 1842, Fairlawn had another important visitor. James Drummond arrived on a botanical expedition to collect 'Swan River' plants and seeds for dispatch to growers in England. The specimens were destined for famous flowerbeds like the ones at the Royal Botanic Gardens, but there were many other enthusiasts eagerly awaiting news about the latest floral discoveries. Drummond published his diary of the Vasse journey to great acclaim. He stayed with the Molloys and their country home featured significantly in the next volume of the *London Journal of Botany* that graced the drawing room tables of high society in London later that year. His descriptions of Georgiana's garden vividly recreate the fragrant profusion of lush climbing plants that weighed down the roof of her verandah, including the same *Maurandya barclayana* that had covered the thatched roof of the house in Augusta, grown from seeds that Mangles sent her. Drummond also described Mrs Molloy's intimate knowledge of the botany of the region and assumed his readers' prior awareness of her growing reputation in Britain.

> You may have heard Capt. Mangles speak of Mrs. Molloy, who has sent him many seeds and specimens of the productions of this country; she has long been ardently attached to Botany, and cultivates plants with great success.[567]

Once again, John Molloy's knowledge of the local flora appeared in print. Molloy took Drummond to see 'a beautiful Convolvulus, growing on his grant of land near Toby's Inlet' and they collected the seeds. Molloy agreed to let Drummond plant *Dasypogon hookeri* and an *Asphodelous* in the garden at Fairlawn and said he would arrange to transport them back to England when they were 'in a state of vegetation'. When Drummond left, he took with him a gift from Georgiana: dried specimens of a new plant.

> By far the finest species of Boronia I have ever observed in Western Australia, grows on the banks of swampy brooks between the Vasse

and Augusta. Captain Molloy informs me he has seen it as high as his head, when riding on horseback. Its foliage is generally pinnated with four pairs of leaflets and an odd one, an inch long; the footstalks and the flowers solitary, large, and of a deep rose colour, springing from the axils of the leaves, on petioles about half an inch in length, each furnished with two minute opposite bracteas. The plant varies, in having its foliage and stems smooth or hairy. Under the belief that this truly beautiful species is new, I have given it the name of Boronia molloyi, after the lady of Capt. Molloy, late of the Rifles and now Government-Resident of the Vasse District.[568]

Perhaps writing in haste and forgetting that he was referring to the lady and not the captain, Drummond made a mistake in naming 'the lovely *Boronia molloyi* by giving it the Latin suffix 'i' for a man's name instead of 'ae' for a woman's. He wrote to William Hooker, recently appointed director of the Royal Botanic Gardens at Kew, and asked for the plant which 'stood as high as a man on horseback' to be named after Georgiana Molloy but two years later another botanist, Friedrich Bartling, described the same plant using the name *Boronia elatior*, which was adopted. More than a hundred years later, Drummond's original request was honoured and his mistake rectified when the plant was renamed *Boronia molloyae*.

In September 1842, Georgiana wrote to her friend Mary Dunlop, now Mrs Stewart Ker, to ask a great favour. Georgiana knew it was unlikely she would survive childbirth again and she had made a decision about what would be best for her children if she died; they would need a mother.

Another daughter, Georgiana, was born on 7 December 1842 and Reverend Wollaston baptised her. Her mother suffered fevers and loss of blood and it took many hours for medical help to arrive. Instead of the best they all might have prayed for, a slow recovery, her condition quickly deteriorated and serious infection left her so weak that she could not leave her bed. In the second week of January 1843, Wollaston rode from Picton again to call on Mrs Molloy and

Georgiana Molloy, née Kennedy (born near Carlisle, Cumberland, England, 23 May 1805; died at the Vasse, Western Australia, 7 April 1843). Married Capt. John Molloy 6 Aug. 1829. Arrived Fremantle, Western Australia, 13 Mar. 1830; settled at Augusta May 1830; moved to the Vasse (near Busselton) May 1839. Collected specimens and seed for James Mangles, England.

J.E. Tonkin ABLO 2006-07, 20th April, 2007

? PARALECTOTYPE

Drosera pallida Lindley
Swan River Append. XX (1839

Although label data indicates Captain James Mangles as the collector, this could not be so as he never collected in Australia. He commissioned others such as Georgiana Molloy and James Drummond to make collections on his behalf. Given the locality is Swan River, it is possible that this was collected by James Drummond (1784-1863), first Government Botanist for the Swan River Distict which now equates to Perth and its surrounds.

J.E. Tonkin, 22nd April, 2007

LECTOTYPE

Drosera pallida Lindley
Swan River Append. XX (1839).
(Selected as lectotype as the other specimen on the sheet is possibly also type material.
1968. N. Marchant & P.D. Sell

© Cambridge University Herbarium

Georgiana's collections included sundews, which are carnivorous plants. This *Drosera pallida* specimen, collected on the Vasse River (Busselton), became part of the personal herbarium of Professor John Lindley and is held today at the Herbarium of Cambridge University.

Pale rainbow (*Drosera pallida*) is not always easy to notice growing in the bush before it flowers, twining secretively up towards the light until its white petals suddenly become evident. The plant in this photograph used a grass tree (*Xanthorrhoea*) for support.

The leaves capture its insect prey by using a sticky enzyme on the ends of the 'tentacles' and allowing the plant to digest the nutrients.

Pale rainbow
(*Drosera pallida*)

© Botanical Museum, Berlin-Dahlem

Opposite is a specimen collected by Georgiana Molloy, now held at the herbarium of the Botanic Garden and Botanical Museum, Berlin-Dahlem. This Pink rainbow (*Drosera menziesii*) shows her usual skill and attention to detail.

Georgiana's Western woody pear (*Xylomelum occidentale*) specimen is in the Herbarium of Cambridge University. It includes unopened buds as well as fully open flowers.

The Western woody pear grew in fragrant groves near the Molloys' home on the Vasse. Georgiana described it as 'a tree of great beauty' and thought the buds (shown here) were even more attractive than the 'full blown' flowers.

The hard, woody, pear-shaped fruits have given this plant its common name.

What Georgiana called the 'native clematis' (*Clematis pubesecens*) was one of the first indigenous plants she used in her own garden. She noticed its vigorous growth and liked the effect of the white flowers mingled with other climbers.

In the winter of 1830, when she must have seen *Hardenbergia comptonia*, the 'native wisteria' flower for the first time, Georgiana thought the local plants were too small to be of much horticultural interest. She was still only just beginning to notice the delicate beauty of Augusta's indigenous flora in 1832 when she described this 'blue vine' in a letter to her sister, Eliza.

White bunny orchid (*Eriochilus dilatatus*)

This dainty orchid was photographed in Augusta in May, the same month the settlers landed there in 1830. It was probably the first local orchid Georgiana saw in flower, usually appearing soon after the first heavy rain of autumn in the southwest.

Tall Boronia *(Boronia molloyae)*. In the nineteenth century it was uncommon, though not unknown, for a species to be named after a woman. Even though botanist James Drummond requested that this plant should be named after her a year before she died, Georgiana did not receive this formal recognition until the 1970s when *Boronia elatior* was renamed *Boronia molloyae* to acknowledge her important contribution as a collector of West Australian plants.

found she had completely lost the use of one leg. He also found that her 'beloved husband', veteran of so many military campaigns and a man of such emotional strength, could not bear to watch his wife suffering. Wollaston was 'deeply concerned for Captain Molloy'.[569]

High summer arrived, the weather turned stormy and there were bushfires around the homestead. Georgiana's discomfort was not just physical. In the first few weeks of 1843, *Nuytsia floribunda* flowered like flames on the Vasse plains. She had planned for months how she would mark the trees, monitor the progress of the flowers and then capture the unpredictable eruption of the precious seeds by tying bags made of cloth around the winged, papery fruits, but she could not walk.

On 15 February a letter from Drummond was published in the Western Australian newspaper, the *Inquirer*. Perhaps his spelling error had already been noticed; publicly identifying John Molloy as the original collector of *Boronia molloyi* would quickly resolve the problem.

> The road from the Vasse to Augusta is a mere footpath, made by the soldiers, two men and a corporal being stationed there; it crosses many swampy valleys with streams of water; some of them, as MacLeod's Creek, the Chapman River, and the Rapids, are of considerable size; the banks of several of these swampy brooks produce one of the most beautiful plants I have ever seen in any country; it belongs to the natural order Rutaceae and the genus Boronia; it occurs in two remarkable forms – the upright hairy, and the smooth drooping: the first grows 8 or 10 feet high, with pennate leaves, and deep rose-coloured or pink flowers; this plant I observed in the valleys to the north of Mount William. Varieties, some of which are snow white, just tipped with crimson, are exceedingly beautiful. This elegant plant was first discovered by Mr Molloy who has paid much attention to the botany of this district.

Even in her fever, Georgiana must have known that all was lost. The vibrant orange of the *Nuytsia floribunda* flowers disappeared again and the seeds ripened on the trees believed by the Noongar people to be the resting places of the dead before their spirits travel onward to the ocean. At night, an unusually brilliant and long-tailed comet lit up the sky above Fairlawn like an omen.[570]

Still unhappy about the medical care his wife was receiving, Molloy sent for a doctor from Australind and on 18 March he wrote a note to Wollaston: 'Mrs Molloy will lose her life for want of nursing.'[571] He was desperate to save her and constructed a water-bed to reduce pressure on the agonising sores that covered the back of her body.

On 23 March she asked to receive Holy Communion and when Wollaston called again four days later he found her barely conscious. The ship's carpenter from a whaler built a more effective water-bed and Wollaston gave Molloy his new mackintosh to insert between the water and the blankets. This waterproof 'mac' that gave Georgiana some temporary relief was invented by a business partner of the man she had once thought of as a father, Alexander Dunlop of Keppoch.[572]

As Georgiana lay in her bedroom, drifting between conscious pain and peaceful sleep, her name was being circulated in print on family breakfast tables, in the gentlemen's clubs and at ladies' reading circles in Perth and across the southwest in another newspaper article. It named her as the first to discover the red Kennedia that rambled over the roof and verandah of her cottage in Augusta.[573]

ON THE BOTANY OF WESTERN AUSTRALIA.
Letter to the Editor
Sir,
In the Journal I sent you of our journey to the south, I observed a fine large dark red Kennedya, growing near the spring on Mr. Turner's land at Augusta, I should have stated that the plant was first discovered by Mrs. Molloy and long cultivated in Captain Molloy's garden at Augusta, where it now remains.
JAMES DRUMMOND Hawthornden, Feb. 16, 1843.

The fever tightened its grip on Georgiana's body but she prayed with Wollaston each time she regained consciousness for a few minutes and before he left she took Holy Communion with Molloy.[574] Heavily sedated to manage the pain, she could see her garden through the window but knew she would never walk there again. The bush and its glories that had captured her heart and mind so securely were memories that gave her comfort in the last days but they were not the last ones she spoke of. In her final lucid moments Georgiana talked to her husband about the friends she had left on the quay at Greenock in Scotland in 1829. She told him she could still see them as clearly in her mind as she had when she waved goodbye. Georgiana was thirty-seven when she died on Saturday, 8 April.[575] Her mother never received the news. Mrs Kennedy died in Cheltenham four weeks later and two sad letters in black-edged envelopes crossed somewhere at sea.[576,577]

Fanny and Charlotte Bussell helped eleven-year-old Sabina and eight-year-old Mary to sew black mourning fabric onto their dresses for the funeral.

> 38 years have passed since I was with you & your dear sisters ministering all the help & consolation I could under your first great sorrow – Oh how I well remember, how Aunt Fanny and I with a workwoman sat stitching away at your little mourning garments to be worn the next day at your dear Mother's funeral – while you & Mary sat side by side on a low seat working with equal diligence, silent tears falling down your cheeks.[578]

Georgiana was buried at Fairlawn on Sunday, 9 April. Less than a year later when work started on laying the foundations of St Mary's church in Busselton, her grave was moved and she was reunited at last with her first daughter, Elizabeth, and her only son John, from Augusta. Mother and children were reinterred beneath the church under the original earth floor of the nave.[579,580,581] In the north of England, one of her Augusta seedlings was flowering for the first time in the garden of horticulturalist George Hailes. He believed the 'pretty *Sisyrinchium cyaneum*' to have been lost to British gardeners for some time.[582]

People bereaved are at their most real. The polished surfaces of politeness usually rub away, but in his grief John Molloy was controlled. He was a father, a settler and a soldier and he had seen too much of life and death to do anything but carry on. Eighty-six years later, a local newspaper article included a historical account of Georgiana Molloy's death and quoted Wollaston's 1843 journal describing the events of the next few days.

> This story of pioneer sacrifice may well close with a sketch of the bereaved husband ten days later – a gentleman and a soldier. 'Captain Molloy came with Dr. Landor on his way to Perth. He looks ill, poor man, but he was tolerably cheerful. He wore his military jacket with his Waterloo medal at the shoulders.'[583]

St Mary's Church, Busselton 1898

JS Battye Library SLWA b3305391_1 (with permission)

LIFE AFTER GEORGIANA

Two weeks before Georgiana died, an old friend in Scotland sat down to write her a long letter.[584] Mary Ker was the Dunlop sister with the deepest Christian faith and Georgiana had asked her to take on the spiritual and educational guidance of her five daughters. Even the most loving and capable father would find it impossible to run a large farm, fulfil his government duties, educate four girls and care for a small baby.

> I have just been taking Molloy's promise that if anything happens to me, he will take all the children to Britain and put them under your care, their father can maintain them bodily but you must take the whole disposal of their education.[585]

When Mary realised her reply to Georgiana's letter had arrived too late, she wrote to John Molloy to say she was ready to care for the children as she did for her own.[586] But Molloy did not want to send his daughters away. Eleven-year-old Sabina took over the domestic management of the home and was responsible for Mary, Amelia and three-year-old Flora, but she could not meet the needs of the baby.

Captain Molloy was guardian to Mary Layman's children after her husband's death. In 1842 she married Robert Heppingstone, the same 'Bobby' that newlywed Mrs Molloy was teaching to read on board the *Warrior* in 1829. Their first child was born days before baby Georgiana arrived. Mary was breastfeeding him, and she lived just a few kilometres away at Wonnerup. To Sabina, the kind Mary Heppingstone who looked after her youngest sister would always be 'Mrs Layman', but she also became known as little Georgiana's 'foster mother'.[587]

Within days of his wife's death, Molloy purchased a new licence for the farm dogs.[588] Life had to go on and there were duties to the community and the family to be seen to. In November, he was chairperson at the first local meeting about the building of St Mary's church, held at Fairlawn. He presided over the Busselton court sittings in a small building known as the Herbery, between the house and the stockyard.[589] He was collector of customs for the Sussex District so his home was very busy when whaleboats and other ships arrived in Geographe Bay. His interest in horse breeding never waned, and at the races he was a dramatic sight in a heavy, two-wheeled cape wagon pulled by his strong horses, Duke and Prince. There were new business ventures too. In 1844 he purchased the hull of a wrecked whaler, the *Halcyon*, and was soon involved in rebuilding it as the *Conservative*. But luck did not go his way.[590] Four years later, after he had spent £1000 on the work, a storm blew the ship off her moorings and Molloy lost everything.[591]

The two Jacks – John Bussell and John Molloy – were close neighbours, their homes on either side of the narrow Vasse River, but Molloy rarely took the quick route to Cattle Chosen on the opposite bank. Like many sailors he never learned to swim and he hated crossing the river on the wobbly tree trunk he called 'Waterloo Bridge'.[592] The two men did not always see eye to eye and there were times when they fell out over stock that roamed across boundaries, but their mutual respect and friendship lasted a lifetime. Both worked tirelessly to further the same cause so close to their hearts: the prosperity of the southwest.

In 1844, Alfred Green married Nancy McDermott, fifteen years after he first met her on board the *Warrior* as eighteen-year-old Ann Turner. The only remaining settlers in Augusta were her father, James Woodward Turner, and John Herring, who had taken on the job of district postmaster. Turner never gave in. His sons moved to the Vasse in 1840 and he moved to Perth in 1850 taking with him and rebuilding on Adelaide Terrace, brick by brick, the Augusta house he had transported from London. He owned his property by the Blackwood until he died.

While Busselton was becoming known as far away as Perth for the quality of its cheese and butter, the route to Augusta from the Vasse was little more than a pathway.[593,594] The government began reclaiming land grants in Augusta, including the block registered to Georgiana Molloy, 'on account of non-performance of the conditions of assignment'. But she was not forgotten. When Mathew Blagden Hale, the new Archdeacon of Adelaide, visited Busselton for the consecration of St Mary's in November 1848, he found Mrs Molloy still alive in people's memories and in the character of her daughters.[595] He noted that 'every one speaks of her in terms of the most unbounded praise' and Wollaston regarded her 'as the best informed, the most accomplished, the most elegant, and the most ladylike woman that ever came into this colony'.[596]

Hale was surprised to find Busselton so undeveloped, 'a Townsite merely in name being in reality a piece of uncleared scrub in a low wet position', but at Fairlawn he was impressed by the peaceful household and the simple, refined lifestyle of the family who lived there.[597]

> When leaving this most interesting house, my companion asked one of the little girls to accompany us over the River, which we had to cross in order that she might bring back the punt, and the return over the river after we had crossed would form a picture worthy of a painter's skill.[598]

> Across the stream the old & leaky boat wended its way towards the opposite bank. On one of the 'thwarts' stood the form of faultless symmetry of our little boat-woman balancing the rude punt pole & pushing her way across with singular grace & skill. In another part of the boat were her little sister Georgie about 6 or 7 and a little native girl.[599]

The influences on the girls were underpinned by the lasting effect of their mother's example, the daily Christian structure of their lives and the overwhelming impact of freedom in the bush around their home. Although they lived in 'the most complete seclusion', Hale saw in them 'a grace & dignity & ease of manner which would do honour to the most refined society, to say nothing of their being, both great & small, strikingly handsome'.

> In fact to come through a Bush settlement & then to find oneself suddenly in the midst of such a family, produces within one no ordinary sensations – One is touched with admiration & delight on the one hand & at the same time one laments that the circle of their acquaintance should be so limited.[600]

Like so many others before him, Hale was struck by the engaging character of Captain Molloy, but in those spring days of 1848, and perhaps for the first time ever, the imposing presence of the old Rifleman with the 'most striking countenance' was outshone by the intelligence and beauty of one of his daughters. Archdeacon Hale confirmed Sabina during the consecration service at St Mary's a week before her seventeenth birthday. Eight weeks later she married him in the same church. They left immediately after the wedding just as her parents had done twenty years earlier, but the couple did not set off for Perth alone. Hale took Sabina's four sisters into his care so that Captain Molloy could make the long-planned visit to Britain.

Sabina Dunlop Hale née Molloy

JS Battye Library SLWA ACC 3674B / 1

Molloy needed to resolve the six-year delay of allocating assets from the complicated trust funds in his mother-in-law's will. Georgiana was a beneficiary, but as she had died within days of her mother and the nature of trust funds in Mrs Kennedy's will meant there were legal complications about who should inherit each share of the estate, with Mary, Dalton, and Georgiana's daughters all having potential claims. The last remaining piece of Mrs Kennedy's fortune was the 'genteel and commodious' house that her father, George Dalton, built in Abbey Street a hundred years earlier. She mortgaged it to keep herself going financially in her final years but refused to sell, holding on to it like a fading heirloom that reminded her of a life she might have lived. She relented just in time, and wrote a new will in 1842.[601]

> In a former letter I named to you my wish that you would not sell the house in Abbey St. but I reverse that wish and shall have my Will altered as soon as I return, & leave it in your power to do what you please.[602]

The whole property on its large corner plot was advertised in June 1844 but it was still for sale in July 1849.[603] Legal fees were eating into the capital and no-one apart from the lawyers was benefitting. Molloy was also keen to see his few remaining military colleagues but there was one big problem: finding the funds for such an expensive journey. On 28 March 1849, a surprising advertisement appeared in the *Perth Inquirer*. Captain Molloy was holding an auction at Fairlawn, selling off almost everything he owned including bed linen, paintings, furniture, books, livestock and fine wine.

On 3 March 1850, he left Western Australia on what turned out to be a 'long and disastrous voyage'.[604] Age was beginning to catch up with him. He celebrated his sixty-fourth birthday on board and by the time he landed six months later, was greatly troubled by swollen legs. A cough he developed during the voyage became so bad he was forced to spend the first two weeks resting, before he continued his recovery enjoying the hospitality of the Reverend Horace Chavasse and his wife Margaret, the same Maggie Dunlop who had waved goodbye to him and his new bride twenty-two years earlier.[605]

Molloy travelled around Britain for eighteen months. He attended the Duke of Wellington's annual banquet on the anniversary of the Battle of Waterloo and finally received the medal commemorating each battle he fought in during the Peninsular War. He stayed with Sir James and Lady Ellen Stirling at their home on the south coast, with Reverend Besley and his second wife in Plymouth, and was a guest of the Reverend and Helen Story at the new manse in Roseneath. The most heart-warming time of all was the week he spent on the coast in Worthing with Jonathan Leach. The two old soldiers felt as if they had never been apart and relived a store of shared memories.[606] Jonathan had been with 'dear old Jack' on the day Molloy met Georgiana in the garden at Crosby. It was all a lifetime away.

The world was changing and Molloy had spent the last twenty years in a developing colony. By 1850 there was a network of railways across England connecting major towns and cities, a far cry from the two-wheeled wagon he used at home. The arrival of rail had transformed the city of his childhood and he found new buildings where once there had been familiar territory. He had never seen a railway station and now he encountered the huge structures of Euston, Paddington, Fenchurch Street, Waterloo and Kings Cross. Just before he set sail for home in October 1851, Molloy paid a visit to The Great Exhibition, housed in an enormous glass building. Made off-site and constructed quickly in Hyde Park using new machinery, the Crystal Palace was the most innovative building of its time. The designer was Joseph Paxton, the same gardener who had grown flowers for the Duke of Devonshire from Georgiana Molloy's seed collection. Molloy bought souvenirs for his children including a glass toy that was a replica of the building.

When he returned to Fairlawn in March 1852 with his four youngest daughters, John Molloy found that things had changed on both sides of the river. Alfred Bussell was married to Ellen, Robert and Ann Heppingstone's daughter.[607] The Fairlawn household and farm were not in good order. Georgiana's little piano was damaged so he ordered a replacement from England and then began a period of building, perhaps instigated by a new awareness of how basic his rural homestead was in comparison with the innovations he had seen in London. Wherever the money came from after such an expensive trip, it was not from an inheritance. After Molloy had spent weeks with lawyers trying to bring the whole matter to a conclusion, there was a complication when the executors examined Georgiana's marriage settlement and discovered her small share of Mrs Kennedy's estate was left, not to John Molloy or his children, but to Sabina's.

In 1854, Mary Dorothea Molloy met Edmund DuCane, an officer in the Corps of Royal Engineers who was stationed at Guildford, near Perth, with responsibility for managing convict labour on public works. In July the following year, John Molloy made the long journey to the city for their wedding and the DuCanes spent their last summer in Australia at Fairlawn with him before they left for England. Soon afterwards, Mary received an unexpected parcel from Captain James Mangles. In it were copies of his letter books bound in cloth, their pages edged with gilt, and there was an inscription: 'Mrs DuCane formerly Miss Mary Molloy with many thanks for her early and zealous services in his behalf.'[608] The letters from her mother that he had transcribed told the story of Mary's childhood in Augusta, her parents' struggles in the fledgling settlement, Georgiana's contributions to the world of botany and her own childlike efforts as a collector.

The waves of change were unstoppable. In July 1857, Amelia married William Richardson-Bunbury and, two years later, Flora was married to William Brockman. In 1859, after thirty years of continued service to the British government as an army captain on half pay, Molloy received two back-dated promotions at the same time and became known as 'the Colonel', although he sold the commission on the same day he received it.[609] By 1860, seventeen-year-old Georgiana had moved to Perth to live with the Hales and for the first time since his marriage, the seventy-four-year-old was living alone. He had fought fearlessly in some of the fiercest battles of the century but there was still one more enemy to face. Time was catching up with him.

Sabina's husband, Mathew Hale, now Bishop of Perth, had two children from his previous marriage, Amy and Mary. In December 1860 he and Sabina were staying at Fairlawn and he wrote to Mary Hale about his growing concerns for the ageing John Molloy.

> We have been much concerned about poor dear grandpapa. His ailments have of late assumed a serious character for one of his age. We have at last persuaded him to resign his office of Government resident, but we cannot induce him to give up Fairlawn or to leave it except for limited times.
>
> ...
>
> He is in excellent spirits generally but much weaker and more stiff in his movements and more confused and unconnected in his old stories.[610]

Molloy reluctantly agreed to hand over responsibility for the running of Fairlawn and Marybrook to Richard Gale, Flora and William Brockmans' farm manager, but the old soldier did not find it easy to sit back and enjoy his retirement. Gale was doing a good job but 'Grandpapa' would not stop interfering.[611] Sabina visited Fairlawn when she could but it was clear that the Colonel needed a more permanent companion, so his youngest daughter, Georgiana, moved home again to care for their father and the Hales went back to Perth. They had known their own tragedies in the first years of marriage. Their first child, John Molloy Hale, was born in July 1850 and lived for only three days. Grandpapa's response to the sad news had not changed from the time when he first became a father and experienced the same loss. Childbirth was a dangerous time for mother and baby. Resignation and faith seemed to be the best safeguards against despair.

> I am this moment in receipt of both your letters of July 9 & Sept 3rd. It gave me unfeigned & heartfelt gratification to find that under providence you had been reconciled to the Almighty Will in removing your dear infant to his heavenly mansion.[612]

When the couple were returning from a visit to England in April, 1860, a second son was born on board ship and Sabina named him, too, for her father, John Molloy Hale.[613] He died seven months later. Soon after she returned home from Fairlawn again in early 1861, Sabina knew she was expecting another baby and Georgiana Theodosia Hale was born on 9 December. The child was named after her two grandmothers, Georgiana Molloy and Lady Theodosia Hale.

When she was not yet three years old, this third Georgiana, little Georgie Hale, began to show the 'Molloy wit' inherited from both her grandparents, even in the very serious company of an elderly John Bussell.

Perth. February 24th 1864

Georgie is a most intelligent little thing ... She has a great collection of Nursery Rhymes which she remembers wonderfully, but sometimes jumbles them gloriously together. One day she stuck herself up in front of John Bussell & repeated two or three times over 'My son John went to bed with his stockings on.' Bussell said in his genial way, 'I'm afraid you're personal' which of course made us laugh all the more.[614]

As an adult, Georgie moved back to Britain with her parents when Bishop Hale retired in 1885 and she developed a strong interest in her family history. Between 1880 and 1890 she was writing to relatives who had known her grandparents, the Molloys, and in the 1890s she was visiting places where Georgiana had lived. In Crosby-on-Eden Georgie questioned villagers and, on a visit to Western Australia, she went to Augusta and walked in the bush collecting wildflowers with Percy Willmott, the local lighthouse keeper at Cape Leeuwin.

Georgiana Theodosia Hale (Bisdee)

JS Battye Library SLWA ACC BA 657 / 145

When she discovered that George Walpole Leake QC had known John Molloy, she began a long correspondence with him that rescued many stories for the future.[615] Leake was eight when he met Molloy in Perth, and their friendship continued for three decades. Georgie encouraged Leake to share details of the long conversations he remembered. As a boy, he read books to the old man whose recall from the distant past was still as sharp as a sword. In March 1881, Leake wrote to Georgie about her grandfather and sent her a copy of *English Battles and Sieges in the Peninsula* by William Napier.[616]

> I cannot put to paper the many or indeed some of the anecdotes which fell from his lips, which were the delight of my boyhood and mature age.
>
> The volume I send you is a mere extract. Read it and be proud of him.[617]

The stories that George Leake passed on to Georgie Hale provide the final pieces in the jigsaw of Molloy's career as a Rifleman. As an elderly man, Leake referred her to a particular section he had once read aloud to her grandfather.[618]

> The actions in the Pyrenees were numerous and hard fought as you will see on reading the book and it was on reading to him the account on p 323 of Echallar and Nantelly that the grand old man's eyes brightened and the color [sic] came to his cheek when he said 'Read that again'.
>
> I read it again and he said so proudly, 'I led up that hill'.

Georgie wrote to the *West Australian* newspaper in 1925, rising fiercely to the defence of her grandfather when an article queried his ancestry and raised questions about his actions at the time of the Layman murder.[619] In 1901, she was the first to attempt full transcriptions of her grandmother's letters to Captain Mangles, recording them

1838

this they constantly remind me of the laurestinus. I do not know the name of any one of them for dear Augusta is quite out of the world & even the limited society of S. W. Australia & very few has too a thought on flowers.

The only person I ever met with here, that I durst speak to on this Subject was our lamented Mr Collie & his visits were so transient I had little opportunity.

Grubbing, Hoes, Beef, Pork, Potatoes, Onions, Anchors - & Anchorage - Whaling - Harpooning - are the chief topics of Conversation: Therefore I am well persuaded any observations respecting a flower garden would be ill timed & not agreable to the generality of my guests.

I have not sent you every flower we have worth sending - & many I fear you will consider worthless. But having obeyed the "golden rule" I have ventured to introduce some literal weeds.

Often in hearing of foreign countries. I have wished to be acquainted with the most

Transcription in the handwriting of Georgiana Hale. The original letter from her grandmother, Georgiana Molloy, was written in 1838 and transcribed by Mangles into his own letter book.

Augusta Historical Society (Molloy collection)

meticulously in a notebook and in letters of her own, along with a personal commentary on their content.

> 'I was engaged in disentangling some closely penned and much crossed letters written 'home' from Western Australia by one who was among its first settlers – my grandmother Mrs Molloy.
>
> The contrast was striking between the accounts in my letters of the difficulties and disappointments inseparably bound up with the life of a pioneer in a new country – & the advanced civilization revealed in the speeches of the present representatives of the same colonies which now in their settled prosperity have become firm pillars of the British Empire.[620]

Somehow, her writing ended up lost for decades in the Long Benton vicarage, where Reverend Besley continued to live after the death of his first wife, Eliza, Georgiana Molloy's sister. In 1985 the house was a private home and its owners sent the dusty bundle of papers they discovered in their roof to the Augusta Historical Society.[621]

* * *

As I travelled on the research pathway, it was not long before I began treading in someone else's footsteps, someone who had gone just ahead of me to clear the way. Where I searched, Georgie Hale had searched before and where I went looking, she had already explored. It was years before I realised that she is the mysterious 'Goggilorum' signature, the 'Gg' of old letters held by the Augusta Historical Society (AHS), the one who not only asked questions but also treasured and kept the answers she found, allowing them to be discovered again. Georgie's transcriptions are not complete, but her memories and reflections have led me to some of the most moving discoveries of all.

The notes added to young Georgiana Kennedy's diary are in Georgie Hale's handwriting, a list of the questions she wanted to ask about her grandmother: 'What was her "secret sorrow"?' A brief anecdote passed on about an ageing grandfather when she was a small child, and remembered later: 'Ship "Hindostan", JM on board abt. 14', the same words that revealed John Molloy's naval career and led me to his adventures on board a burning ship off the coast of Spain.

At Wonnerup, the nineteenth-century home of the Layman family, there is a rosewood- and brass-inlaid lady's sewing box in the care of the National Trust.[622] Owned by Georgiana Molloy's daughter Mary Dorothea DuCane, it once belonged to her mother and dates from around 1820 to 1825. The embossed leather decoration on the containers inside the box indicates a date close to 1825, when Georgiana Kennedy was twenty years old.[623] An object of such craftsmanship and value would have been a typical twenty-first birthday gift for a young lady officially entering adult life.

The sewing box's story was finally confirmed in 2010 when I sat in the reading room of the AHS and transcribed Georgie Hale's writing more carefully. She described her memories of looking through the items hidden away in 'an old rosewood workbox belonging to Mrs Molloy'. There are so many tiny compartments and hidden places in Georgiana's sewing box that it seems to give up new secrets on every viewing. She tucked away two of her pink, handwritten visiting cards: one with her maiden name and one with her married name. Another treasure was her brother George's ticket for the opening ceremony of the Carlisle Canal in March 1823, just before his tenth birthday. A secret compartment in the lid holds a simple silk and linen sampler embroidered by the fifteen-year-old girl who had already lost her father and met the man she would marry.

Hoarding small things that mark life's moments is a habit that did not die with the eighteenth century. The things we keep may be tiny but they are not trivia. They reveal what matters most to each of us along the way. Georgie Hale recognised that the jumble of little things in the Wonnerup sewing box capture in their smallness the great sweep of her grandparents' lives, but it was not until she was an adult that she understood the significance of all the treasures. What had once looked like a useless tangle of old sewing threads became evidence of the hardships of a settler's life. As a young woman, Georgiana Kennedy grew up in a household with servants to dress her and silk gowns made to order. She sewed for amusement and bought new clothes each season. As Mrs Molloy, she bought plain, durable cotton cambric and made not only her own dresses but those for her children and servants as well. When the fabric was completely worn out, she cut these garments down for household rags but not before she had painstakingly unpicked the precious threads so they could be used again.

> A striking feature in those letters is the value placed on objects so common in a civilized country that the poorest can possess them – as needles and threads – It was not until I had read this correspondence that I understood the meaning of a little bundle of used threads – ... The threads now yellow with age have grown to have an interest of their own among the many relics which the old box contains.[624]

In another velvet-lined compartment beneath Mrs Molloy's lace-making tools and a collection of baby-sized white buttons, there is another tiny treasure, which Georgie Hale recognised as 'not the least among them'. The first time I saw the contents of the box, a crumpled note inside revealed that it had once been wrapped around the bullet taken from John Molloy after the Battle of Waterloo.[625] I had searched for it before in vain and I assumed that such a precious family heirloom had been passed on. But I had been looking for the wrong thing.

A few years later Mike did some research into military history and told me, just as the box was being opened once again for viewing, that we should be looking not for a bullet-shaped object but a round musket ball as used by the French army. He also mentioned that it would be made of lead and therefore probably whitened with age. In the centre compartment was a chalky marble with a tiny, delicately carved case made from a hazelnut shell. As I placed the musket ball on my gloved palm I felt its leaden heaviness. It was not perfectly round, but dented slightly on one side where it had met the bone in Captain Molloy's leg in June 1815, just before the final shots were fired at the Battle of Waterloo. An object of no great beauty or usefulness can carry as much resonance for those who find it generations later as it did on the day its owner chose to keep it.

* * *

The collection of farm and household records in the JS Battye Library shows that life at Fairlawn was simple and uneventful for Molloy and his nineteen-year-old daughter Georgiana, but his health problems were becoming more evident. Friends noticed that he could still retell old stories but found it difficult to recall anything recent. On Christmas Day, 1865, Mathew Hale wrote: 'Poor grandpapa has become quite unable to attend to his own business through the entire failure of his memory. He cannot remember anything.'[626]

In the end, time robbed John Molloy of his private memories too and the true story of his long life was gone. Rumours about when and where he was born and theories about his mysterious ancestry continue today. The *Australian Dictionary of Biography* states that he was born of 'unknown parentage' and that 'the Molloy from whom he took his name and his upbringing was Captain AJ Pye Molloy RN, a tyrannical captain dismissed from his ship for cowardice in 1795'. He chose a lifetime of silence that cost him his public past but ensured his family the best future he could give them. John and Georgiana's daughter Mary Dorothea became Lady DuCane. When their granddaughter, Georgie Hale, married John Hutton Bisdee of Tasmania in 1904, there was a lavish reception at the home of Senator Macfarlane and newspapers reported it as the Australian high society wedding of the year. Bisdee was a lieutenant in the 2nd Imperial Bushmen and the first Australian to receive the Victoria Cross.[627]

LIFE AFTER GEORGIANA

John Molloy, Georgiana's 'excellent husband and best friend', died of old age, sitting in his chair at home on 6 October 1867 and he was buried in the graveyard of St Mary's church in Busselton two days later. The cart arrived from Fairlawn pulled by two of his horses in funeral mantles. His fine, mahogany coffin was trimmed with local lace and lined with pitch to protect 'the gallant old Colonel' from the water that contributed to such floral profusion at the Vasse. The service was 'very largely attended'.

> There were many moist eyes around the graveside, as he was beloved by all classes of the community. The Rev. H. W. Brown, who had known him for many years, completely broke down, and it was some time before he could continue the burial service.[628]

John Molloy was eighty-one when he died, not eighty-seven as inscribed on his tombstone. He was the sixty-eighth entry in the burial record book that he began in his own handwriting, in a tent on the beach at Augusta in 1830.

* * *

After seven years of research and several attempts at shaping a mountain of notes into the framework for a biography, I realised that my attempts to use a purely logical planning structure were not working. I decided to begin again and started looking for a phrase that felt like an emotional signpost, a subtitle that would steer my writing and keep it focused on the very heart of the story. I spent an afternoon re-reading a copy of the little book that Georgiana brought with her to Western Australia, the collection of Robert Burns's poetry that was a gift on her wedding day. That book was one of the first clues there was more to Georgiana than history had revealed, and it represented so many of the themes, places and ideas that were important to her. When I came to the poem 'On Cessnock Banks', I knew I had found the words I needed to be my guide. Although she had many attributes, it is still Georgiana's 'mind that shines' so brightly.

With that refrain from the poem pinned next to the computer screen I started writing once again. A year later I typed a full stop at the end of the first complete draft of the manuscript and went online to check my references. One of the searches brought up the link to the botanical book that Captain Mangles sent to Georgiana in 1840, and I saw it myself for the first time as images on the screen.

> There is a language in each flower
> That opens to the eye
> A voiceless – but a magic power
> Doth in earth's blossoms lie.[629]

The Language and Sentiment of Flowers was based on the idea of emotions conveyed by particular flowers, such as myrtle for love, ivy for friendship and hawthorn for hope. But the book went further and made a direct connection between the plants and the immortal hand that made them: 'God gave to each a language of its own and bade the simple blossom teach where'er its seeds are sown'.

I wondered which flower Georgiana would have looked up first when the precious book arrived, and I guessed it would have been the red Kennedia that she loved so much. It was her namesake. It weighed down the rafters of her verandah by the river in Augusta. The botanist James Drummond remembered her for it publicly in the last days of her life at Fairlawn.

I found it between Juniper and Larkspur; Class Diadelphia, Order Decandria, a plant 'of rare delicacy and beauty'. In the language of flowers, Kennedia is the floral messenger for mental beauty.[630]

Dunbartonshire, Scotland 1829

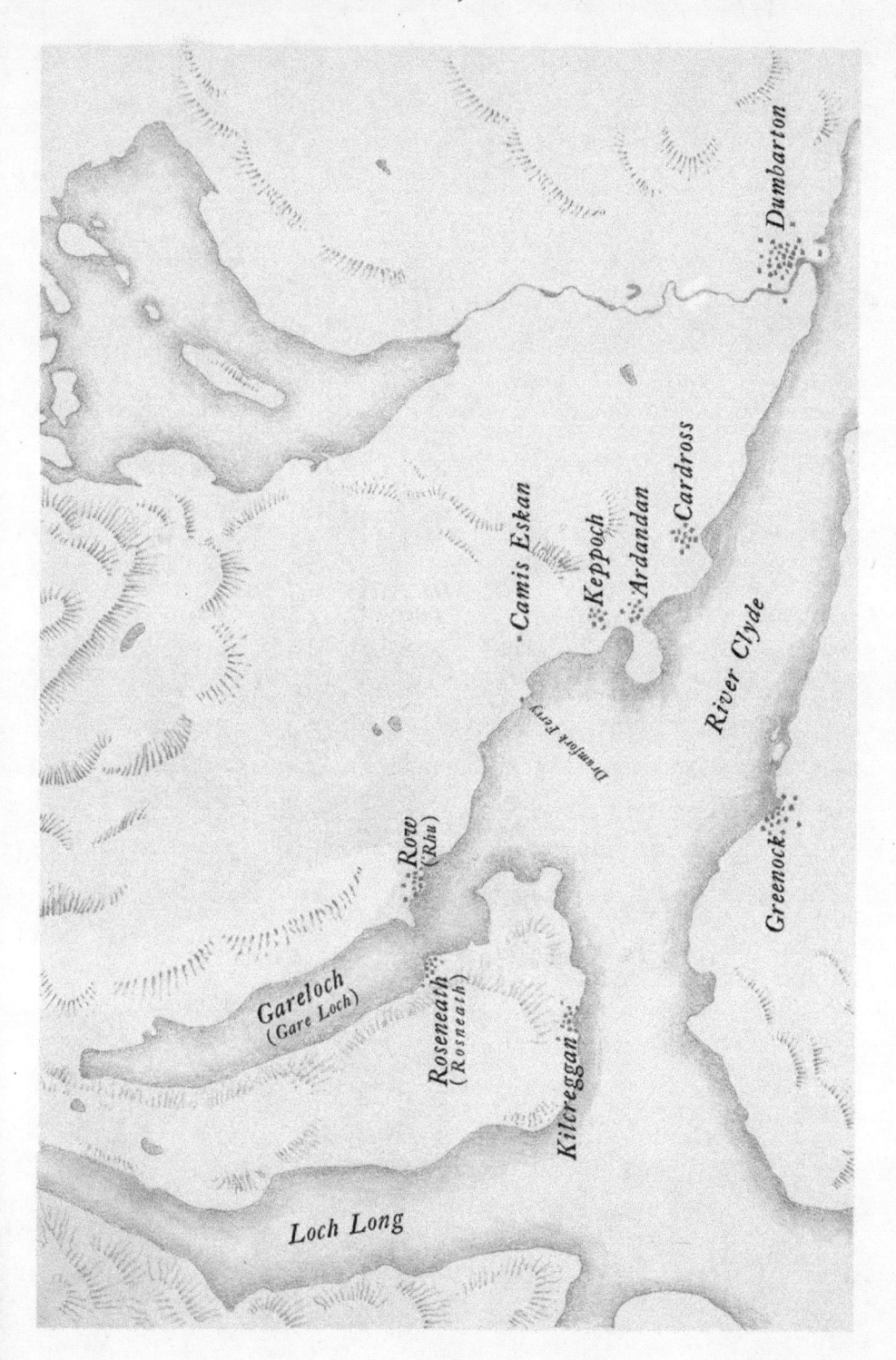

Augusta, Western Australia 1830

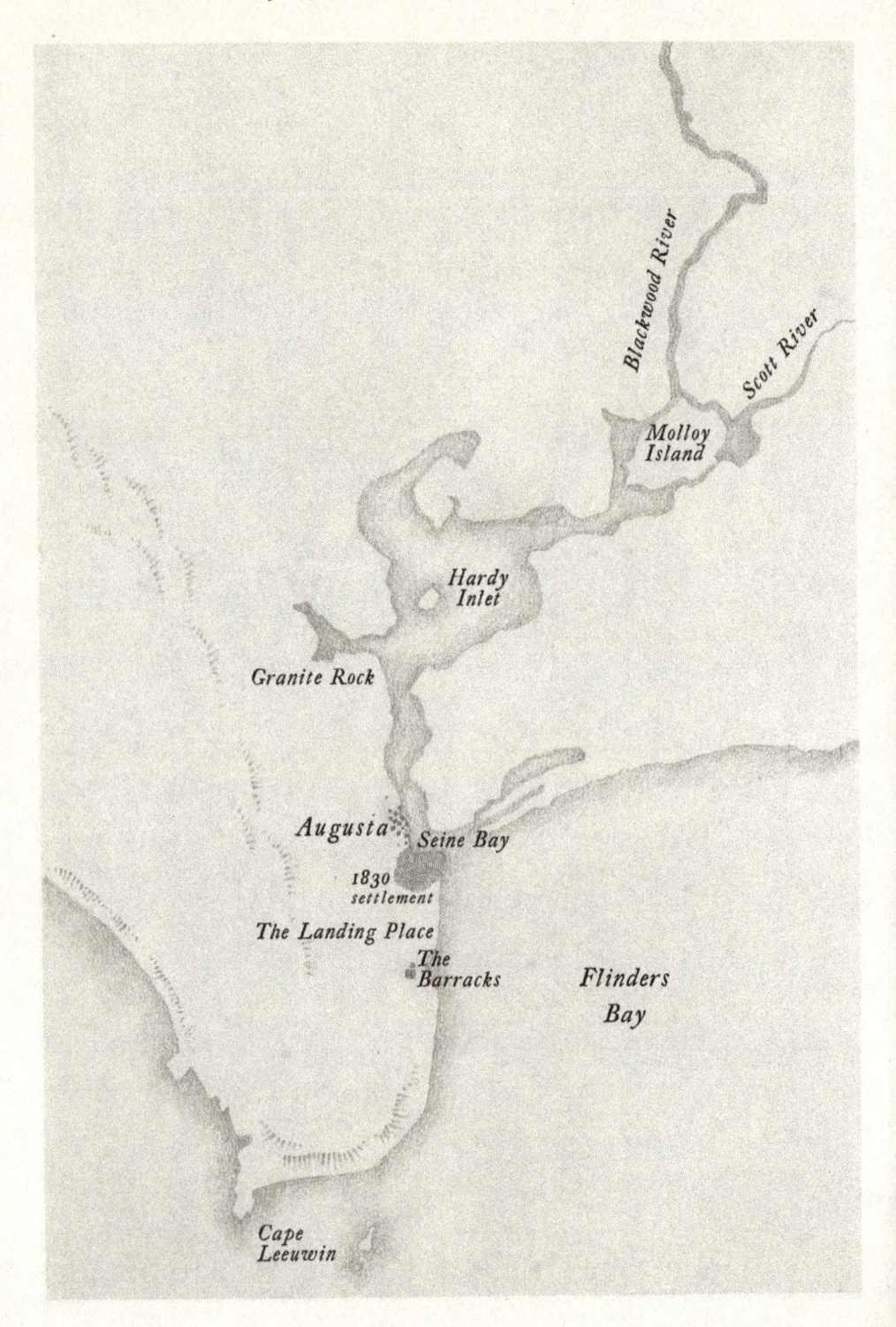

Endnotes

AHS   Augusta Historical Society, Augusta, WA
BLP   JS Battye Library, State Library of Western Australia, Perth, WA
CAC   Cumbria Archive Centre, Carlisle, UK
NA   National Archives, Kew, UK

1. The title and wording of Burns's poem varied in different publications. This quote is from 'On Cessnock Banks' in Georgiana Molloy's own copy, *The Songs of Robert Burns*, John Sharpe, London 1824

A childhood in Eden

2. Handwritten text in a Dalton family Bible, copy acquired by Patrick Richardson-Bunbury, transcribed by the author.
3. *An All Consuming Passion: Origins, modernity and the Australian life of Georgiana Molloy*, William J. Lines, Allen & Unwin 1994.
4. *Holy Bible*, Printed by John Archdeacon, Cambridge 1792; *The Force of Truth* by Thomas Scott, Printed by J Seeley, Buckingham 1811; *Sacred Poetry*, 7th edition, Wm Oliphant; *Letters on the Elementary Principles of Education* by Elizabeth Hamilton, Vol. 1, 3rd edition.
5. *The British Album* in two volumes, John Bell, London 1793.
6. John Sharpe, London 1824. Poem written by Robert Burns 1759–96.
7. Records of Carlisle Grammar School.
8. *The History and Antiquities of Carlisle*, Samuel Jefferson, Whittaker and Co. 1838.
9. Library and Museum of Freemasonry, London GBR 1991 HC 1/G/4.
10. *A roll of honour of over 17,000 men and women who have collected manuscripts and printed books from the XIVth to the XIXth century*, William Carew Hazlitt 1908; and *Contributions Towards a Dictionary of English Book-Collectors* by Bernard Quaritch and Edward Burbidge, 1892.
11. *The Forgotten Army: Fencible Regiments of Great Britain 1793-1816*, Ron McGuigan.
12. Colonel Andrew McDowell (McDouall), List of the officers of the several regiments and corps of fencible cavalry.
13. Lines written to Elizabeth Dalton by David Archibald Kennedy, 29 June 1800, H. M. O. Hale family collection.
14. The area used as St Mary's parish church was a separate area of the nave in 1805 and is used today as the regimental chapel.
15. CAC D KEN 4/13/10
16. CAC D KEN 4/23/1
17. CAC D KEN 4/13/3
18. CAC D KEN 4/13
19. Dalton family Bible.

20 CAC D KEN 3/7/8 Letter from John De Whelpdale to David Kennedy, February 1809.
21 Letter from Georgiana Hale, 28 December 1897, AHS.
22 CAC D KEN 4/13/6 Memorandum.
23 CAC D KEN 4/3
24 AHS Molloy collection Letter from Georgiana Hale.
25 CAC D KEN 3/7/8 Letter to David Kennedy from his father, David Kennedy, senior, April 1809.
26 CAC D KEN 3/56/1 Note written by Mrs Kennedy to her daughter Elizabeth and any future daughters, Undated c. 1801.
27 AHS Molloy collection Letter from Georgiana Bisdee née Hale.
28 Letter from Elizabeth Boyle Cunningham née Dunlop to Margaret Chavasse, her niece, December 1888 H. M. O. Hale family collection 11a.
29 BLP Journal of Frances Louisa Bussell, Augusta 1835, MN586 6926A.
30 *Principal Inhabitants of Cumberland and Westmoreland 1829.*
31 *The Letters of Sara Hutchinson from 1800 to 1835*, Ed. Kathleen Coburn, University of Toronto Press 1954.
32 Extract from 'Lines composed a few miles above Tintern Abbey, on revisiting the banks of the Wye during a tour. July 13, 1798', William Wordsworth.
33 Letter from Edmund DuCane to Georgiana Hale, 14 July 1889, H. M. O. Hale family collection (Bunbury Index No 35). Transcription by Patrick Richardson-Bunbury.
34 CAC Letters to David Kennedy and Mrs Kennedy, D KEN 3/6/2 1806 and 1810; D KEN 3/7/6 1800–1815 D KEN 3/9/1 1819.
35 Letter from Edmund DuCane to Georgiana Hale, 14th July 1889, H. M. O. Hale family collection.
36 AHS Molloy collection Letter from Georgiana Bisdee née Hale.
37 CAC D KEN 3/28/2 Diary of Georgiana Kennedy, June 1829.

John Molloy, London boy

38 Herald of Arms in Ordinary 1982–1997, Thomas Woodcock, Esq. research for Patrick Richardson-Bunbury. College of Arms; Pallot's Marriage Index for England: 1780–1837.
39 Letter from Sir Edmund DuCane to Georgiana Hale, 7 December 1892, H. M. O. Hale family collection.
40 *The Gentleman's Magazine*, John Nichols, Vol. 62 1787, Meteorological Table for October 1786.
41 *Georgiana Molloy: Portrait with background*, Alexandra Hasluck, OUP Melbourne 1955; 'The Irish RM: Capt. John Molloy of the Vasse', Gil Hardwick, first published April 2000 in Reece R. H. W. (ed.), *The Irish in Western Australia* (Studies in Western Australian History, Vol. 20), Centre for Western

Endnotes

Australian History, Department of History, University of Western Australia, 2000, Pages 1–20.

42   Old Bailey proceedings, 20 Feb 1799 17990220; Records of the Sun Fire Office, Guildhall Library London, MS 11936/401/624352, 6 January 1794.

43   Sun Fire insurance records, Guildhall Library, MS 11936/440/800420, 24 February 1807.

44   Letter from Sir Edmund DuCane letter to Georgiana Hale, 7 December 1892, H. M. O. Hale family collection.

45   John Molloy to his daughter Mary, quoted in a letter from Edmund DuCane to Molloy's grand-daughter Georgiana Hale, 1 December 1892. DuCane was John Molloy's son-in-law. He married Mary Dorothea Molloy. H. M. O. Hale family collection.

46   Herald of Arms in Ordinary 1982–1997, Thomas Woodcock, Esq. research for Patrick Richardson-Bunbury.

47   Sun Fire insurance records, Guildhall Library, MS 11936/401/624353, MS 11936/401/621967, MS 11936/401/624733, MS 11936/401/624354, MS 11936/401/626890, MS 11936/401/628035, MS 11936/401/630177, MS 11936/407/655256, MS 11936/407/655287, MS 11936/407/658962, MS 11936/398/619246

48   Old Bailey proceedings, 2 December 1801, 18011202.

49   *The Times* newspaper Notices, 12 September 1801.

50   An archaic term meaning 'late'.

51   William Molloy, Old Bailey proceedings, 20 February 1799, 17990220.

52   *London*, Volume 3 by Charles Knight, created from the 1842 edition. From the Edwin C Bolles papers (MS004), Digital Collections and Archives, Tufts University, Medford.

53   ibid.

54   Recollections by George Leake, November 1890, H. M. O. Hale family collection.

55   BLP ACC 2877, Georgiana Bisdee née Hale, daughter of Sabina Hale née Molloy.

56   *Narratives of shipwrecks of the Royal Navy between 1793 and 1849*, W Gilly (ed.) 1850.

57   NA ADM 36/15145

58   Georgiana Bisdee née Hale, Letter to the Editor, *Western Mail*, Perth 27 August 1925.

59   No 63A, Transcription by Georgiana Hale, H. M. O. Hale family collection.

60   Letter from Sir Edmund DuCane to Georgiana Hale, 7 December 1892, H. M. O. Hale family collection.

61   NA HMS *Penguin* Ship's muster records, 1801/1802 ADM 36/15145.

62   NA HMS *Hindostan* Ship's muster records, 1802 ADM 36 15292.

63   NA HMS *Hindostan* Ship's muster records, 1803/1804 ADM 36/15417.

64 Letter from Sir Edmund DuCane to Georgiana Hale, 1 December 1892, H. M. O. Hale family collection.
65 Admiral Horatio Nelson, letter to Lord St Vincent, 19 April 1804.
66 Recollections of George Leake, November 1890, H. M. O. Hale family collection.
67 NA William Molloy Probate, 11/1419 Folio 37, John Molloy's father also left an allowance to his mother, Ann, and brother, Neale Molloy.

Sisters and secrets
68 Advertisements in the *Carlisle Patriot*, September and October 1819.
69 CAC D KEN 4/8/6
70 CAC D KEN 4/13/15
71 CAC D KEN 3/20/2 Account sent to Mrs Kennedy; Guildhall Library London, Records of Sun Fire Office, January 1808.
72 Extract from *A Topographical Survey of the Parish of Kensington*, Joshua Rhodes, 1766. Courtesy of the Royal Borough of Kensington and Chelsea Local Studies and Archives.
73 CAC D KEN 3/8/14
74 Transcription by Patrick Richardson-Bunbury of the handwriting of Georgiana Hale. H. M. O. Hale family collection.
75 CAC D KEN 4/13/11 1822-24
76 *The History of the Town and School of Rugby*, Nicholas Harris Nicolas Esq FSA, Merridew & Son, Coventry, and E. Pretty, Northampton MDCCCXXVI 1828; *The History, Topography and Directory of Warwickshire*, William West Birmingham 1830.
77 CAC D KEN 3/59/6 Letter from J Martinday to Mrs Kennedy.
78 Abraham and John Caldecott were related to the local nobility, the Boughtons, and their stepmother was a daughter of the Senhouse family from Netherhall.
79 NGR SP4763876687 English Heritage P47NE 3/29 06/10/60- II
80 CAC D KEN 3/28/9 Letter from Georgiana Molloy to Mrs Kennedy, 12 January 1830.
81 CAC D KEN/3/59/6 Letter from J Martinday to Mrs Kennedy, 1826.
82 *An All Consuming Passion: Origins, modernity and the Australian life of Georgiana Molloy*, William J. Lines, p28, Allen & Unwin 1994.
83 CAC D KEN 3/26 Letter from W S Phillips to Mrs Kennedy, 5 February 1828.
84 CAC D KEN 3/35 /8 Undated notes from 'AC' to Georgiana Kennedy.
85 CAC D KEN 3/35/3 Letter from W S Phillips to Mrs Kennedy, 1827.
86 CAC D KEN 3/26 Note from Georgiana Kennedy to Mrs Kennedy, April 1827.
87 CAC D KEN 3/26 Letter from Ann Caldecott to Mrs Kennedy, 23 April 1827.
88 Besley was a Fellow of Balliol College, Oxford, at the same time as William Phillips was next door at Trinity.

Endnotes

89   CAC D KEN 3/12 Letter from Reverend John Besley to Mrs Kennedy.
90   CAC D KEN 3/12 Letter from Ann Caldecott to Mrs Kennedy.
91   Letter from M. C. Chavasse to Georgiana Hale, 7 June No 11b, H. M. O. Hale family collection.
92   CAC D KEN /3 Letter from William Phillips to Mrs Kennedy, 22 January.
93   CAC D KEN 3/11; D KEN 3/12 1825; D KEN 3/13 1828–1830 Letters from William Butlin to Mrs Kennedy.
94   CAC D KEN 3/26 Letter from 'Wm B' to Mrs Kennedy.
95   CAC D KEN 3 /26 Letter from 'Wm B' to Mrs Kennedy.
96   CAC D KEN 3 /26 Letter from William Phillips to Mrs Kennedy, 5 February 1828.
97   CAC D KEN 3/26 Letter from William Phillips to Mrs Kennedy.
98   Letter from Mrs E. B. Cunningham (née Elizabeth Dunlop) to Margaret Chavasse, December 1888. H. M. O. Hale family collection No 11a.
99   CAC D KEN 3/27 List of clothes and equipment needed by a lady going to India.
100   Transcribed letter from Margaret Chavasse to Georgiana Hale, 7 June Undated. H. M. O. Hale family collection No 11b.
101   BLP ACC 2877A/1 Diary of Georgiana Kennedy, Monday 9 February 1829.
102   CAC D KEN 3/26 Letter from William Butlin to Mrs. Kennedy, 1828.
103   BLP ACC 2877 A/1 Diary of Georgiana Kennedy, 27 February 1829.
104   BLP ACC 2877 A/1 Diary of Georgiana Kennedy, 28 February 1829 and 7 March 1829.
105   CAC D KEN 3/63/12 Letter from John Caldecott to Mrs Kennedy, May 1827.
106   Warwickshire County Record Office CR 1106/1 1824-30.

An unbroken spirit

107   *Annals of Garelochside*, William Charles Maughan, London 1897.
108   *Minute Book of the Board of Green Cloth 1809–1820*, privately printed, Glasgow 1891.
109   *The Dunlop Papers* Volume 2, J. G. Dunlop, privately printed, Frome and London 1939.
110   Maughan, *op. cit.*
111   BLP ACC 2877 A/1 Diary of Georgiana Kennedy, 24 February 1829.
112   BLP ACC 2877 A/1 Diary of Georgiana Kennedy.
113   BLP ACC 4730A/18 and ACC 4730A/17 Augusta Historical Society, MN 1648; Notebook in the handwriting of Georgiana Kennedy, July 1828. Original transcription by H. M. W.ilson revised 1995 by Patrick Richardson-Bunbury in collaboration with Graham Hopner, Local Studies Librarian, Dumbarton ACC 4730A/18 and ACC 4730A/17.
114   A small hired carriage.

115 BLP ACC 2877 A/1 Diary of Georgiana Kennedy, Sunday 11 January 1829.
116 *An All Consuming Passion: Origins, modernity and the Australian life of Georgiana Molloy*, William J. Lines, Allen & Unwin 1994.
117 BLP ACC 4730A/18 and ACC 4730A/17; AHS MN 1648, Notebook diary in the handwriting of Georgiana Kennedy, July 1828.
118 ibid.
119 This chapter draws on A. S. Byatt's explanation (Chapter 7, Landscape) in *Unruly Times: Wordsworth and Coleridge in their time*, Vintage 1997.
120 ibid.
121 ibid.
122 William Wordsworth's Preface to the 1802 edition of *Lyrical Ballads*.
123 *Lyrical Ballads with a Few Other Poems*, William Wordsworth and Samuel Taylor Coleridge, London 1798.
124 Samuel Taylor Coleridge in Biographia, cited by Byatt *op. cit.*
125 BLP ACC 4730A/18 and ACC 4730A/17 Notebook in the handwriting of Georgiana Kennedy, July 1828.
126 Probably David Hutcheson of Greenock. Hutcheson Dunlop, a son of Alexander Dunlop, was also on board.
127 CAC D KEN 3/26 Letter from Mrs Kennedy to Georgiana Kennedy, c1828.
128 CAC D KEN 3/26 Letter from Georgiana Kennedy to Mrs Kennedy, c1828.
129 ibid.
130 BLP ACC 4730A/18 and ACC 4730A/17 Notebook in the handwriting of Georgiana Kennedy, July 1828.
131 Maughan, *op. cit.*
132 *Statistical Account of 1791–99, Parish of Roseneath*, Reverend George Drummond, Volume 4.
133 *Statistical account of 1845 Parish of Roseneath*, Reverend Robert Story.
134 Drummond, *op. cit.*
135 Maughan, *op cit.*
136 ibid.
137 *Caledonia: Or an account, historical and topographic, of North Britain*, Volume 3, George Chalmers, Cadell and Davies 1824.
138 *Memoir of the life of the Rev. Robert Story*, Robert Herbert Story, Macmillan and Co London 1862.
139 Maughan London 1897, *op. cit.*
140 Story, *op. cit.*
141 Maughan, *op. cit.*
142 Story, *op. cit.*
143 *Roseneath Past and Present*, William Charles Maughan, London 1893.
144 BLP ACC 3278 A Letter from Georgiana Molloy to Helen Story, 8 December 1834.

145 BLP ACC 3278 A/2 Letter from Georgiana Molloy to Helen Story, 1 October 1833.
146 BLP ACC 2877 A/1 Diary of Georgiana Kennedy, April 13 1829.
147 BLP ACC 3278 A/2 Letter from Georgiana Kennedy to Helen and Robert Story, 25 January 1830.
148 *The Dunlops of Dunlop*, J. G. Dunlop, Butler & Tanner, London 1939.
149 Story, *op. cit.*
150 *Georgiana Molloy: Portrait with background*, Alexandra Hasluck, OUP Melbourne 1955.
151 Story, *op. cit.*
152 *John McLeod Campbell: The extent and nature of atonement*, James C. Goodloe IV, Princeton Theological Seminary.
153 *Peace in Believing*, Reverend Robert Story, 1829.
154 ibid.
155 Lines, *op. cit.*
156 *Annals of Garelochside*, *op. cit.*
157 BLP ACC 2877 A/1 Diary of Georgiana Kennedy, 29 March 1829.

King George commands

158 A line from a traditional seventeenth-century ballad popular with the Rifle Brigade, probably published in 1706 as a song called 'The Recruiting Officer': 'Over the hills and o'er the Main, To Flanders, Portugal and Spain, Queen Ann commands and we'll obey, Over the hills and far away'.
159 NA WO 13/1710
160 NA WO 31/242; Journal of the House of Commons Appendix, Volume 64, July 1807–July 1809.
161 *Sunday Times*, Perth 22 May, 1921, 'Links with the Past' by Horace Stirling, cited by Alexandra Hasluck in *Georgiana Molloy: Portrait with background*, Oxford University Press 1955.
162 Moretonhampstead History Society: Silvester Treleaven's diary 1806.
163 CAC D KEN 3/28 Letter from Georgiana Molloy to George Kennedy, 16 May 1836.
164 NA WO 13/1710
165 *Rough Sketches of the Life of an Old Soldier*, Jonathan Leach, Longman London 1831.
166 *The Recollections of Rifleman Harris*, Benjamin Harris, ed. Henry Curling, H. Hurst London 1848.
167 *The History of the Rifle Brigade (The Prince Consort's Own) formerly the 95th*, Sir William H. Cope, Chatto & Windus 1877.
168 Letter from Edmund DuCane to Georgiana Hale, 1 December 1892, H. M. O. Hale family collection No 15.
169 Metropolitan Archive Burials, St Giles-in-the-Fields Camden, 8 May 1809.

170 State Library NSW Mitchell Library B 988, Bishop Hale's letters, November 1848, Volumes 1–2, original in Stirling House (RWAHS). Newspaper cutting c. 1924 in the Maud Sanderson née Parry papers. Via H. M. Wilson article 'Memory Echoes' by 'H The Father of the South West'.

171 Recollections by George Leake, November 1890, H. M. O. Hale family collection; No. 17 copied by H. M. O. Hale and G T Hale from Sir Edmund DuCane's original.

172 *The Soldiers Whom Wellington Led: Deeds of chivalry, daring and renown*, Edward Fraser, Methuen & Co Ltd London 1913.

173 Peninsular Journal of Charles Crowe, Volume 2, transcribed by Michael Heath-Caldwell, March 2 1814.

174 *English Battles and Sieges in the Peninsula*, Sir William Napier, KCB John Murray London 1879.

175 *Rough Sketches of the Life of an Old Soldier*, Jonathan Leach, Longman London 1831.

176 *Waterloo: The battle for modern Europe*, Andrew Roberts, HarperCollins London 2005.

177 *The Vision of Judgement*, George Gordon, Lord Byron.

178 Recollections by George Leake, November 1890, H. M. O. Hale family collection, No. 17 copied by H. M. O. Hale and G T Hale.

179 Sharp-shooter.

180 *Georgiana Molloy: Portrait with background*, Alexandra Hasluck, Oxford University Press 1955.

181 Recollections by George Leake, *op. cit.*

182 BLP ACC 4732 A/ 3 A/4 Warrants appointing John Molloy as Deputy Judge Advocate 1815 and 1816 signed by the Duke of Wellington.

183 *A Statistical Account of the British Empire*, John Ramsay McCulloch, Charles Knight Comp. 1839.

184 *The Soldiers Whom Wellington Led: Deeds of daring, chivalry and renown*, Edward Fraser, Nabu Press 2010.

185 Colonel Jonathan Leach, cited in Fraser, *op. cit.*

186 *The Royal Naval and Military Calendar; and National Record for 1821*, Sir George Mackenzie.

187 Letter from John Molloy to Sabina Hale, 18 September 1853, H. M. O. Hale family collection.

188 Letter from Edmund DuCane to Georgiana Hale, 7 December 1892, H. M. O. Hale family collection.

189 *Edinburgh Gazette*, June 1824.

190 *The Times*, 17 January 1829.

191 *The Gentleman's Magazine* Volume 99 Part 2, July 1829.

192 *Belle Assemblée or Court and Fashionable Magazine*, J. Bell, 1829.

May the end be blest

193 Notes written by Georgiana Hale, H. M. O. Hale family collection 63A.
194 Letter from Margaret Chavasse, daughter of Margaret Chavasse née Dunlop, to Georgiana Hale, 7 June, H. M. O. Hale family collection, H. M. W. Index No 11b.
195 Letter from Elizabeth Boyle Cunningham née Dunlop to Margaret Chavasse, December 1888, H. M. O. Hale family collection, H. M. W. Index No 11a.
196 Kirkman Finlay was a wealthy Member of Parliament who lived in Glasgow. He was the most prominent cotton merchant at the time when Molloy was stationed there with the 95th Regiment to control an uprising of cotton weavers. Molloy stayed at Finlay's country home, Toward Castle, in 1824.
197 *Rough Sketches of the Life of an Old Soldier*, Jonathan Leach, Longman London 1831.
198 *The Copepodologist's Cabinet: A biographical and bibliographical history*, Volume 1, David M. Damkaer, American Philosophical Society 2002.
199 *Dacelo leachii* (the blue-winged kookaburra) was named for Elford Leach. A bird that some sailors believe forewarns them of bad weather is known as Leach's Storm-petrel.
200 *Rifle-Green by Nature*, Keith Harrison and Eric Smith, The Ray Society 2008.
201 *The Royal Naval and Military Calendar; and National Record for 1821*, Sir George Mackenzie.
202 CAC D KEN 3/59/3 Letters from George Leach to Mrs Kennedy.
203 Notes written by Georgiana Hale, H. M. O. Hale family collection No 63A.
204 CAC D KEN 3/9/4 Letter from George Leach junior to Mrs Kennedy, 22 October 1820.
205 CAC D KEN 3/28/9 Letter from Georgiana Molloy to Mrs Kennedy, 4 December 1831.
206 CAC D KEN 3/32/3 Letter from John Molloy to Mrs Kennedy, 1827.
207 CAC D KEN 3/46/5 Letter from Dalton Kennedy to Mrs Kennedy, 11 November 1837. Transcribed by Patrick Richardson-Bunbury.
208 Handwritten notes transcribed by Patrick Richardson-Bunbury, Richardson-Bunbury family archive. The Crawfurds and Kennedys were related. Dalton Kennedy married Margueretta, a daughter of his guardian, ACB Crawfurd of Ardmillan House, Girvan, Ayrshire, in 1840.
209 BLP ACC 3278 A/1 Letter from Eliza Kennedy to John Molloy, previously attributed to Georgiana Kennedy.
210 BLP ACC 2877 A/1 Diary of Georgiana Kennedy, 1 January 1829.
211 BLP ACC 2877 A/1 Diary of Georgiana Kennedy, February 1829.
212 BLP ACC 2877 A/1 Diary of Georgiana Molloy, January 1829.
213 BLP ACC 2877 A/1 Diary of Georgiana Molloy, January 1829.
214 Letter from Elizabeth Boyle Cunningham née Dunlop to Margaret Chavasse, December 1888, H. M. O. Hale family collection, H. M. W. Index 11a.

215 BLP ACC 3278 A/2 Letter from Georgiana Molloy to Helen Story, 12 September 1829.
216 CAC D KEN 3/34/11828 Letter to Mrs Kennedy from Dalton Kennedy; D KEN 3/35/7 D KEN 3/36/2 1829 Letter to Mary Kennedy from Dalton Kennedy, 1828; D KEN 3/37/2 Draft letter from Mrs Kennedy to Dalton Kennedy; D KEN 3/40/1/1 Letter to Mrs Kennedy from Hugh (Draper), 1829.
217 BLP ACC 2877 A/1 Diary of Georgiana Kennedy, 2 March 1829.
218 BLP ACC 2877 A/1 Diary of Georgiana Kennedy, 25 April 1829.
219 BLP ACC 2877 A/1 Diary of Georgiana Kennedy, May 1829.
220 BLP ACC 2877 A/1 Diary of Georgiana Kennedy, June 1829.
221 Burials in the Parish of St Giles, Bishop's transcript, 1829; Herald of Arms in Ordinary 1982–1997 Thomas Woodcock, Esq., LVO, FSA research for Patrick Richardson-Bunbury.
222 BLP ACC 2877 A/1 Diary of Georgiana Kennedy, 17 January 1829.
223 Inland Revenue records Volume 1 Folio 24: copy of typed note given to H. M. Wilson, 30 December 1983, provided by Patrick Richardson-Bunbury.
224 BLP ACC 2877 A/1 Diary of Georgiana Kennedy, January to August 1829.
225 *The Gardener's Magazine and Register*, Volume 5, 1829.
226 *A brief sketch of the long and varied career of Marshall MacDermott of Adelaide, South Australia*. W. K. Thomas, written for private distribution amongst relatives and special friends Marshall MacDermott, 1874. MacDermott established the first bank in Western Australia and managed the Bank of Australasia.
227 CAC D KEN 3/28/9 Letter from Georgiana Molloy to Mrs Kennedy, 4 December 1831.
228 BLP ACC 2877 A/1 Diary of Georgiana Kennedy, 1829.
229 BLP ACC 227 A Letters of John Molloy.
230 ibid.
231 BLP ACC 2877 A/1 Diary of Georgiana Kennedy, 1829.
232 BLP ACC 3278A Letters of Georgiana Molloy from an original letter to Helen Story, 8 December 1834.
233 BLP ACC 2877 A/1 Diary of Georgiana Kennedy, 26 July 1829.
234 *The Evening Times* 16 May 2007.
235 CAC D KEN 3/45/2 Marriage certificate 6 August 1829.
236 Reverend Robert Story recorded the marriage on the certificate of Banns because Cardross was not his own parish.
237 BLP ACC 2877 A/1 Diary of Georgiana Kennedy 6 August 1829.
238 CAC D KEN 3/28/9 Letter from Georgiana Molloy to Mrs Kennedy, November 1830, and BLP ACC 501A Letter from Georgiana Molloy to Eliza Besley, November 1832.
239 BLP ACC 2877 A/1 Diary of Georgiana Kennedy, 6 August 1829.

Adieu, my native land!

240 BLP ACC 2877 A/1 Diary of Georgiana Molloy, 7 August 1829.
241 BLP ACC 2877 A/1 Diary of Georgiana Molloy, 8 August 1829.
242 CAC D KEN 3/9 Letter from Mrs Kennedy to Dalton Kennedy, 16 April 1828.
243 CAC D KEN 3/28/9 Letter from Georgiana Molloy to Mrs Kennedy, 4 December 1831.
244 BLP Diary of Georgiana Molloy, 16 August 1829, ACC 2877 A/1.
245 BLP ACC 2877 A/1 Diary of Georgiana Molloy, 16–17 August 1829.
246 BLP ACC 3278A Letter from Georgiana and John Molloy to Mary Dunlop, postmark 14 August 1829.
247 A pelerine was worn over a dress like a long, pointed collar or shawl.
248 BLP ACC 2877 A/1 Diary of Georgiana Molloy, 24 August 1829.
249 BLP ACC 3278A
250 ibid.
251 BLP ACC 2877 A/1 Diary of Georgiana Molloy, 8 September 1829.
252 http://apps.kew.org/herbcat/navigator.do
253 BLP A/1 ACC 2877 Diary of Georgiana Molloy, 31 August 1829.
254 Knowing looks or glances.
255 BLP ACC 3278 A/2 Letter from Georgiana Molloy to Helen Story, 12 September 1829.
256 BLP ACC 2877 A/1 Diary of Georgiana Molloy, 19 September 1829.
257 BLP ACC 2877 A/1 Diary of Georgiana Molloy, 5 September 1829.
258 *The Gentleman's Magazine* Reviews, July 1829.
259 *The Leicester Journal*, 26 November 1829.
260 BLP ACC 3278 A/2 Letter from Georgiana Molloy to Helen Story, 12 September 1829.
261 WO12/10059 summarised at www.captainbrown.net/stories_01.shtml by Louise Prescott.
262 Notes of Georgiana Hale, recorded from the recollections of Sabina Hale, H. M. O. Hale family collection No 63A.
263 CAC D KEN 3/28/9 Letter from Georgiana Molloy to Mrs Frances Birkett via Mrs Kennedy, 15 April 1831.
264 *The Colony of Western Australia: A manual for emigrants*, Nathaniel Ogle, London 1839.
265 CAC D KEN 3/28/2 Georgiana Molloy's journal, 19 October 1829.
266 From *Childe Harold's Pilgrimage* by George Gordon, Lord Byron Canto the First, XIII
267 CAC D KEN 3/28/2 Georgiana Molloy's journal, 23 October 1829.
268 Diary of James Woodward Turner, 18 October 1829–12 January 1830, *Journal and proceedings* (Western Australian Historical Society), Volume I Pt. X (1931) 994.1.b13704953.

269 CAC D KEN 3/28/9 Letter from Georgiana Molloy to Mrs Birkett via Mrs Kennedy, 15 April 1831.
270 CAC D KEN 3/28/2 Georgiana Molloy's journal of the voyage on the *Warrior*, 17 November 1829.
271 ibid. 30 November 1829.
272 BLP MN 350 Turner Family papers. James Woodward Turner's journal on board the *Warrior*, 24 October 1829.
273 BLP ACC 337A/170 Diary of Charles Bussell on board the *Warrior* 1829 in *The Voyage Out: 100 years of sea travel to Australia*, Bryce Moore, Helen Garwood, Nancy Lutton, eds. Fremantle, WA: Fremantle Arts Centre Press in association with the Library Board of Western Australia 1991.
274 CAC D KEN 3/28/9 Letter from Georgiana Molloy to Mrs Birkett among letters from Georgiana Molloy to Mrs Kennedy.
275 CAC D KEN 3/28 /9 Letter from Georgiana Molloy to Mrs Kennedy, 12 January 1830.
276 CAC D KEN 3/28/9 Letter from Georgiana Molloy to Mrs Birkett.
277 BLP ACC 2877 A/2 Diary of Georgiana Molloy, 1830.
278 CAC D KEN 3/28/9 Letter from Georgiana Molloy to Mrs Kennedy, 11 March–4 April 1830.
279 ibid.
280 'Settlement of The Swan: the birth of Perth', Ruth Marchant James, *Australian Heritage*, March 2007.
281 CAC D KEN 3/28/9.
282 CAC D KEN 3/28/9 Letter from Georgiana Molloy to Mrs Kennedy, 11 March–4 April 1830.
283 ibid.
284 CAC D KEN 3/28/9 Letter from Georgiana Molloy to Mrs Kennedy, undated c1830.
285 ibid.
286 BLP ACC 2877 A/2 Diary of Georgiana Molloy, 1830.
287 ibid. and CAC D KEN 3/28/9 Letter from Georgiana Molloy to Mrs Kennedy, November 1830.
288 CAC D KEN 3/28/9 Letter from Georgiana Molloy to Mrs Kennedy, undated c1830.
289 Captain Currie was the first Fremantle harbour master. He arrived with Stirling on the *Parmelia* in 1829.
290 BLP ACC 2877 A/2 Diary of Georgiana Molloy, 1830.
291 Notes of Georgiana Bisdee née Hale from the reminiscences of her mother Sabina Hale. Copy from Patrick Richardson-Bunbury, H. M. O. Hale family collection.

Endnotes

Cottage on the Killiter

292 From documents in the office of the Hon. J. S. Roe Esquire, Surveyor General. His Excellency Lieutenant-Governor Stirling, 11 May 1833; *Perth Gazette*, 5 October 1833.

293 BLP 2877 A/2 Diary of Georgiana Molloy, 7 May 1830, *Redwood: A tale in two volumes*, Maria Sedgwick 1824.

294 BLP ACC 2877 A/2 Diary of Georgiana Molloy, 1830.

295 BLP ACC 1345A Records of St Mary's Church Busselton from 1830.

296 CAC D KEN 3/28/9

297 CAC D KEN 3/28/9

298 *Cattle Chosen: The story of the first group settlement in Western Australia 1829 to 1841* Chapter 2, E. O. G. Shann, UWA Press 1926.

299 James Turner is recorded as 'carpenter' on some documents but the description was used for the owner of a carpentry business as well as an individual carpenter.

300 London Metropolitan Archives MS, July and August 1824.

301 By a remarkable coincidence, J G Bussell's tutor at Oxford was William Phillips.

302 Du Bois Agett and John Dawson arrived on the *Egyptian* in February 1830.

303 Notes of Georgiana Bisdee née Hale from the reminiscences of her mother, Sabina Hale. Copy from Patrick Richardson-Bunbury, H. M. O. Hale family collection.

304 CAC D KEN 3/28/9 Letter from Georgiana Molloy to Mrs Kennedy, 4 December 1831.

305 CAC D KEN 3/28/9

306 *Encyclopaedia Britannica* 6th Edition, ed. Charles Maclaren, May 1823.

307 Georgiana told her mother that the baby's name was 'Elizabeth Mary' and the same name was used to announce the birth in Carlisle newspapers. When John Molloy recorded his daughter's birth and death in the Parish records he wrote her name as 'Mary Elizabeth'.

308 CAC D KEN 3/28/9 Letter from Georgiana Molloy to Mrs Kennedy c1830.

309 ibid.

310 CAC D KEN 3/28/3 Georgiana Molloy's personal account.

311 CAC D KEN 3/28/9 Letter from Georgiana Molloy to Mrs Kennedy, November 1830.

312 Anne Heppingstone

313 An eighteenth-century English folk song popular with soldiers during the Napoleonic Wars and a Spanish folk song, with words meaning 'Little one, what's the matter?'

314 Notes of Georgiana Hale recorded from the recollections of her mother, Sabina Hale. From Patrick Richardson-Bunbury, H. M. O. Hale family collection 63A.

315 James Stirling, Lt. Governor: Instructions to Mr John Kellam, Assistant Surveyor, Memo, Augusta, 11 May 1830. Royal Western Australian Historical Society, 4308A/HS 450, typed transcript.
316 Notes of Georgiana Hale, recorded from the recollections of her mother, Sabina Hale. Copy from Patrick Richardson-Bunbury, H. M. O. Hale family collection 63A.
317 CAC D KEN 3/28/9 Letter from Georgiana Molloy to Mrs Kennedy, c1830.
318 BLP ACC 337A/333 Letter from Frances Louisa (Fanny) Bussell junior to her mother Mrs Frances Louisa Bussell, 20 April 1833.
319 CAC D KEN 3/28/9
320 ibid.
321 ibid.
322 BLP 994.12 AUG Letter books of Captain John Molloy, 29 August 1830–5 July 1841, H. M. O. Hale family collection inherited by Mr H. M. O. Hale from his aunt, Georgiana Bisdee, brought to Western Australia by Patrick Richardson-Bunbury and presented to the JS Battye Library for transcription. Copy provided by Patrick Richardson-Bunbury. Official correspondence of Colonel Molloy (1830–41).
323 CAC D KEN 3/28/9 Letter from Georgiana Molloy to Mrs Kennedy, 25 February 1833.
324 CAC D KEN 3/28/9 Letter from Georgiana Molloy to Mrs Kennedy, 15 February 1837.
325 CAC D KEN 3/28 /9 Letter from Georgiana Molloy to Mrs Kennedy, c. November 1830.
326 CAC D KEN 3/28/9 Letter from Georgiana Molloy to Mrs Kennedy, 4 December 1831.
327 BLP ACC 3278 A Letter to the Rev. Robert Story and Helen Story from Georgiana Molloy, 22 January 1830.
328 CAC D KEN 3/28 9 Letter from Georgiana Kennedy to Mrs Kennedy.
329 BLP ACC 6926A/3 Letter book of Joseph Vernon Bussell. Letter to Capel Carter, 22 December 1832.
330 CAC D KEN 3/28/9 Letter from Georgiana Molloy to Mrs Frances Birkett via Mrs Kennedy, 15 April 1831.
331 'Ciliter' on John Thomson's Atlas of Scotland 1832, National Library of Scotland BLP ACC 3278A, Diary of Georgiana Molloy, 30 May 1833; ACC 3278A/2 Letter to Helen Story, 8 December 1834.
332 CAC D KEN 3/28/9
333 CAC D KEN 3/28/9 Letter from Georgiana Molloy to Mrs Kennedy, 16 July 1832.
334 D KEN 3/28/9
335 The new addressee is 'Mrs Dalton Kennedy'. The person who changed the address had known her long enough to use her family name.

Endnotes

Mending and making

336 BLP ACC 6926A/3 Letter book of Joseph Vernon Bussell. Letter to Capel Carter, 22 December 1832.
337 CAC D KEN 3/28/9 Letter from Georgiana Molloy to Mrs Kennedy, 4 December 1831.
338 CAC D KEN 3/28/9 Letter from Georgiana Molloy to Mrs Kennedy, 16 July 1832.
339 BLP ACC 3278A Letter from Georgiana Molloy to Helen Story, 1 October 1833.
340 CAC D KEN 3/28/29 Letter from Georgiana Molloy to Mrs Kennedy, 4 December 1831.
341 *Cattle Chosen: The story of the first group settlement in Western Australia 1829 to 1841* by E. O. G. Shann, Chapter 2, quoting a letter from J. G. Bussell to C. Wells, July 1831, MA UWA Press 1926.
342 *The Colony of Western Australia: A manual for emigrants* (Mr Bussell's journal, p227) Nathaniel Ogle, London 1839
343 BLP ACC 6926 A/3 Letter book of Joseph Vernon Bussell Two Letters to Capel Carter, 22 December 1832.
344 ibid.
345 BLP ACC 3278A Letter from Georgiana Molloy to Margaret Dunlop, January 1832.
346 BLP ACC 6926A/3 Letter book of Joseph Vernon Bussell. Letter to Capel Carter, 22 December 1832.
347 BLP ACC 2553A From Swan River Letters by the Du Cane family based on the original letters of Georgiana Molloy, ACC 3278A.
348 BLP 994.12 AUG Letter books of Captain John Molloy, 29 October 1832, Letter to J S Roe, 29 August 1830–5 July 1841. H. M. O. Hale family collection. Official correspondence of Colonel Molloy (1830–41).
349 BLP ACC 3278A Letter from Georgiana Molloy to Margaret Dunlop, 12 January 1832.
350 BLP ACC 3278A Letter to Helen Story, 8 December 1834.
351 Colonel Hanson's pamphlet *Perth Gazette*, 19 January 1833.
352 BLP 501A/1 Letter from Georgiana Molloy to Margaret Chavasse née Dunlop, 12 January 1833.
353 *Perth Gazette* Shipping Intelligence, 9 March 1833.
354 CAC D KEN 3/28/9 Letter from Georgiana Molloy to Mrs Kennedy, 25 February 1833.
355 CAC D KEN 3/63/18 Letter from Mrs Kennedy to Mr Fife, c. June 1832.
356 CAC D KEN 3/63/18 Letter from Eliza Besley to Mrs Kennedy, 14 June 1832.
357 CAC D KEN 3/63/18 Letter from Mrs Kennedy to Mr Fife.
358 CAC D KEN 3/63/18 Letter from Eliza Besley to Mrs Kennedy.

359 CAC D KEN 3/28/9 Letter from Georgiana Molloy to Mrs Kennedy, 29 May 1833.
360 BLP 3278A/2 Letter from Georgiana Molloy to Elizabeth Besley, 1833–34.
361 ibid.
362 CAC D KEN 3/28/9 Letter from Georgiana Molloy to Mrs Kennedy, 26 June 1834.
363 CAC DKEN3/63/18 Letter from Eliza Besley to Mrs Kennedy, 23 December 1833.
364 *Carlisle Journal*, Births, Deaths and Marriages, 8 March 1834.
365 Longbenton Church Register burials, 1834.
366 BLP ACC 3278A/2 Letter from Georgiana Molloy to Helen Story, October 1833.
367 CAC D KEN 3/28/9 Letter from Georgiana Molloy to Mrs Kennedy, November 1830.
368 CAC D KEN 3/28/9 Letter from Georgiana Molloy to Mrs Frances Birkett via Mrs Kennedy, 15 April 1831.
369 *Hampshire Chronicle*, 24 April 1820.
370 BLP ACC 3908/A Letter in the Edward Rodon Huggins collection relating to Mrs Frances Bussell's sisters, Emily Huggins née Yates and Mary Beckford Bowker née Yates, and Thomas Legall Yates senior, their father.
371 *The Gardeners Magazine* Volume 9, John Loudon, 1833.
372 BLP 3278A/2 Letter from Georgiana Molloy to her sister Elizabeth Besley, 1833–34.
373 BLP ACC 4305A Three leaves from Mrs John Molloy's Journal, 1 May–26 September 1833, found by the late Mr Walter Gale at Busselton.
374 CAC D KEN 3/28/9 Letter from Georgiana Molloy to Mrs Kennedy, 16 July 1832.
375 CAC D KEN 3/28/9 Letter from Georgiana Molloy to Mrs Kennedy, 29 May 1833.
376 CAC D KEN 3/28/9 Letter from Georgiana Molloy to Mrs Kennedy, 4 December 1831.
377 CAC D KEN 3 /28/9 Letter from Georgiana Molloy to Mrs Kennedy, 29 May 1833.
378 CAC D KEN 3/28/9 Letter from Georgiana Molloy to Mrs Kennedy, May–October 1833.
379 'A Most Singular Man: Robert Lyon Milne', Reece, B., *Early Days: Journal of the Royal Western Australian Historical Society*, Volume 13, pp. 585–606, 2011.
380 Stirling arrived on the *James Pattison*, on 19 August 1834.
381 A wave of charitable intervention in the early 1830s sent children who were deemed potential vagrants to the British colonies and indentured them to 'masters' as agricultural 'apprentices'. Mainly boys, they were aged between twelve and fifteen.
382 BLP 3278A/2 Letter from Georgiana Molloy to Eliza Besley, 1833–34.

ENDNOTES

383 BLP ACC 1648 A/5 Typescript from an original manuscript, *South West Aboriginal Language Or Dialect: What the Aboriginals Term 'Dornderup Wongie', and Other Things Concerning Australia Generally*, Alfred John Bussell, 1930.
384 BLP 994.12 AUG Official correspondence of Colonel Molloy (1830–41) Letter to the Colonial Secretary, 12 October 1833.
385 BLP 3278A/2 Letter from Georgiana Molloy to Eliza Besley, 1833–34.
386 CAC D KEN 3/28/9 Letter from Georgiana Molloy to Mrs Kennedy, 29 May 1833.
387 BLP ACC 5909A/58 Diary of Frances (Fanny) Louisa Bussell, 16 November 1833.
388 BLP ACC 6926A/5 Diary of Frances (Fanny) Louisa Bussell, 3–16 November 1833.
389 BLP ACC 337A/795 Letter from Frances (Fanny) Louisa Bussell to John Garrett Bussell, 24 November 1834.
390 CAC D KEN 3/28/9 Letter from Georgiana Molloy to Mrs Kennedy, 29 May 1833.
391 ibid.
392 BLP ACC 4305A Three leaves from Mrs John Molloy's Journal, 1 May–26 September 1833. Found by the late Mr Walter Gale at Busselton.
393 CAC D KEN 3/28/9 Letter from Georgiana Molloy to Mrs Kennedy, 29 May 1833.
394 BLP ACC 6926A/5 Diary of Frances (Fanny) Louisa Bussell, 3–16 November 1833.
395 BLP ACC 3278A/2 Letter from Georgiana Molloy to Eliza Besley, 1833–34.
396 BLP 3278A/2 Letter from Georgiana Molloy to Eliza Besley, 1833–34.
397 George Layman arrived in Augusta early in 1830 with the government contract to build the first barracks. Mary Layman was Ellen Stirling's maid in Perth. In 1837 the family moved to their grant at the Vasse and called the homestead Wonnerup.
398 *Perth Gazette*, 25 January 1834.
399 BLP ACC 3278A Letter from Georgiana Molloy to Helen Story, 8 December 1834.
400 ibid.
401 BLP ACC 337A/266 Letter from Elizabeth Capel (Bessie) Bussell to Capel Carter, 13 April 1834; and in ACC 337A/266 *Cattle Chosen: The story of the first group settlement in Western Australia, 1829 to 1841*, Edward Shann. Compiled by Patience Barnard for use by Professor Shann, UWA Press 1926. Transcriptions collected by Patience Barnard and assistants, Shann Papers ACC 337A.
402 BLP ACC 3278A Letter from Georgiana Molloy to Helen Story, 8 December 1834.
403 *Perth Gazette*, 6 December 1834, By His Excellency's Command, Peter Brown, Colonial Secretary. Government notice, Surveyor General's Office Perth, 5 December 1834.
404 *Perth Gazette*, Survey Office Western Australia, 24 October 1834.

405 BLP ACC 3893A Letter from Frances (Fanny) Louisa Bussell to Emily Pakenam Huggins, 19 October 1834. Original transcription by H. M. W.ilson, Private MN 0586/24.
406 BLP ACC 3278A Letter from Georgiana Molloy to Helen Story, 8 December 1834.
407 ibid.
408 CAC D KEN 3/53/6 Letters to Mrs Kennedy relating to Dalton Kennedy's imprisonment for debt, 1834.
409 Letter from Mrs Kennedy to Mrs Frances Birkett, 6 July 1836. Transcribed by Patrick Richardson Bunbury, checked by H. M. W.ilson and Constance Berryman. Copy from Patrick Richardson-Bunbury. H. M. O. Hale family collection.
410 *Perth Gazette*, 20 September 1834.
411 *Tracts Relative to the Aborigines. Published by Direction of the Meeting for Sufferings from 1838 to 1842*, Society of Friends London 1838.
412 BLP 3278A/2 Letter from Georgiana Molloy to Eliza Besley, 1833–34.
413 BLP ACC 3278A Letter from Georgiana Molloy to Helen Story, 8 December 1834.
414 Narrative account of the colony of Western Australia *The Sydney Gazette*, 1 August 1835.
415 CAC D KEN 3/28/9 Letter from Georgiana Molloy to Mrs Kennedy, 22 December 1835.
416 ibid.
417 BLP ACC 6927A/1 Molloy Journal, April 1836. In 2007, the Battye Library acquired a nineteenth-century journal believed to have been written by members of the Bussell family. Analysis of the text by Patrick Richardson-Bunbury showed that it belonged to John Molloy. The handwriting and content reveal that when Molloy was away, entries were made by Georgiana Molloy. Containing records from February 1835 to February 1840, the journal provides a detailed picture of life in Augusta and also makes it possible to adjust dates previously attached incorrectly to some events.
418 BLP ACC 6927A/1 Molloy Journal, 1836.
419 ibid.
420 BLP ACC 6927A/1 Molloy Journal, 1836–37 (not chronologically ordered).
421 BLP ACC 6927A/1 Molloy Journal, 1837.
422 BLP ACC 6927A/1 Molloy Journal, 1836.
423 BLP ACC 6927A/1 Poisonous lead shot. Molloy Journal, 1837.
424 BLP ACC 6927A/1 Molloy Journal, 1836.
425 ibid. A tradition in Dunmow, Essex donated a gammon or 'flitch' of bacon to a married couple who had not argued once during the previous year.
426 BLP ACC 6927A/1 Molloy Journal, 1837.
427 BLP ACC 6926A/9 Diary of Frances (Fanny) Louisa Bussell, May 1836.
428 *Perth Gazette* and *West Australian Journal*, 24 December 1836.
429 BLP ACC 6927A/1 Molloy Journal, 1836.

430 BLP ACC 6927A/1 Molloy Journal, 1838.
431 BLP ACC 6927A/1 Molloy Journal, 1837.
432 Mary Molloy was often called 'Dora' when she was a child.
433 CAC D KEN 3/28/29 Letter from Georgiana Molloy to Mrs Kennedy, 13 February 1837.

Botany by the Blackwood River

434 *Gardening Women: Their stories from 1600 to the present*, Catherine Horwood, Hachette UK 2010
435 Commonly known today as the Augusta kennedia, it was later given the botanical name *Kennedia macrophylla* and is now *Kennedia lateritia*.
436 *The Young Lady's Book: A manual of elegant recreations, exercises and pursuits*, Vizetelly, Branston & Co. London 1829.
437 CAC D KEN 3/28/9 Letter from Georgiana Molloy to Mrs Kennedy, 23 November 1829.
438 BLP ACC 479A Letter books of James Mangles. Transcription of a letter from Georgiana Molloy to James Mangles, 25 January 1838.
439 BLP ACC 3278A/2 Letter from Georgiana Molloy to Eliza Besley, 7 November 1832. Georgiana was referring to a holly-leaved Hovea and Hardenbergia.
440 CAC D KEN 3/28/9 Letter from Georgiana Molloy to Mrs Kennedy and Mary Kennedy, 22 April 1833.
441 Notes of Georgiana Hale, H. M. O. Hale family collection No 63A.
442 BLP ACC 479A Letter books of James Mangles. Transcription of a letter from Georgiana Molloy to James Mangles, 25 January 1838.
443 BLP ACC 3278A/2 Letter from Georgiana Molloy to Eliza Besley, 1833–34.
444 *The British Flower Garden*, Volume 6, Robert Sweet, James Ridgeway & Sons London 1838.
445 *Paxton's Magazine of Botany and Register of Flowering Plants*, Volume 6, W. S. Orr & Co. London 1839.
446 BLP ACC 479A Letter books of James Mangles. Letter from James Drummond to James Mangles, July 1835.
447 BLP ACC 479A Letter books of James Mangles. Transcription of a letter from Georgiana Molloy to James Mangles.
448 BLP ACC 6927A/1 Molloy Journal, 1836.
449 *Perth Gazette* Shipping Intelligence departures, 1 August 1835.
450 BLP ACC 6927A/1 Molloy Journal, 1837.
451 ibid.
452 ibid.
453 ibid. Drinking Roman (or Romany) style tea on the green plateau.
454 Colonists used European orthography to spell Aboriginal words phonetically, even though English and Aboriginal languages do not have exactly matching

phonemes. This resulted in a variety of different spellings recorded for the same words, including Aboriginal names and place names: Gaywal, Gaware, Gayware, Goewar.

455 BLP ACC 337A/795 Journal of Elizabeth (Bessie) Bussell, April–December 1837.
456 Elijah Dawson's report to Molloy states that he was speared by 'the chief of this tribe'.
457 BLP ACC 6926A/10 Copy by Frances (Fanny) Louisa Bussell of letter written by Elizabeth (Bessie) Bussell, 15 September 1837.
458 State Records Office of WA ACC 488/12 Colonial Secretary's Office inward correspondence, 1834–1845 Letter from Lenox Bussell to the Colonial Secretary, 19 August 1837.
459 ibid. 27 September 1837.
460 BLP ACC 6926A/10 Copy by Frances (Fanny) Louisa Bussell of letter written by Elizabeth (Bessie) Bussell, 15 September 1837.
461 *Perth Gazette*, 13 May 1837.
462 British House of Commons Select Committee on Aborigines (British Settlements) Report, House of Commons Parliamentary Paper 425, July 1837, 84. House of Commons digitised archival images: Ref HL/PO/JO/10/8/1203 Session 1837: 809–898.
463 BLP ACC 2877 A/1 Diary of Georgiana Kennedy, 1 January 1829.
464 BLP ACC 4732A/2 Letter from Mary Ker née Dunlop to Georgiana Molloy, March–April 1843.
465 BLP ACC 6927A/2 Molloy Journal, 1837.
466 Notes of Georgiana Hale, H. M. O. Hale family collection No 63A.
467 BLP ACC 479A Letter books of James Mangles. Transcription of a letter from Georgiana Molloy to James Mangles, 25 January 1838.
468 BLP ACC 6927A/2 Molloy Journal, 1837.
469 BLP ACC 479A Letter books of James Mangles. Transcription of a letter from Georgiana Molloy to James Mangles, 25 January 1838.
470 ibid.
471 ibid. A silique is a type of fruit, a long seed capsule or pod.
472 ibid.
473 BLP ACC 6927A/2 Molloy Journal, 1838.
474 ibid.
475 BLP ACC 479A Letter books of James Mangles. Transcription of a letter from Georgiana Molloy to James Mangles, 25 January 1838.
476 J. R. Gowen was head gardener at Highclere Castle, Hampshire. Highclere was used as the setting for the television series *Downton Abbey*, Carnival Films UK and WGBH Boston USA.

477 BLP ACC 479A Transcription of a letter from J R Gowen to James Mangles, 17 August 1838.
478 BLP ACC 479A Letter books of James Mangles. Transcription of a letter from Georgiana Molloy to James Mangles, January–November 1838.
479 ibid.
480 ibid.
481 BLP 6927A/2 Molloy Journal, 1838.
482 ibid.
483 BLP ACC 479A Letter books of James Mangles. Transcription of two letters from Georgiana Molloy to James Mangles, 1 and 21 November 1838.
484 BLP ACC 479A Letter books of James Mangles. Transcription of a letter from Dr John Lindley to James Mangles, 15 September 1838.
485 Digitised images of the Molloy journals are available to view on the website of the State Library of Western Australia at www.slwa.wa.gov.au/resources/bussell_diaries/molloy_diary_01
486 BLP ACC 479A Letter books of James Mangles. Transcription of a letter from Georgiana Molloy to James Mangles, June 1840.
487 BLP ACC 6927A/2 Molloy Journal, 1839.
488 CAC D KEN 3/28/9 John Molloy's postscript to a letter from Georgiana Molloy to Mrs Kennedy, 16 July 1832.
489 BLP ACC 6927A/2 Molloy Journal, 1839.
490 Memories of Sabina Hale recorded as notes by her daughter Georgiana Hale, H. M. O. Hale family collection No 63A.
491 BLP ACC 6927A/2, Molloy Journal, 1839.

A garden in Busselton

492 Memories of Sabina Hale recorded as notes by her daughter Georgiana Hale, H. M. O. Hale family collection No 63A.
493 CAC D KEN 3/28/1 Sketch maps signed by John Molloy, c.1830.
494 BLP ACC 479A Letter books of James Mangles. Transcription of a letter from Georgiana Molloy to James Mangles, January 1840.
495 ibid.
496 ibid.
497 BLP Molloy Journal, May 1839, MN 1726 ACC 6927A/2.
498 Heppingstone, Ian D. and Wilson, H. Margaret, '"Mrs John": The Letters of Charlotte Bussell of Cattle Chosen.', *Early Days*, Journal and Proceedings, Volume VII, Part V, Perth: Royal Western Australian Historical Society, 1973.
499 John was a brother of Thomas Salkilld. He arrived from England in 1838 to work for Turner and a third brother, Benjamin, joined them at some stage.
500 BLP ACC 6927A/2 Molloy Journal, 1839.
501 Molloy's journal notes 'erroneous dates' for this entry.

502 BLP 994.12 AUG Official correspondence of Colonel Molloy, 1830–41. Letter from John Molloy to the Colonial Secretary accompanying witness depositions, 15 December 1839.
503 BLP ACC 4730A/1B Letter from Mrs Kennedy to John Molloy, 18 July 1839. Transcribed by Patrick Richardson-Bunbury.
504 Mrs Kennedy seems to have forgotten that the Molloys named their firstborn 'Elizabeth'.
505 CAC D KEN 3/62/7 Agreement between Mrs Kennedy and Messrs Newman and Gwinnett, 4 June 1836.
506 CAC D KEN 4/23/1 Letter to Mrs Kennedy from William Morley, her land agent, September 1836.
507 CAC D KEN 4/23/4 Letter to Mrs Kennedy from William Morley, June 1837.
508 CAC D KEN 3/65/4 Letter from Mary Birt née Kennedy to Mrs Kennedy, 1842.
509 CAC D KEN 3/63/29 Letters to Mrs Kennedy relating to the lease of a house in Carlisle to Ellen Carlyle, 1838.
510 Eleanor Carlyle was related to Mrs Lodge, the previous tenant. Also known as 'Ellen', she was the daughter of Mrs Lodge's cousin Joseph Dacre Carlyle, a Chancellor of Carlisle.
511 Mary Kennedy's arrival was three or four months earlier than the date given in other biographies: *Georgiana Molloy: Portrait with background*, Alexandra Hasluck, Oxford University Press 1955; *An All Consuming Passion: Origins, modernity and the Australian life of Georgiana Molloy*, William J. Lines, Allen & Unwin 1994.
512 John Molloy's handwriting so presumably he had never seen the written name, Preiss.
513 Notes of Sabina Hale to her daughter Georgiana Bisdee née Hale. H. M. O. Hale family collection, copy from Patrick Richardson-Bunbury.
514 CAC D KEN 3/56/6 Letter from Mary Birt née Kennedy to Mrs Kennedy, October 1841.
515 CAC D KEN 3/65/4 Letter from Georgiana Molloy to Mrs Kennedy, 19 October 1840.
516 Memories of Sabina Hale told to her daughter Georgiana Hale. H. M. O. Hale family collection No 63A.
517 Photocopy of front cover and inscription on fly-leaf: 'Mrs Molloy the gift of James Mangles, 1839', from Patrick Richardson-Bunbury, from the collection of John Coote.
518 BLP ACC 479A Letter books of James Mangles. Transcription of a letter from Georgiana Molloy to James Mangles.
519 ibid.
520 ibid.
521 The Department of Plant Sciences at the University of Cambridge holds twenty-five items collected by Georgiana Molloy including sundews.

522 *The Greenhouse, Hot house & Stove*, Charles McIntosh FHS, head gardener to His Grace the Duke of Buccleugh, Wm. S. Orr & Co London 1838.
523 BLP ACC 479A Letter books of James Mangles.
524 *The American Gardener's Magazine and Register of Useful Discoveries and Improvements in Horticulture and Rural Affairs* Volume 2, Boston 1836.
525 BLP ACC 479A Letter books of James Mangles. Transcription of a letter from John Lindley to James Mangles, 1839.
526 ibid. Transcription of a letter from Joseph Paxton to James Mangles 3 September 1839.
527 Dr John Ryan provides an interesting discussion on this topic in 'Values and Evaluations: Reading for Beauty in John Lindley's *A Sketch of the Vegetation of the Swan River Colony* (1839–40)', J. Ryan, (2010), *The New Critic*, Issue 13, 1–17, Crawley, Western Australia.
528 Georgiana used 'Ward's glazed box' herself to pack plants for Mangles in 1842. BLP ACC 479A.
529 ibid. Transcription of a letter from Georgiana Molloy to James Mangles.
530 ibid.
531 ibid.
532 Recollections of Amy Wilkinson née Hale, a daughter of Mathew Hale by his first marriage. H. M. O. Hale family collection, copy from Patrick Richardson-Bunbury.
533 BLP ACC 479A Letter books of James Mangles. Transcription of a letter from Georgiana Molloy to James Mangles, June–July 1840. After ten years in Australia, Georgiana still referred to the seasons using their English equivalent, with May as spring rather than autumn.
534 ibid. The 'notices' section contained the latest news and information.
535 *The Floriculture Magazine and Miscellany of Gardening* Vol V. Notices, 1840–41.
536 *The Floricultural Cabinet and Florists' Magazine* Vol IX, 1841. All four plants are indigenous to the Vasse area where Georgiana was collecting botanical specimens. The common name for *Babingtonia camphorosmae* is Camphor Myrtle. Common names for the 'bloodwood' *Eucalyptus calophyll*, also known as *Corymbia calophylla*, are Marri and Port Gregory Gum. *Pultenaea* are often referred to as 'bush peas' and *Euthales macrophylla* is an archaic name for *Velleia macrophylla*, large-leaved velleia.
537 BLP ACC 479A Letter books of James Mangles. Transcription of a letter from Georgiana Molloy to James Mangles, January–November 1838.
538 Extract from 'Lines composed a few miles above Tintern Abbey on revisiting the banks of the Wye during a tour 13 July 1798', William Wordsworth
539 BLP ACC 479A Letter books of James Mangles. Transcription of a letter from Georgiana Molloy to James Mangles, August–October 1840.
540 BLP ACC 479A Letter books of James Mangles. Transcription of a letter from Georgiana Molloy to James Mangles, June–July 1840.

541 BLP ACC 6926A Diary of Frances (Fanny) Louisa Bussell, 1840.
542 Memories of Sabina Hale told to her daughter Georgiana Hale. Transcribed by Patrick Richardson-Bunbury, 1982. H. M. O. Hale family collection No 63A.
543 CAC D KEN 3/50 Certificates of Marriage between Mary Gertrude Kennedy and William Henry Birt, 1840 and 1841.
544 *South African Commercial Advertiser*, Birt–Kennedy marriage, 20 January 1841.
545 *Schola regia cantuarensis: a history of Canterbury School, commonly called the King's School*, Charles Eveleigh Woodruff and Henry James Cape, Mitchell, Hughes & Company 1908; CAC D KEN 3/65 Letters from Mary Kennedy to Mrs Kennedy, 1841.
546 BLP ACC 479A Letter books of James Mangles. Transcription of a letter from Georgiana Molloy to James Mangles, June–July 1840.
547 *OCBIL theory: towards an integrated understanding of the evolution, ecology and conservation of biodiversity on old, climatically buffered, infertile landscapes*, Stephen D. Hopper, Plant Soil, 2009. Published online by Springer Science + Business Media B. V. 2009.
548 BLP ACC 479A Letter books of James Mangles. Transcription of a letter from Georgiana Molloy to James Mangles, August–October 1841.
549 The citation is Georgiana's own reference to the numbering in a *hortus siccus* she sent to Mangles.
550 An upturned tub on a tall post, used as a landmark for ships in Geographe Bay.
551 ibid. 20 January 1841.
552 ibid. 6 February 1841.
553 ibid. 9 April 1841 1841.
554 *Cattle Chosen: The story of the first group settlement in Western Australia, 1829 to 1841*, Chapter 8 Wild Justice, Edward Shann, UWA Press 1926.
555 CAC D KEN 3/56 Letter from Mrs Kennedy to her daughter, Mary Birt, recounting the content of a letter from Georgiana Molloy, October 1841. The letter does not identify which three of the Bussell brothers it referred to.
556 Elizabeth Senhouse became Mrs Pocklington when she married Joseph Pocklington. They both later adopted the surname 'Pocklington-Senhouse'.
557 ibid.
558 Court proceedings show that John Molloy was not involved in the trial of Charles Bussell nor was he associated in any way with the verdict or punishment. The case was tried in the Perth Quarter Sessions on 1 July 1842, before W. H. Mackie and a bench of magistrates.
559 *The Inquirer*, Perth 13 July 1842.
560 Recollections of Amy Wilkinson née Hale, a daughter of Mathew Hale by his first marriage. H. M. O. Hale family collection, copy from Patrick Richardson-Bunbury.
561 ibid.
562 BLP ACC 479A Letter books of James Mangles. Transcription of a letter from Georgiana Molloy to James Mangles, 6 February 1842.

ENDNOTES

563 *Wollaston's Picton Journal* (1841–1844), Volume 1 of the Journals and diaries (1841–1856) of Reverend John Ramsden Wollaston, M. A. collected by Canon A. Burton; ed. Canon Burton and Percy U. Henn.
564 BLP 3278A/3 Letter from Mrs Kennedy to Mary Molloy, 14 February 1842.
565 Wollaston was an Anglican clergyman who later became Archdeacon of Western Australia.
566 BLP ACC 479A Letter books of James Mangles. Transcription of a letter from Georgiana Molloy to James Mangles, 11 April 1842.
567 *London Journal of Botany* Volume 2: Swan River Botany, James Drummond.
568 ibid.
569 *Wollaston's Picton Journal, op. cit.*
570 C/1843 D1, the unusually bright 'Great March Comet of 1843' was last observed on 19 April.
571 *Wollaston's Picton Journal, op. cit.*
572 Charles Macintosh and Alexander Dunlop were Glasgow partners in Tennant, Knox & Co.
573 *The Inquirer* Perth, Wednesday 22 March 1843.
574 *Wollaston's Picton Journal, op. cit.*
575 Transcription by the author of copies provided by Patrick Richardson-Bunbury, in Mrs Kennedy's handwriting, originally copied from a Dalton family Bible.
576 Mrs Kennedy died on 25 May 1843. *Carlisle Journal* BMD, 10 June 1843. Her executors, W. S. Phillips and W. H. Gwinnett, noted in the final accounts of her estate that a monthly bond payment due to her during her lifetime from Mrs Arden (George Kennedy's widow, Amelia, who had remarried) was due up to 25 May 1843. Her funeral expenses were paid in July 1843. Her death is recorded in the register of death in Cheltenham for March–May 1843.
577 Letter from Charlotte Bussell to Fanny Bussell, 16 October 1848. Transcription provided by Patrick Richardson-Bunbury.
578 Letter from Charlotte Bussell to Sabina Hale, May 1881. H. M. O. Hale family collection
579 *WA Country Cemeteries, Headstones and Registers* recorded on microfiche H/S St Mary's Anglican Cemetery, Busselton, 1841–1967, Series 1, 5, Battye Library. Transcribed by Elise de Munck and *South-Western News*, 8 April 1932. Heritage Council of Western Australia.
580 BLP ACC 3594A/48/63 Letter from Georgiana Bisdee née Hale to Mr Prinsep, 12 August 1907.
581 The first church service was held on 11 April 1845.
582 BLP ACC 479A Letter books of James Mangles. Transcription of a letter from George Hailes to James Mangles, June 1844.
583 'A Waterloo Veteran' by A. B. in *The West Australian* Perth, quoting from John Ramsden Wollaston's *Picton Journal*, 28 September 1929.

Life after Georgiana

584 BLP ACC 4732A/2 Letter from Mary Stewart Ker née Dunlop to Georgiana Molloy, 29 March/27 April 1843. H. M. O. Hale family collection.
585 Georgiana Molloy's letter quoted in a letter from Mary Stewart Ker née Dunlop to John Molloy, 20 March 1844. Transcribed by Georgiana Hale. H. M. O. Hale family collection.
586 ibid.
587 Words of Sabina Hale née Molloy written by Georgiana Hale, H. M. O. Hale family collection No 63A.
588 *Perth Gazette*, 15 April 1843.
589 BLP ACC 4553A/89 Reminiscences of Charlotte Josephine Prinsep née Bussell daughter of John G Bussell, interviewed by Paul Hasluck, 1928.
590 The *Halcyon* was wrecked at Toby's Inlet. John Molloy paid £60 for it on 11 September 1844, *Perth Gazette*, 21 September 1844.
591 *The Enquirer* Perth, July 1848.
592 BLP ACC 4553A/89 Reminiscences of Charlotte Josephine Prinsep née Bussell interviewed by Paul Hasluck, 1928.
593 State Library of New South Wales B 988 Mathew Blagden Hale papers, 1848–1875: letters and diaries.
594 James Drummond in *London Journal of Botany*, 1842.
595 Mathew Blagden Hale became Archdeacon of Adelaide 1847, first Bishop of Perth in 1857 and Bishop of Brisbane in 1875.
596 Extract from 'Perth's First Bishop' by A. B. in *The West Australian*, 25 July 1936.
597 State Library of New South Wales B 988 Mathew Blagden Hale papers, 1848–75. Letter 2 November 1848.
598 Either Amelia ten years or Flora Molloy eight years.
599 State Library of New South Wales B 988 Mathew Blagden Hale papers, 1848–1875. Letter, 2 November 848.
600 ibid.
601 NA Records of the Prerogative Court of Canterbury PROB 11/1987/35: probate 4 October 1843.
602 BLP ACC 4730A/1B Letter from Mrs Kennedy to John Molloy, 18 July 1839, Transcribed by Patrick Richardson-Bunbury.
603 CAC DB 3/65 Advertisement. Eleanor (Ellen) Carlyle, the original tenant, was still renting the house as Mrs Ellen Maclean with her husband Major H. D. Maclean, High Sheriff of Cumberland.
604 Letter from John Molloy to Sabina Hale, 31 January 1851. H. M. O. Hale family collection.
605 Census for England, 30 March 1851. John Molloy was recorded as a visitor at the Vicarage in Rushall, Staffordshire.

ENDNOTES

606 BLP ACC 4730A and AHS listing. Letter from Jonathan Leach to John Molloy Plymouth, 16 August 1851.
607 Alfred and Ellen Bussell went on to build Ellensbrook and Wallcliffe House near Margaret River.
608 *Royal Engineer: A life of Sir Edmund DuCane*, Alexandra Hasluck, Angus and Robertson Sydney 1973.
609 *The Edinburgh Gazette*, 19 April 1859, and *The London Gazette*, 15 April 1859.
610 State Library of New South Wales B 988 Mathew Blagden Hale papers, 1848–75: letters and diaries.
611 ibid.
612 Letter from John Molloy to Sabina Hale, from Edinburgh Scotland, 31 January 1851. H. M. O. Hale family collection.
613 *Perth Gazette*, 20 April 1860.
614 State Library of New South Wales B 988 Mathew Blagden Hale papers, 1848–1875: letters and diaries.
615 The first Crown Solicitor for Western Australia, George Leake arrived with his mother in 1833 on the same ship as Fanny and Bessie Bussell.
616 *English Battles and Sieges in the Peninsula*, Sir William Napier KCB, London, 1879.
617 Letter from G. W. Leake to Georgiana Hale, Perth, 26 March 1881. H. M. O. Hale family collection No 17.
618 ibid.
619 *The West Australian*, 1 August 1925.
620 AHS Molloy collection.
621 ibid.
622 National Trust of Western Australia ACC 2008.11.
623 Email to the author from English Furniture Department, Sotheby's London, February 2009.
624 AHS Molloy collection. Letter from Georgiana Bisdee née Hale.
625 National Trust of Western Australia ACC 2008.11.
626 State Library of New South Wales B 988 Mathew Blagden Hale papers, 1848–1875: letters and diaries.
627 *Western Mail* Perth, 7 May 1904.
628 *Western Mail* Perth, 12 August 1920, 'Grand Old Man', Hugh Kalyptus, 'Old Time Memories: Busselton's.
629 *Flora's Lexicon: an interpretation of the Language and Sentiment of Flowers with an outline of botany and a poetical introduction*, Catherine H. Waterman, Hooker and Claxton, Philadelphia, 1839.
630 ibid.

Image Credits

All images copyright Mike Rumble and Bernice Barry, unless otherwise indicated. Thank you to those listed below for permission to use the following images:

1st section
    Photo page 1a, 2c-e – Mrs Dorothy Margaret Blaasch nee Richardson-Bunbury
    Photos page 1b, 2a, b – Patrick Richardson Bunbury
    Photos page 3a, 5a, 6a, 7b – Cumbria Archive Centre
    Photo 6b – Mrs Patricia Sedgwick

2nd section
    Photos page 3, 6 – J.S. Battye Library
    Photo page 7 - Cumbria Archive Centre
    Photos page 8 – National Trust of Western Australia

4th section
    Photo page 3c – Herbarium B, Botanical Museum Berlin-Dahlem, Freie Universität Berlin

Index of Names

References are to page numbers and Endnote numbers.

AGG, Amelia, 233
BAKER, William, 264
BANKS, Joseph, 134
BENTHAM, George, 134
BESLEY, Elizabeth *see also Elizabeth Margaret Kennedy*, 180, 181-183
BESLEY, John, 51, 180, 286, 293
BIRKETT, Frances *senior*, 23, 170, 173
BIRKETT, Frances *junior*, *Lady Grant*, 23, 143
BIRKETT, Henry, 23
BIRT, Mary *see also Mary Gertrude Kennedy*, 264, 269
BIRT, William Henry, 264
BISDEE, Georgiana Theodosia *see also Georgie Hale*, 290, 296
BISDEE, John Hutton, 296
BOBBINGOOT, 216
BOWER, Phoebe, 184
BOWKER, Mary *see also Mary Beckford Yates*, Endnote 370
BROCKMAN, Flora *see also Flora Molloy*, 288
BROCKMAN, William Locke, 288
BULL, Henry, 265
BUNBURY, Henry, 202
BURNS, Robert, 10, 297

BUSSELL, Alfred Pickmore, 156, 190, 216, 269, 271, 287
BUSSELL, Charles, 142, 156, 176, 194, 199, 200, 216, 269, 271
BUSSELL, Charlotte *previously Charlotte Cookworthy*, née Spicer, 240, 279
BUSSELL, Elizabeth Capel (Bessie) 184, 185, 192, 194, 216
BUSSELL, Ellen *see also Ellen Heppingstone*, 287
BUSSELL, Frances Louisa *senior*, née Yates, 156, 197, 199
BUSSELL, Frances Louisa *junior* (Fanny) 184, 185, 192, 194, 217, 258, 279
BUSSELL, John Garrett, 149, 155, 156, 158, 161, 176, 194, 195, 202, 216, 240, 242, 265, 282, 289
BUSSELL, Joseph Vernon, 156, 216
BUSSELL, Lenox, 156, 184, 194, 216, 217
BUSSELL, Mary Yates *see also Mary Taylor*, 184, 195, 219
BUSSELL, William, 156

BUSSELL, William Marchant, 156, 184
BUTLIN, William, 47, 54, 56, 130
BYRNE, Anna-Matilda, 135, 136, 140
BYRNE, Francis, 114, 120, 135, 137
CALDECOTT, Abraham, 48
CALDECOTT, Ann née Stephens, 48, 49, 51, 53, 57, 130
CALDECOTT, John, 48
CALVERT, Mary née Mitchinson, 24
CALVERT, William, 24
CAMPBELL, Helen, 76, 77
CAMPBELL, Henry, 263
CAMPBELL, Isabella, 80
CAMPBELL, John McLeod, 79
CAMPBELL, Mary, 81
CARLYLE, Eleanor, 245
CARTER, Capel, 194
CARUS, Jane, 56, 62
CHAPMAN, George, 156, 193, 215, 216
CHAPMAN, Henry, 156, 193, 215, 216
CHAPMAN, James, 156, 193

CHAVASSE, Horace, 286
CHAVASSE, Margaret see also Margaret Dunlop, 286
COLERIDGE, Samuel Taylor, 15, 23, 70
COLERIDGE, Sara née Fricker, 23
CUMANGOOT, 271
CUNNINGHAM, Elizabeth see also Elizabeth Dunlop, Endnotes 28, 98, 195, 214
DALTON, Elizabeth see also Elizabeth Kennedy, 13, 15, 16
DALTON, George, 13, 15
DALTON, Margaret née Graham, 13
DALTON, Thomas, 13
DAWSON, Ann, 138, 154, 157, 169, 182, 195, 217
DAWSON, Elijah, 138, 150, 162, 193, 194, 195, 200, 216, 217
DAWSON, George, 154
DAWSON, John, 157
DAWSON, Richard, 150, 185
DENNISTOUN, James, 65, 112, 120, 121, 141, 170
DuCANE, Edmund, 287, Endnotes 33, 35, 39, 44, 45, 60, 64, 168, 171, 188
DuCANE, Mary see also Mary Dorothea Molloy, 287, 288, 294, 296

DRUMMOND, James, 169, 211, 213, 255, 266, 275, 276, 278, 298
DUNDAP, 241
DUNLOP, Alexander, 56, 57, 61, 63, 79, 113, 119, 278
DUNLOP, Elizabeth Boyle see also Elizabeth Cunningham, 55, 56, 63
DUNLOP, Helen Boyle see also Helen Story, 62, 74
DUNLOP, Hutcheson, 66
DUNLOP, Margaret Colquhoun (Maggie) 62, 66, 103, 111, 120, 130, 179
DUNLOP, Mary, see also Mary Ker, 62, 73, 78, 131, 158, 219
ELIOT, George, 265
GALE, Richard, 289
GALYPERT, 190
GAYWAL, 216, 217, 263, 265, 268, 269
GIUSTINIANI, Louis, 218
GRAHAM, James, 13
GRAHAM, John, 18
GRAHAM, Margaret (Peggy) see also Margaret Dalton, 13
GRANT, Frances see also Frances Birkett junior, 23, 143, 144
GRANT, James Robert, 23

GREEN, Alfred, 174, 192, 195, 214, 216, 221, 225, 229, 233, 239, 283
HAILES, George, 280
HALE, Amy, 288
HALE, Georgie see also Georgiana Theodosia Bisdee, 289-296
HALE, Mary, 288
HALE, Mathew Blagden, 283, 284, 288, 290
HALE, Sabina Dunlop see also Sabina Molloy, 264, 284, 287, 289
HEPPINGSTONE, Ann, 138, 160, 161, 201, 282
HEPPINGSTONE, Charlotte, 138, 160, 161, 201, 282
HEPPINGSTONE, Elizabeth, 138
HEPPINGSTONE, Ellen, 287
HEPPINGSTONE, Robert senior, 138, 199
HEPPINGSTONE, Robert junior, 138, 281
HERRING, John, 156, 163, 174, 195, 202, 241, 242, 283,
HOOKER, William, 266, 276
HUGGINS, Edward Rodon, 185
HUGGINS, Emily see also Emily Packenham Yates, Endnotes 370, 405

INDEX

HUTCHINSON, Mary *see also Mary Wordsworth*, 23
HUTCHINSON, Sara, 23
INJANGOOT, 216
HUTT, John, 242, 263
IRVING, Edward, 74, 77, 78, 80, 81, 134
IRWIN, Thomas, 245
KELLAM, John, 150, 156, 191
KENNEDY, David *senior*, Endnote 25
KENNEDY, David, 15, 16, 18-21, 25-27
KENNEDY, (David) Dalton, 21, 106, 109, 110, 112, 119, 121, 130, 134, 180, 197, 242, 243
KENNEDY, Elizabeth *see also Elizabeth Dalton*, 16, 21-24, 27, 42, 45-48, 50-57, 72, 103, 105, 107-112, 129-130, 159, 173, 180, 181, 185, 197, 198, 242-245, 269, 274, 279, 285
KENNEDY, Elizabeth Margaret *see also Elizabeth Besley*, 17, 49-54
KENNEDY, George, 21, 27, 47, 51, 87, 106, 180, 189, 233, 244
KENNEDY, Georgiana *see also Georgiana Molloy*, Birth: 7
Marriage: 123, 126
KENNEDY, Jane, 21
KENNEDY, Mary, 17

KENNEDY, Mary Gertrude *see also Mary Birt*, 18, 43, 48, 130, 180, 181, 197, 198, 242, 245, 246, 258, 261, 264
KENNY, 216, 269, 271
KER, Mary *see also Mary Dunlop*, 276, 281
LAYMAN, George, 168, 193, 198, 215, 217, 233, 268, 269
LAYMAN, Mary, *see also Mary Heppingstone*, 193, 282
LEACH, George *senior*, 105, 106
LEACH, George *junior*, 42, 45, 106-108
LEACH, Jonathan, 94, 96, 105, 106, 286
LEACH, William Elford, 106
LEAKE, George Walpole, 94, 291
LINDLEY, John, 212, 231, 234, 247, 252, 254, 255, 257, 259
LODDIGES, George, 212, 254
LODGE, Sarah, 245
LOWRY, John, 197, 198
LYON MILNE, Robert, 189
MACDERMOTT, Marshall, 114
MANGLES, Ellen *see also Ellen Stirling*, 148, 149
MANGLES, James, 205,

211-214, 231, 234, 247, 249, 250, 252, 253-258, 267, 274, 275, 288, 298
MANGLES, Robert, 211, 212, 253, 255
MARRYATT, Charlotte, 207, 254
McDERMOTT, James, 156, 178, 197
McDOUALL, Andrew, 16, 27, 43
McLEOD, Donald Hume, 169
MILER, Merth, 92
MITCHINSON, John, 15, 24, 26, 110
MOLLOY, Amelia Georgiana *see also Amelia Richardson-Bunbury*, 229, 238, 240, 246, 258, 281, 288
MOLLOY, Elizabeth Mary, 158-162
MOLLOY, Flora Elizabeth *see also Flora Brockman*, 257, 273, 281
MOLLOY, Georgiana *see also Georgiana Kennedy*,
Marriage: 123
Started collecting for James Mangles: 205
Death: 279
MOLLOY, Georgiana *junior*, 276, 282, 288, 289
MOLLOY, John,
Birth: 29
Marriage: 123
Death: 297

MOLLOY, John *junior*, 201, 202, 204, 205, 221, 222, 224
MOLLOY, Mary née Conner, 29, 31, 92
MOLLOY, Mary Dorothea *see also Mary DuCane*, 195, 197, 201, 202, 204, 205, 227, 232, 237, 258, 279, 287
MOLLOY, Sabina Dunlop *see also Sabina Hale*, 103, 174, 175, 182, 185, 188, 190, 192, 193, 198, 199, 201, 220, 226, 227, 229, 232, 236, 237, 246, 254, 273, 279, 281, 282, 284
MOLLOY, Susannah, 31, 41, 86, 113
MOLLOY, William, 29, 30-32, 41
MOULD, Emma, 184, 199
MORLEY, William, 244
MUNGO, 269, 271
NICHOLSON, William, 18, 21
NUGUNDUNG, 216, 263, 265
PAXTON, Joseph, 212, 213, 253, 254, 257, 287
PEARCE, Edward, 156, 176
PHILLIPS, William Spencer, 49-51, 54-57, 232
PLASKETT, William, 267, 269, 271

PREISS, Johann Ludwig, 246, 256
PYE MOLLOY, Anthony James, 35, 296
NIXSON, Paul, 18
RICHARDSON-BUNBURY, Amelia *see also Amelia Molloy*, 288
RICHARDSON-BUNBURY, William, 288
SALKILLD, John, 241
SALKILLD, Thomas, 155
SAUL, George, 245
SENHOUSE, Elizabeth, *Mrs Pocklington-Senhouse*, 10, 11, 121
SIMMONS, Charles, 169, 170, 174
SMITH, Harry, 142
STAPLES, James, 138, 154, 165, 166, 169, 188, 195, 209
STORY, Helen *see also Helen Dunlop*, 75, 120, 136, 175, 286
STORY, Robert, 74-77, 79-81, 113, 123
STIRLING, James, 99, 114, 116, 148, 149, 150, 154, 165, 178, 179, 189, 190, 197, 202, 210, 211, 213, 263, 286
STIRLING, Ellen *see also Ellen Mangles*, 149, 205, 210, 212, 213, 234, 286
SOUTHEY, Edith née Fricker, 23

SOUTHEY, Robert, 15, 23
TAYLOR, Mary *see also Mary Bussell*, 219
TAYLOR, Patrick, 219
TROUTBECK, George, 18, 108, 109, 176, 180
TROUTBECK, William, 18
TURNER, (McDERMOTT / GREEN) Elizabeth Ann (Nancy), 178, 197, 214, 283
TURNER, George, 199, 215, 241
TURNER, James Woodward, 142, 149, 155, 163, 169, 178, 186, 197, 233, 241, 278, 283
TURNER, John, 199, 215
TURNER, Maria née Rockley, 155, 178
TURNER, Thomas, 155, 199, 241
WEST, Richard, 241
WOBERDUNG, 269, 271
WORDSWORTH, Mary née Hutchinson, 23
WORDSWORTH, William, 15, 23, 24, 70, 71, 261
WELLINGTON, Arthur Wellesley, Duke of, 89, 92, 94-96, 286
WILLMOTT, William 'Percy', 290

INDEX

WOLLASTON, John Ramsden, 274, 276-280, 283

YATES, Emily Packenham *see also Emily Huggins*, Endnotes: 370

YATES, Frances Louisa *see also Frances Louisa Bussell senior*, 185

YATES, Mary Beckford *see also Mary Bowker*, Endnote 370

YATES, Thomas Legall *senior*, 185

Acknowledgements and Sources

When using handwritten texts as sources, I have transcribed from original documents, or copies of them, wherever possible, even if they have been transcribed and published before. If a previous transcriber misreads a word or misses out a sentence, meaning can change and an error is recycled when later researchers work from that version rather than the original. My transcriptions of the sources referenced here may still include some errors, but I hope this new layer of interpretation will be useful to those who take the research further. If shared publicly, the accumulated outcomes of continued research enrich the evidence base available for future study. For this reason, I have included a detailed collection of endnotes so that others can refer to the sources and build on this work. There is always more to learn: 'History always has a few tricks up its frayed sleeve. It's been around a long time.' *Mort*, Terry Pratchett.

After a decade of investigation in archives, libraries and museums, and exploration in cities, towns, villages and bush locations, it would be an impossible task to thank every individual who has helped me along the way but I hope each person will recognise the significance of their contribution somewhere within the pages of this book. My sincere thanks go to the following, for the important roles they have played on my research journey:

Patrick Richardson-Bunbury, for sharing his own extensive knowledge and personal insights into the history of his great-great-grandparents, and for his guidance, enduring support and encouragement.

Patricia and the late Michael Sedgwick, for their generosity of time and access to the nooks and crannies of their home.

Andrew Bunbury, for undertaking on my behalf the research into his great-great-grandfather's history with such enthusiasm and for the long days he spent at the National Archives, Kew.

Robert Hale, for making the H. M. O. Hale family collection

available to Patrick Richardson-Bunbury and for giving permission for it to be included.

Dorothy Margaret Blaasch née Richardson-Bunbury for sharing her knowledge of the Molloy family history and for access to her collection of portraits.

Margaret Wright, for her hours of research on naval documents at the National Archives, Kew.

The Cumbria Archive Centre, for years of five-star customer service.

Francesca Halfacree, Conservation Unit, Cumbria Archive Centre, for managing my rambling requests.

Kay Craze of Augusta, for introducing me to her cousin Mel Whinnen who fell into the Augusta well, and thanks to Mel for his childhood story.

Mairi Gallagher, for arranging our visit to Keppoch House and the Brodie family for their hospitality.

Jane Scott, for botanical advice and expertise.

Petra Mitchinson, for transcriptions of eighteenth- and nineteenth-century Carlisle newspapers and for information about John Mitchinson.

Lyndon Johnson, for research at the University of Toronto.

Glenda Downing, for her meticulous, accomplished, warm-spirited editing.

I am also grateful to many individuals and organisations who provided information and answered questions, including: the 95th Rifles Living History Society; John Alferink; Augusta Historical Society; the JS Battye Library of West Australian History; the Bodleian Library, Oxford; the British Library; Jeremy Bruhl; Busselton Historical Society; Richard Clark of Geographe Community Landcare Nursery; Roma Kail, Research Librarian at Victoria University in the University of Toronto; Pam Charlton and Judith Crimmins of Heythrop College, Kensington; Dr Alexander George; Steve Howell, JS Battye

Library; Noreen Hackett, AHS; Harrow School library; Dr Neville Marchant; Margaret River Historical Society; Andrew James Baxter McAdam; the National Trust of Western Australia; Louise Prescott of Wisconsin, USA; Tom Robson, Senior Archivist at Cumbria Archive Service; the Royal Western Australian Historical Society; Susan Snell, Archivist and Records Manager at the London Library and Museum of Freemasonry; Dave Walker and Tim Reid, Kensington Central Library, RBKC; Warwickshire County Records Office; the Western Australian Herbarium; Stephen White, Local Studies Librarian at Carlisle Library.

To my wise and wonderful agent, Martin Shaw, thank you for everything right from the very beginning.

Huge and heartfelt thanks go to the many bookshops and other retailers who supported the self-published book in 2015 and started its journey. I'm indebted to my publisher Alex Craig for her empathy and enthusiasm, to Rebecca Hamilton and my patient editor Jodi De Vantier, and to the whole team at Picador, in whose safe hands Georgiana's story is travelling on.

My greatest debt of all is to Mike Rumble, my partner in all life's adventures for more than three decades. He told me to start writing, provided every single thing I needed to keep going, and carried me across the finish line.

Bernice Barry lives on Western Australia's southwest coast near the place where Georgiana Molloy arrived in 1830. She closed the door on a career in international curriculum innovation in 2011, deciding to focus on her lifelong interest in writing, literature and history. Bernice has a BA in English, French and Spanish, an Advanced Diploma in the teaching of reading, a MA in Education, and has written many publications on education, from language development software for young children to new national curricula for students and student teachers. She has been researching the lives of Georgiana and John Molloy for twelve years, travelling in Australia and Europe to access original sources and historical sites.